TRUTH REVEALED

"Studying goes before knowledge"

BY

GARY WENDELL STANFIELD SR.

Matthew 10: 36 And a man's foes shall be they of his own household.

The Lie- "The ones living the lie, don't realize the lie they are living."

Studies done by Gary Wendell Stanfield

All poems written by Gary W. Stanfield

Quote on the book cover by Gary W. Stanfield.

DEDICATION

This book's dedication goes to all those who have lost all hope in believing in a Higher Power. That has caused your disbelief from maybe being in any of the world religions and have found yourself wanting, so you just gave up and became an Atheist or even from the life you had been dealt. This book, as well as my other ones, will give you the encouragement to not give up because the truth will renew your mind of that future hope to keep looking forward to that coming hope of a new and forever life that will become available to you, where all these Satanic earthly woes will be no more and a completely new future that life on this earth will never compare to the riches and righteousness of living on the New Earth with our Creator and Savior Yahweh.

PREFACE

This book is a treasure trove of studies uncovering the truth behind the brainwashing perpetuated by Christian lies. It is a valuable resource for learning truths not taught within Christianity and for guiding you onto the path of salvation. Once Yahweh fills a person with His Spirit, which grants salvation, there is no such thing as backsliding. His Spirit is poured out again, and the truth is taught before the Tribulation Period and His return at the end of it. No one can be judged without hearing the whole truth and having the opportunity for salvation. Yahweh has made a way for everyone to hear the full truth, whether they died after Constantine's 11th Roman Emperor persecution, never having heard the truth with salvation available, up to the Papacy's 7-Year Peace Plan. Those still alive during the Peace Plan will also have the opportunity at that time.

Through this book, you will discover that, despite what was done to Yahweh's Word, enough truth remains for people to find their way to Him and His salvation. However, salvation is not available to anyone today, dating back to Constantine's time. Only through Yahweh's love and mercy does He desire all men to receive, though the scriptures make it clear this will not happen due to individual choice.

Table of Contents

CHAPTER 1
MILLENNIAL KINGDOM

What is the Millennial Kingdom for?

Latin Word

Mille = A Thousand

Annum = Years

More proof that the King James root was Jerome's Latin Vulgate which has a lot of Latin words in it.

A.   TO FULFILL HIS PROMISE TO THE ELECT.

Revelation 5: 10

And **hast made us unto our Yahweh kings and priests:** and <u>we shall reign on the earth.</u>

And I saw thrones, and they sat upon them, and judgment was given unto them: and <u>**I saw the souls of them that were beheaded for the witness of Jesus/Yahweh, and for the Word of God/Yahweh, and which had not worshipped the beast, neither his image, neither had received his mark upon their foreheads, or in their hands;**</u> and <u>**they lived and reigned with Christ/Yahweh a thousand years.**</u>

14 Blessed are those who wash their robes, so that <u>**they may have the right to the tree of life and may enter the city by its gates.**</u>The truth must be taught once again or Yahweh cannot judge anyone that never heard the truth with the opportunity to have salvation, that goes back to Constantine. Many people believe that they will be able to plead ignorance. Yahweh will never let that happen. To teach all those that had died and never heard the truth with the opportunity to have salvation.

Before the 11 Roman Emperor Persecutions:

1 **Thessalonians 1: 5**

"For our Word came not unto you in word only, but also in power, and in the Spirit, and in much assurance; as ye know what manner of men we were among you for your sake."

After Constantine's 11th Roman Persecution:

Proverbs 1: 28 Then they will call on me, but I will not answer; they will earnestly seek me, but will not find me.

Daniel 7: 12 As concerning the rest of the beasts, they had **their dominion taken away: yet their lives were prolonged for a season and time.**

Zechariah14: 16

"Then it will come about that any who are left of all the nations that went against Jerusalem/Zion will go up year to year to worship the King."

THE REASON THE NATIONS LIVES WERE PROLONGED FOR A SEASON AND A TIME IS BY ALL THOSE THAT NEVER HEARD THE TRUTH FROM ALL THESE NATIONS AND THEY WILL REPOPULATE THE NATIONS BY HAVING CHILDREN DURING THE MILLENNIAL KINGDOM TO REPOPULATE THE WORLD. A THOUSAND YEARS IS A LONG TIME TO KEEP REPRODUCING AND WILL END UP AS THE SAND OF THE SEA. THESE ARE THOSE DURING SATAN'S SHORT SEASON WILL BE LIKE THE SAND OF THE SEA SHOWN BELOW:

15 But **outside are** the dogs, the sorcerers, the sexually immoral, the murderers, the idolaters, and everyone who loves and practices falsehood.

Now, why would Yahweh be teaching that type of people if they could not be forgiven? Verse 15 are the ones that never heard the truth; these are those that Yahweh is teaching and are not allowed to enter the gates of the city; only the Elect are allowed to, and not those that died as transgressors. You should be able to see the difference between the two. It will be their choice who they will serve when all is said and done.

The reason if you are a murderer or those that have had Abortions and even homosexuals can be forgiven, Prostitutes, or what have you. Everyone will die, somehow, some way, someday. The reason is this is fully Satan's world and is all about death, immorality, and many other of Satan's vices to make people feel that there is no hope for certain people when Yahweh has made a way for everyone to have salvation and why everyone will have forgiveness offered to them, so never lose hope no matter what you have done. The only thing that is not forgivable and will put a person in the Lake of Fire is when a person is given salvation, which is the infilling of Yahweh's Spirit with power and a person turns their back on Yahweh and walks away from the good thing that makes a person his. Many denominations in Christianity teach that you can backslide all you want and still be able to receive salvation and hope that you don't die before you do. The deceit comes with believing that so many have been taught that they are Spirit-filled, like when they get baptized or at other times. Even the Pentecostals don't realize the deceit that they are in, but Satan is a deceiver and wants people to burn with him.

2 Corinthians 11: 14

And no marvel; for Satan himself is transformed into a messenger of light. I am not out to get anyone saved, there is no salvation attainable in this Satanic world, but what I am out to do is to wake people up to the truth that will lead to their salvation. There is no religion on this Earth that can save anyone, it is your choice

to believe or not to believe when the time comes whether if you die or still living at the time it is given again, each person is responsible for their own salvation. If you are in any of these world religions the best thing for now is to get out of them and wait for when salvation is taught and given again. Christianity gives people a false since of security, just as the other world religions do.

Isa 25: 9

And it shall be said in that day, Lo, this is our God/Yahweh; we have waited for him, and he will save us: this is **the Lord/Yahweh**; we have waited for him, **we will be glad and rejoice in his salvation.**

Isaiah 66: 23

And it shall come to pass, that **from one new moon to another, and from one sabbath to another, shall all flesh come to worship before me, saith Yahweh**.

Isaiah 12: 3 Therefore with joy shall ye draw water out of the wells of salvation.

Isaiah 14: 7 **The whole earth is at rest and is quiet**: they break forth into singing.

Zachariah 13: 2 And it shall come to pass in that day, saith **the LORD/YAHWEH of hosts**, that I will cut off the names of the idols out of the land, and they shall no more be remembered: and also, I will cause the prophets and the unclean spirit to pass out of the land.

Zech 14: 4,16

4 And his feet shall stand in that day upon the mount of Olives, which *is* before Zion on the east, and the mount of Olives shall cleave in the midst thereof toward the east and toward the west, *and there shall be* a very great valley; and half of the mountain shall remove toward the north, and half of it toward the south.

Matthew 6: 9-10

9 **After this manner therefore pray ye: Our Father which art in heaven, Hallowed be thy name.**

10 **Thy kingdom come, thy will be done on earth, as it is in heaven.**

Micah 4: 3

"And he shall judge among many people, and rebuke strong nations afar off; and they shall beat their swords into plowshares, and their spears into pruninghooks: nation shall not lift up a sword against nation, neither shall they learn war anymore."

Those who are left of all the nations are those who had died and never heard the truth with salvation available. All the rest were burned up at his coming, they had their chance and did not accept it. The second Lake of Fire is at the White Throne Judgement, the second Gog and Magog war against Satan and the wicked and Yahweh and his Elect when Yahweh sends fire down from heaven and burns them all up with this earth and the heavens, then will create a New Heaven and a New Earth and the former will not be remembered.

Revelation 20: 3

And cast him into the bottomless pit, and shut him up, and set a seal upon him, that he should deceive the nations no more, till the thousand years should be fulfilled: and after that he must be loosed a little season. SATAN WAS KILLED AND PUT IN THE GRAVE, HIS PRISON.

REVELATION 20: 7-11

7 And when the thousand years are expired, Satan shall be loosed out of his prison,

8 And shall <u>go out to deceive the nations which are in the four quarters of the earth, Gog and Magog, to gather them together to battle:</u> the number of whom is as the sand of the sea.

9 And they went up on the breadth of the earth, and compassed the camp of the elect about, and the beloved city: **and** <u>fire came down from Yahweh out of heaven, and devoured them.</u>

10 And the devil that deceived them was cast into the lake of fire and brimstone...

11 "And **I saw a great white throne**, and him that sat on it, from whose face the earth and the heaven fled away; and there was found no place for them."

THIS WAS THE WHITE THRONE JUDGEMENT ON ALL THE WICKED.

<u>THERE ARE A COUPLE OF VERY INTERESTING VERSES THAT MAY BE THE PROPHECY ABOUT THIS FIRE COMING DOWN FROM HEAVEN AND DEVOURING THEM IN II EZDRAS, SEEN IN A DREAM.</u>

<u>**II Esdras 13: 10-11**</u>

10 But only **I saw that he sent out of his mouth as it had been a blast of fire, and out of his lips a flaming breath, and out of his tongue he cast out sparks and tempests.**

11 And <u>they were all mixed together; the blast of fire, the flaming breath, and the great tempest; and fell with violence upon the multitude which was prepared to fight, and burned them up everyone, so that upon a sudden of an innumerable multitude nothing was to be perceived, but only dust and smell of smoke:</u> when I saw this I was afraid.

<u>**Revelation 8: 5**</u>

And the Messenger took the censer, and filled it with fire of the altar, and cast it into the earth: and there were voices, and thunderings, and lightnings, and an earthquake.

31 **And ye my flock, the flock of my pasture, are men, saith Yahweh.**

CHAPTER 2

LIFE DURING THE MILLENNIUM

A. YAHWEH MESSIAH WILL BUILD THE THIRD HOUSE OF YAHWEH DURING THE MILLENNIUM.

Zachariah 6: 12-13

12 And speak unto him, saying, Thus speaketh the LORD/**Yahweh** of hosts, saying, Behold **the man whose name *is* The BRANCH;** and he shall grow up out of his place, and **he shall build the** temple/**House of** the LORD/**Yahweh**:

13 Even **he shall build the** temple/**House of** the LORD/**Yahweh**; and he shall bear the glory/**Righteousness**, and **shall sit and rule upon his throne; and he shall be a priest upon his throne: and the counsel of peace shall be between them both. All this building a third Temple in Jerusalem/Zion is a Christian lie. The Temple being spoken of is no other than the one inside the Facade of the Dome of the Rock, built by Constantine in the 4ᵗʰ century, called the "Temple of God" built on the site of the pagan Temple of Jupiter a name for Nimrod, in the worship of Nimrod.** \

EVERLASTING KINGDOM.

Ezekiel 34: 31 And ye my flock, the flock of my pasture, are men, saith Yahweh.

Daniel 7: 13-14

[13] I saw in the night visions, and behold, one like the Son of man came with the clouds of heaven, and came to the Ancient of days, and they brought him near before him.

14 **And there was given him dominion, and glory/esteem, and a kingdom, that all people, nations, and languages, should serve him: his dominion is an everlasting dominion, which shall not pass away, and his kingdom that which shall not be destroyed.**

27 **And the kingdom and dominion, and the greatness of the kingdom under the whole heaven, shall be given to the people of the** saints/**Elect of the most High, whose kingdom is an everlasting kingdom, and all dominions shall serve and obey him.**

Isaiah 65: 9 And I will bring forth a seed out of Jacob, and out of Judah an inheritor of my mountains: and mine elect shall inherit it, and my servants shall dwell there.

Isaiah 2: 2-3,5

2 And it shall come to pass in the last days, *that* the mountain of the LORD'S/**Yahweh's** house shall be established in the top of the mountains and shall be exalted above the hills; and all nations shall flow unto it.

3 And many people shall go and say, come ye, and let us go up to the mountain of the LORD/**Yahweh**, to the house of Yahweh of Jacob; and he will teach us of his ways, and we will walk in his paths: for out of Zion shall go forth the law, and the word of the LORD/**Yahweh** from Jerusalem/**Zion**.

5 O house of Jacob, come ye, and let us walk in the light of the LORD/**Yahweh.Isaiah 9: 7** Of the increase of his government and **peace there shall be no end,** upon the throne of David, and upon his kingdom, to order it, and to establish it with judgment

Isaiah 65: 24

And it shall come to pass, that before they call, I will answer; and while they are yet speaking, I will hear.

Ezekiel 34: 24 And I the LORD/**YAHWEH** will be their God/**Mighty One,** and my servant David a prince/**King** among them; I the LORD/**YAHWEH** have spoken it.

Luke 1: 32-33 He shall be great and shall be called **the Son of the Highest**: and the Lord/Yahweh shall give unto him the throne of his father David: 33 And he shall reign over the house of Jacob forever; and of his kingdom there shall be no end.

Zach 13: 2 And it shall come to pass in that day, saith **the LORD of hosts**, that I will cut off the names of the idols out of the land, and they shall no more be remembered: and also, I will cause the prophets and the unclean spirit to pass out of the land.

Isaiah 60: 21 <u>**Thy people also shall be all righteous: they shall inherit the land for ever**</u>, <u>the branch of my planting, the work of my hands, that I may be glorified/esteemed.</u>

B.   HARVEST INCREASE.

Zach 8: 12

12 "For the seed shall be prosperous; the vine shall give her fruit, and the ground shall give her increase, and the heavens shall give their dew; and I will cause the remnant of this people to possess all these things."

Ezek 36: 29

I will also save you from all your uncleannesses: and I will call for the corn, and will increase it, and lay no famine upon you.

Amos 9: 13

Behold, the days come, saith the Lord/Yahweh, that the plowman shall overtake the reaper, and the treader of grapes him that soweth seed; and the mountains shall drop sweet wine, and all the hills shall melt.

Ezekiel 34: 26

26 And I will make them and the places round about my hill a blessing; and I will cause the shower to come down in his season; there shall be showers of blessing.

Ezek 34: 27-30

27 And the tree of the field shall yield her fruit, and the earth shall yield her increase, and they shall be safe in their land, and shall know that I am the LORD/YAHWEH, when I have broken the bands of their yoke, and delivered them out of the hand of those that served themselves of them.

29 And I will raise up for them a plant of renown, and they shall be no more consumed with hunger in the land, neither bear the shame of the heathen anymore.

30 And I will multiply the fruit of the tree, and the increase of the field, that ye shall receive no more reproach of famine among the heathen.

C.   NO MORE WAR.

Ezekiel 34: 28

And they shall no more be a prey to the heathen, neither shall the beast of the land devour them; but they shall dwell safely, and none shall make them afraid.

Isaiah 60: 18

Violence shall no more be heard in thy land, wasting nor destruction within thy borders; but thou shalt call thy walls Salvation, and thy gates Praise.

They shall not hurt nor destroy in all my holy/**righteous** mountain: for the earth shall be full of the knowledge of Yahweh, as the waters cover the sea.

D. NO MORE WILD ANIMALS.

25 And I will make with them a **covenant of peace, and will cause the evil beasts to cease out of the land: and they shall dwell safely in the wilderness, and sleep in the woods.**

28 And **they shall no more be a prey to the heathen, neither shall the beast of the land devour them; but they shall dwell safely, and none shall make them afraid.**

Isaiah 65: 25

The wolf and the lamb shall feed together, and the lion shall eat straw like the bullock: and dust shall be the serpent's meat. They shall not hurt nor destroy in all my holy mountain, saith Yahweh.

Isaiah 11: 6-9

6 **The wolf also shall dwell with the lamb, and the leopard shall lie down with the kid; and the calf and the young lion and the fatling together; and a little child shall lead them.**

7 And **the cow and the bear shall feed; their young ones shall lie down together: and the lion shall eat straw like the ox.**

8 And **the sucking child shall play on the hole of the asp, and the weaned child shall put his hand on the cockatrice' den.**

E. YAHWEH WILL GIVE ONE PURE LANGUAGE

Zephaniah 3: 8-9

8 Therefore <u>wait ye upon me, saith the LORD/**Yahweh**, until the day that I rise up to the prey:</u> **for my determination** *is* **to gather the nations, that I may assemble the**

12

kingdoms, to pour upon them mine indignation, *even* all my fierce anger: for all the earth shall be devoured with the fire of my jealousy. Verse 8 is speaking of the Armagedon War when all the armies of every nation goes against Zion.9 For then will I turn to the people a pure language, that <u>they may all call upon the name</u> of the LORD/**Yahweh**, <u>to serve him with one consent.</u> Verse 9, At the end of that war Yahweh returns and collects his Elect and burns up all the wicked, then he starts his Millennial Kingdom. So He most likely gave them a pure language when they were caught up since they were praising him on the Mothership above the earth and did the same for those during the Millennial Kingdom that never heard the truth, the ones that he taught, that were brought up from the grave on this earth to be taught the truth, so during the Millennial Kingdom they will all speak one pure language.

F. WILL ENJOY THEIR OWN LABOR.

Isaiah 65: 21,23

21 **And they shall build houses, and inhabit them; and they shall plant vineyards, and eat the fruit of them.**

23 **They shall not labor in vain, nor bring forth for trouble; for they are the seed of the blessed of** the LORD/YAHWEH, **and their offspring with them.**

During the Millennium everyone will live to be 100 years old before they die, babies, the youth and the old people, the Elect of course will never die.

Isaiah 65: 20 There shall be <u>**no more thence an infant of days**</u>, <u>**nor an old man that hath not filled his days:**</u> for <u>**the child shall die an hundred years old**</u>; but the sinner/**transgressor** being a hundred years old shall be accursed.

Accursed because they did not want to believe when they were being taught so their end is in the Lake of Fire.

You may be thinking I thought those that were given salvation would never die again. They won't, this is those that never heard the truth and had no opportunity for salvation that Yahweh is teaching them himself during this time. These are the ones that are still having children, and they are the ones that came from all the nations on earth, still in their natural celestial bodies.

Daniel 12: 2 And **many of them that sleep in the dust of the earth shall awake,** some to everlasting life, and some to shame _and_ everlasting contempt.

I believe that Daniel 12: 2 is speaking of those that Yahweh raises in their earthly bodies from all nations to be taught by him and they will have children to populate the earth. The everlasting life and everlasting contempt is how they end up after Satan is loosed to deceive them they make the choice which one they will serve after the Millenium.

Isaiah 2: 3

And many people shall go and say, Come ye, and let us go up to the mountain of the LORD/**Yahweh**, to the house of the Yahweh of Jacob; and **he will teach us of his ways, and we will walk in his paths:** for out of Zion shall go forth the law, and the word of the LORD/Yahweh from Jerusalem/**Zion**. **They won't, this is those that never heard the truth and had no opportunity for salvation that Yahweh is teaching them himself during this time. These are the ones that are still having children, and they are the ones that came from all the nations on earth.**

G.   ANIMAL OFFERINGS RESUMED.

The Levite Priests will be reinstituted to do animal offerings again for the transgressions of the people that are being taught by Yahweh during the Millenium.

Ezekiel 40: 39

And in **the porch of the gate** *were* two tables on this side, and two tables on that side, to slay thereon the burnt offering and the transgression offering and the trespass offering.

H. THE ELECT RULE OVER THE NATIONS.

Daniel 7: 18 But the Elect of the most High shall take the kingdom, and **possess the kingdom forever, even for ever and ever.**

Revelation 5: 10 You have made them to be a kingdom to serve our Yahweh, and **they will reign upon the earth."**

Revelation 20: 6 Blessed and righteous is he that hath part in the first resurrection: on such the second death hath no power, **but they shall be** priests/**KINGS of Yahweh and of his Messiah. and shall reign with him for a thousand years.**

I. THOSE NATIONS THAT WILL NOT SERVE YAHWEH.

Psalms 33: 12 - Blessed is the nation whose God/**Mighty One** is the LORD/**Yahweh**; and the people whom he hath chosen for his own inheritance.

Proverbs 14: 34 - Righteousness exalteth a nation: but sin/transgression is a reproach to many people.

Zechariah 14: 16

"Then it will come about that <u>**any who are left of all the nations that went against Jerusalem/Zion will go up year to year to worship the King.**</u>

<u>**REVELATION CHAPTER 17**</u>

<u>**IS ALL ABOUT HOW ZION BECOMES THE CAPITAL CITY OF THE WORLD WHEN THE POPE MOVES HIS THRONE THERE TO RULE THE WORLD FROM ZION AND THE 3 1/2 YEAR TRIBULATION PERIOD WHEN THE PAPACY AND CHRISTIANS WILL**</u>

KILL THE ELECT OF YAHWEH MESSIAH: THE REASON FOR MAKING CHRISTIANITY THE WORLD RELIGION AND KILLING ANYONE THAT WILL NOT COME OVER TO IT. ALONG WITH ENFORCING THE MARK OF THE BEAST (THE CROSS) KNOWING THAT THE SPIRIT FILLED OF YAHWEH, THE ELECT WILL NOT TAKE THE MARK AND THEY ARE KILLED AS A TESTIMONY THAT YAHWEH IS TRUE, EVERYONE ELSE WILL TAKE THE MARK JUST TO SAVE THEIR LIVES, ONLY TO LOSE THEM BY YAHWEH AT HIS COMING.

Revelation 6: 14-17

And the heaven departed as a scroll when it is rolled together; and every mountain and island were moved out of their places. And the kings of the earth, and the great men, and the rich men, and the chief captains, and the mighty men, and every bondman, and every free man, hid themselves in the dens and in the rocks of the mountains; And said to the mountains and rocks, Fall on us, and hide us from the face of him that sitteth on the throne, and from the wrath of the Lamb: For the great day of his wrath is come; and who shall be able to stand?

CHAPTER 3
A LITTLE HISTORY ON ZION

A.   ENCYCLOPEDIA BRITANNICA

"Aelia Capitolina, a city founded in ad 135 C.E. by the Romans on the ruins of Jerusalem/ZION, which their forces, under Titus, had destroyed in 70 C.E. The name was given after the Second Jewish Revolt (132–135), in honor of the emperor Hadrian (clan name, was Aelius) as well as the deities of the Capitoline Triad (Jupiter, Juno, and Minerva). A sanctuary to Jupiter was built on the TEMPLE MOUNT, and statues of Roman deities were erected in the city in intentional violation of Old Covenant law. The area was walled, and a large foreign population was imported; Jews were forbidden entrance to the city. The present walls of the Old City of ZION follow the layout of the Roman walls. The name was used until Christianity became the official religion of the Roman Empire in the 4th century. A temple to Jupiter was constructed right on the Temple Mount, and idols of Roman deities were erected throughout the city in a deliberate and malicious violation of Yahweh's law."

The name Jerusalem is believed by some scholars to come from Uru + Shalem, meaning the foundation of Shalem or founded by Shalem or the city of Shalem[1]. **Shalem was the city deity of the place** before El Elyon (Most High). - From Wikipedia, the free encyclopedia -

Zion was named Jerusalem by the Romans after Aelia Capitolina was built because the present walls of the Old City of ZION follow the layout of the Roman walls. / You are not seeing the same city that Immanuel walked, everything is a Roman deceit and lie. Now you can understand why Yahweh will destroy this Zion because of what was done in a city of lies. Constantine built his churches on old pagan temple sites. (Church means pagan temple). There is a big chance that they are not all Jews that live there being called Jews, just part of the deceit. Yahweh brings back the 10 lost tribes during the 7-Year Peace Plan, so they will be there during the Tribulation part of the Peace Plan for the last 3 ½ years of it, and from these are the 144,000 from the 12 tribes sealed, and they are the ones who will call Yahweh back. What people are in Israel JUDAEA now if they are not Jews?

CONSTANTINE BUILT HIS TEMPLE OF GOD WHERE THE TEMPLE OF JUPITER ONCE STOOD INSIDE THE ANTONIA FORTRESS, ON THE PART CALLED THE TEMPLE MOUNT, FOR JUPITER'S TEMPLE THEN CONSTANTINE'S TEMPLE. THEY KNOW THE HOUSE OF YAHWEH NEVER SAT ON THE TEMPLE MOUNT IT SAT BELOW IT IN THE OLD CITY OF ZION (this is proven by scriptures to be true). PAGAN SUN WORSHIPERS USED TEMPLES. JEWS USED THE HOUSE OF YAHWEH THAT SAT ON MOUNT MORIAH IN THE OLD CITY OF ZION. NOT ON THE PAGAN TEMPLE MOUNT, THEN THE MUSLIMS WHEN THEY TOOK OVER ZION FROM THE PAPACY/CHRISTIANS, THEY BUILT A FACADE AROUND THE TEMPLE OF GOD BUILT BY CONSTANTINE IN THE 4TH CENTURY AND IT WAS NICK NAMED THE DOME OF THE ROCK, THE DOME IS ACTUALLY THE DOME OF THE TEMPLE. THE MORE I LEARN, THE MORE IT SEEMS THAT THE SO-CALLED JEWS ARE PART OF THE DECEIT.

Theodore Hertzl - a Catholic Jew, said that Zionists are Catholic Jews. He worked with the Papacy to convert them so they would be allowed to go back to their homeland. Zionism is a political movement THAT was started so they could end up having their own Jewish State. Herzl was elected President of the Zionist Movement, and they adopted Rothschild Red Hexagram as the Zionist flag, which later became the flag of Israel, the star being called the **Star of David, which is the star of Remphan.**

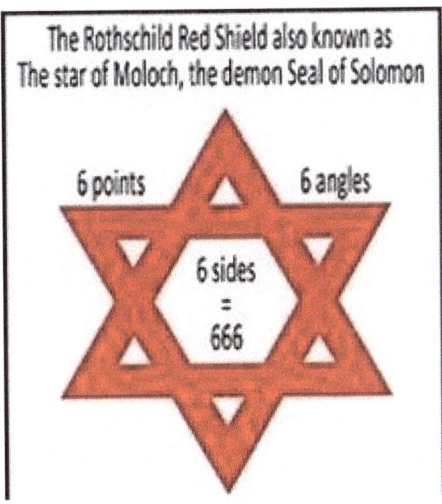

Zionist Movement adopted Rothschild Red Hexagram as the Zionist flag, then called the star "The Star of David."

WE LIVE IN A WORLD OF LIES AND MASS CONFUSION ABOUT EVERYTHING. ALL ABOUT ZION.

THIS WHOLE CHAPTER SPEAKS ABOUT ZION THE CITY CALLED JERUSALEM TODAY:

REVELATION CHAPTER 18

And after these things I saw another Messenger come down from heaven, having great power; and the earth was lightened with his righteousness.

2 And he cried mightily with a strong voice, saying, Babylon the great is fallen, is fallen, and is become the habitation of devils, and the hold of every foul spirit, and a cage of every unclean and hateful bird.

3 For all nations have drunk of the wine of the wrath of her fornication, and the kings of the earth have committed fornication with her, and the merchants of the earth are waxed rich through the abundance of her delicacies.

4 And I heard another voice from heaven, saying, Come out of her, my people, that ye be not partakers of her transgressions, and that ye receive not of her plagues.

5 For her transgressions have reached unto heaven, and Yahweh hath remembered her iniquities.

6 Reward her even as she rewarded you, and double unto her double according to her works: in the cup which she hath filled fill to her double.

7 How much she hath glorified herself, and lived deliciously, so much torment and sorrow give her: for she saith in her heart, I sit a queen, and am no widow, and shall see no sorrow.

8 <u>Therefore shall her plagues come in one day, death, and mourning, and famine; and she shall be utterly burned with fire</u>: for strong is Yahweh who judgeth her.

9 And the kings of the earth, who have committed fornication and lived deliciously with her, shall bewail her, and lament for her, when they shall see the smoke of her burning,

10 Standing afar off for the fear of her torment, saying, Alas, alas that great city Babylon, that mighty city! for in one hour is thy judgment come.

11 And the merchants of the earth shall weep and mourn over her; for no man buyeth their merchandise any more.

12 The merchandise of gold, and silver, and precious stones, and of pearls, and fine linen, and purple, and silk, and scarlet, and all thyine wood, and all manner vessels of ivory, and all manner vessels of most precious wood, and of brass, and iron, and marble,

13 And cinnamon, and odors, and ointments, and frankincense, and wine, and oil, and fine flour, and wheat, and beasts, and sheep, and horses, and chariots, and slaves, and souls of men.

14 And the fruits that thy soul lusted after are departed from thee, and all things which were dainty and goodly are departed from thee, and thou shalt find them no more at all.

15 The merchants of these things, which were made rich by her, shall stand afar off for the fear of her torment, weeping and wailing,

16 And saying, Alas, alas that great city, that was clothed in fine linen, and purple, and scarlet, and decked with gold, and precious stones, and pearls!

17 For in one hour so great riches is come to naught. And every shipmaster, and all the company in ships, and sailors, and as many as trade by sea, stood afar off,

18 And cried when they saw the smoke of her burning, saying, What city is like unto this great city!

19 And they cast dust on their heads, and cried, weeping and wailing, saying, Alas, alas that great city, wherein were made rich all that had ships in the sea by reason of her costliness! for in one hour is she made desolate.

²⁰ Rejoice over her, thou heaven, and ye apostles and prophets; for <u>Yahweh hath avenged you on her.</u>

²¹ And a mighty Messenger took up a stone like a great millstone, and cast it into the sea, saying, Thus <u>with violence shall that great city Babylon be thrown down, and shall be found no more at all.</u>

²² <u>And the voice of harpers, and musicians, and of pipers, and trumpeters, shall be heard no more at all in thee; and no craftsman, of whatsoever craft he be, shall be found any more in thee; and the sound of a millstone shall be heard no more at all in thee;</u>

²³ <u>And the light of a candle shall shine no more at all in thee; and the voice of the bridegroom and of the bride shall be heard no more at all in thee: for thy merchants were the great men of the earth; for by thy sorceries were all nations deceived.</u>

²⁴ <u>And in her was found the blood of prophets, and of elect, and of all that were slain upon the earth.</u>

Revelation 18: 10,17,19,21

^{10.} IN ONE HOUR IS THY JUDGMENT COME.

^{17.} IN ONE HOUR...RICHES COME TO NOUGHT.

^{19.} IN ONE HOUR IS SHE MADE DESOLATE

^{21.} WITH VIOLENCE ZION IS THROWN DOWN.

THE END OF ZION HERE ON EARTH IS CALLED JERUSALEM TODAY.

<u>Revelation 18: 22-23</u>

22 And the voice of harpers, and musicians, and of pipers, and trumpeters, shall be heard no more at all in thee; and no craftsman, of whatsoever craft *he be*, shall be found any more in thee; and the sound of a millstone shall be heard no more at all in thee;

23 And the light of a candle shall shine no more at all in thee; and the voice of the bridegroom and of the bride shall be heard no more at all in thee: for thy merchants were the great men of the earth; for by thy sorceries were all nations deceived.

Jeremiah 4: 6

Set up the standard toward Zion: retire, stay not: for I will bring evil from the north, and a great destruction. **ZION IS THE LAST DAY BABYLON.**

Revelation 18: 2

And he cried mightily with a strong voice, saying, Babylon the great is fallen, is fallen, and is become the habitation of devils, and the hold of every foul spirit, and a cage of every unclean and hateful bird.

SHE LAYS DOWN WITH THE BABYLONIAN RELIGIOUS SYSTEM STARTED BY NIMROD, THE PAPACY, AND WHY THE POPE MOVES HIS THRONE TO ZION TO THE TEMPLE OF GOD INSIDE THE FACADE OF THE DOME OF THE ROCK. THE PAPACY WILL KILL MOSES AND ELIYAH, AND THEIR KILLING IS WHAT STARTS THE TRIBULATION PERIOD, AND THE ELECT WILL BE KILLED AT THIS TIME, AND WHY ZION HAS ALL THEIR BLOOD ON HER HANDS.

THIS WHOLE CHAPTER IS SPEAKING OF THE CITY ZION THEY ARE CALLING JERUSALEM TODAY. SHE IS DESTROYED DURING THE ARMAGEDDON WAR."

Zechariah 14: 17

And it shall be, that whoso will not come up **of all the families of the earth** unto Jerusalem/**Zion** to worship the King, the LORD/**YAHWEH** of hosts, even upon them **shall be no rain.**

All the families of the earth are the ones raised that never heard the truth nor had the opportunity for salvation. They still have Terrestrial bodies, so they were just raised from their graves and not given celestial bodies like the Elect received when they were taken up into spacecraft. These are the ones that are still having children during the Millenium, and they are the ones that came from all the nations on earth.

Isaiah 60: 12 - For **the nation and kingdom that will not serve thee shall perish;** yea, **those nations shall be utterly wasted.**

Micah 4: 3 - And he shall judge among many people, and rebuke strong nations afar off; and they shall beat their swords into plowshares, and their spears into pruninghooks: nation shall not lift up a sword against nation, neither shall they learn war anymore.

5 O house of Jacob, come ye, and let us walk in the light of the LORD/**Yahweh.**

Isaiah 30: 29 **Ye shall have a song,** as in the night when a holy/**righteous** solemnity is kept; and gladness of heart, as when one goeth with a pipe/**song** to come into the mountain of the LORD/**Yahweh,**

Isaiah 66: 23 And it shall come to pass, that from one new moon to another, and from one sabbath to another, shall all flesh come to worship before me, saith Yahweh.

When There Will Be

When will death be no more?
When there is no more war,
When hunger is finally fed,
When blood is no longer shed.

When there are no more tears,
When there are no more fears,
When there is no more pain,
When riches are not for gain.

When there will be a new birth,
When there will be a new earth,
When there will be a new day,
When there will be Yahweh!

There will be death no more,
There will be no more war,
There will be all hunger fed,
There will be no blood shed.

There will be no more tears,
There will be no more fears,
There will be no more pain,
There will be no riches to gain.

By Gary W. Stanfield

Isaiah 25: 8

He will swallow up death in victory; and Yahweh will wipe away tears from off all faces; and the rebuke of his people shall he take away from off all the earth: for Yahweh hath spoken it.

Isaiah 10: 12

Wherefore it shall come to pass, that when the Lord/**Yahweh** hath performed his whole work upon mount Zion and on Jerusalem/**Zion**, **I will punish the fruit of the stout heart of the king of Assyria, and the esteem of his high looks.**

I believe this King of Assyria is no other than Nimrod himself, the last Pope!

There will still be death after the Millennial Kingdom at the White Throne Judgement, which is the second Gog and Magog War against Yahweh and his Elect and Satan with the wicked, that Yahweh will burn up with this Earth. Yahweh will create a New Heaven and a New Earth and live with his Elect on the New Earth, and that is when Heaven on Earth happens, and no more death and everything else the poem speaks about. The Millennial Kingdom will be a glimpse into what the New Earth will be like in many aspects, but not fully. "**He will swallow up death in victory.**"

I cannot stress enough that all the world religions, which includes Christianity, are all of Satan to put people in the Lake of Fire, not to save them from it.

CHAPTER 4

THE NEW HEAVEN AND NEW EARTH

2 Peter 3: 13

Nevertheless we, **according to his promise, look for new heavens and a new earth, wherein dwelleth righteousness.**

Isaiah 66: 22

For as **the new heavens and the new earth, which I will make, shall remain before me, saith Yahweh, so shall your seed and your name remain.**

Isaiah 60: 21

<u>**Thy people also shall be all righteous**</u>: <u>they shall inherit the land for ever,</u> **<u>the branch of my planting, the work of my hands, that I may be esteemed.</u>**

<u>**REVELATION CHAPTER 21 - All about New Zion that will come down on the New Earth.**</u>

1 And I saw a new heaven and a new earth: for the first heaven and the first earth were passed away; and there was no more sea.

2 And I John saw the righteous city, NEW ZION, coming down from Yahweh out of heaven, prepared as a bride adorned for her husband.

3 And I heard a great voice out of heaven saying, Behold, the tabernacle of Yahweh is with men, and he will dwell with them, and they shall be his people, and Yahweh himself shall be with them, and be their Mighty One.

⁴ And Yahweh shall wipe away all tears from their eyes; and there shall be no more death, neither sorrow, nor crying, neither shall there be any more pain: for the former things are passed away.

⁵ And he that sat upon the throne said, Behold, I make all things new. And he said unto me, Write: for these words are true and faithful.

⁶ And he said unto me, It is done. I am Alpha and Omega, the beginning and the end. I will give unto him that is athirst of the fountain of the water of life freely.

⁷ He that overcometh shall inherit all things; and I will be his Father., and he shall be my son.

⁸ But the fearful, and unbelieving, and the abominable, and murderers, and whoremongers, and sorcerers, and idolaters, and all liars, shall have their part in the lake which burneth with fire and brimstone: which is the second death.

These were the ones that were taught by Yahweh, and those that followed satan were burned in the Lake of Fire at the White Throne Judgement when the whole earth burned up with the Wicked and Satan

⁹ And there came unto me one of the seven Messengers which had the seven vials full of the seven last plagues, and talked with me, saying, Come hither, I will shew thee the bride, the Lamb's wife.

¹⁰ And he carried me away in the spirit to a great and high mountain, and shewed me that great city, the righteous ZION, descending out of heaven from Yahweh,

¹¹ Having the righteousness of Yahweh: and her light was like unto a stone most precious, even like a jasper stone, clear as crystal;

¹² And had a wall great and high, and had twelve gates, and at the gates twelve Messengers, and names written thereon, which are the names of the twelve tribes of the children of Judaea:

13 **On the east three gates; on the north three gates; on the south three gates; and on the west three gates.**

14 **And the wall of the city had twelve foundations, and in them the names of the twelve apostles of the Lamb.**

15 **And he that talked with me had a golden reed to measure the city, and the gates thereof, and the wall thereof.**

16 **And the city lieth foursquare, and the length is as large as the breadth: and he measured the city with the reed, twelve thousand furlongs. The length and the breadth and the height of it are equal.**

17 **And he measured the wall thereof, a hundred and forty and four cubits, according to the measure of a man, that is, of the Messenger.**

18 **And the building of the wall of it was of jasper: and the city was pure gold, like unto clear glass.**

19 **And the foundations of the wall of the city were garnished with all manner of precious stones. The first foundation was jasper; the second, sapphire; the third, a chalcedony; the fourth, an emerald;**

20 **The fifth, sardonyx; the sixth, sardius; the seventh, chrysolyte; the eighth, beryl; the ninth, a topaz; the tenth, a chrysoprasus; the eleventh, a jacinth; the twelfth, anamethyst.**

21 **And the twelve gates were twelve pearls: every several gate was of one pearl: and the street of the city was pure gold, as it were transparent glass.**

22 **And I saw no House therein: for the Master Yahweh and the Lamb are the House of it.**

23 <u>And the city had no need of the sun, neither of the moon, to shine in it: for the righteousness of Yahweh did lighten it, and the Lamb is the light thereof.</u>

24 And the nations of them which are saved shall walk in the light of it: and the kings of the earth do bring their esteem and honour into it.

25 And the gates of it shall not be shut at all by day: for there shall be no night there.

26 And they shall bring the glory and honor of the nations into it.

27 And there shall in no wise enter into it any thing that defileth, neither whatsoever worketh abomination, or maketh a lie: but they which are written in the Lamb's book of life.

<u>REVELATION CHAPTER 22</u> A continuation of Chapter 21

22 And he shewed me a pure river of water of life, clear as crystal, proceeding out of the throne of Yahweh and of the Lamb.

2 In the midst of the street of it, and on either side of the river, was there the tree of life, which bare twelve manner of fruits, and yielded her fruit every month: and the leaves of the tree were for the healing of the nations.

3 And there shall be no more curse: but the throne of Yahweh and of the Lamb shall be in it; and his servants shall serve him:

4 <u>And they shall see his **face**</u>; and his name shall be in their foreheads.

5 And there shall be no night there; and they need no candle, neither light of the sun; for the Master Yahweh giveth them light: and they shall reign for ever and ever.

⁶ And he said unto me, These sayings are faithful and true: and the Master Yahweh of the righteous prophets sent his Messenger to shew unto his servants the things which must shortly be done.

⁷ Behold, I come quickly: blessed is he that keepeth the sayings of the prophecy of this book.

⁸ And I John saw these things, and heard them. And when I had heard and seen, <u>I fell down to worship before the feet of the Messenger which shewed me these things.</u>

⁹ <u>Then saith he unto me, See thou do it not: for I am thy fellowservant, and of thy brethren the prophets, and of them which keep the sayings of this book: worship Yahweh.</u>

¹⁰ And he saith unto me, Seal not the sayings of the prophecy of this book: for the time is at hand.

¹¹ He that is unjust, let him be unjust still: and he which is filthy, let him be filthy still: and he that is righteous, let him be righteous still: and he that is righteous, let him be righteous still.

HOLY REPLACED "RIGHTEOUS" IN MANY VERSES OF SCRIPTURE. SO THE ABOVE VERSE SHOWS THE TRUTH WITH THE ADDED LIE. HOLY COMES FROM PAGAN SUN WORSHIP.

¹² And, behold, I come quickly; and my reward is with me, to give every man according as his work shall be.

¹³ I am Alpha and Omega, the beginning and the end, the first and the last.

¹⁴ Blessed are they that do his commandments, that they may have right to the tree of life, and may enter in through the gates into the city.

¹⁵ For without are dogs, and sorcerers, and whoremongers, and murderers, and idolaters, and whosoever loveth and maketh a lie.

¹⁶ I Yahweh have sent mine Messenger to testify unto you these things in the assemblies. I am the root and the offspring of David, and the bright and morning star.

¹⁷ And the Spirit and the bride say, Come. And let him that heareth say, Come. And let him that is athirst come. And whosoever will, let him take the water of life freely.

¹⁸ For I testify unto every man that heareth the words of the prophecy of this book, If any man shall add unto these things, shall add unto him the plagues that are written in this book:

¹⁹ And if any man shall take away from the words of the book of this prophecy, Yahweh shall take away his part out of the book of life, and out of the righteous city, and from the things which are written in this book.

²⁰ He which testifieth these things saith, Surely I come quickly. Even so, come, Master Yahweh.

²¹ The Spirit of our Master Yahweh Messiah be with you all.

They added Amen at the end of the last 2 verses, which should not be there. It is a pagan sun deity name.

Revelation 19: 1-10 Marriage supper of the Lamb takes place on the New Earth.

1 And after these things I heard a great voice of much people in heaven, saying, Halleluyah; Salvation, and honor, and power, unto Yahweh our Mighty One:

2 For true and righteous are his judgments: for <u>He hath judged the great whore, which did corrupt the earth with her fornication, and hath avenged the blood of His servants at her hand.</u>

<u>**THIS IS THE ARMAGEDDON WAR WHEN ZION IS JUDGED.**</u>

3 And again they said, Halleluyah. <u>And her smoke rose up for ever and ever.</u>

4 And the four and twenty elders and the four beasts fell down and worshipped Yahweh that sat on the throne, saying, Halleluyah.

MARRIAGE SUPPER OF THE LAMB verses 5-7 – TAKES PLACE ON THE NEW EARTH NOT THIS ONE.

5 And a voice came out of the throne, saying, Praise our Yahweh, all ye His servants, and ye that fear him, both small and great.

6 And I heard as it were the voice of a great multitude, and as the voice of many waters, and as the voice of mighty thunderings, saying, Halleluyah: <u>for Yahweh Almighty omnipotent reigned.</u>

NOTICE IN THE LAST VERSE IT SAYS THAT HE REIGNED, SO THIS TAKES PLACE AFTER THE MILLENNIAL KINGDOM ON THE NEW EARTH. HIS WIFE IS NEW ZION IN BELOW VERSES.

7 Let us be glad and rejoice, and give honor to Him: for the marriage of the Lamb is come, and his wife hath made herself ready.

8 And to her was granted that she should be arrayed in fine linen, clean and white: for the fine linen is the righteousness of believers.

9 And he saith unto me, Write, Blessed are they which are called unto the marriage supper of the Lamb. And he saith unto me, These are the true sayings of Yahweh.

10 And I fell at his feet to worship him. And he said unto me, See thou do it not: I am thy fellow servant, and of thy brethren that have the testimony of Yahweh: worship Yahweh: for the testimony of Yahweh is the spirit of prophecy.

1 Corinthians 2: 9

"But as it is written, Eye hath not seen, nor ear heard, neither have entered into the heart of man, **the things which Yahweh hath prepared for them that love him.**"

The word "**deceive**" appears 500 **times** in scripture. The word "**deceived**" is used **70 times** in the scriptures. **You have been warned many times, far too many have ignored those warnings.**

Matthew 24: 24

For there shall arise false Christs/**Messiahs, and false prophets, and shall show great signs and wonders;** insomuch that, **if it were possible, they shall** deceive the very elect.

It is not possible with the infilling of Yahweh's Spirit, which is what gives a person salvation.

Matthew 22: 29

Jesus/**Immanuel** answered them, "**You are deceived, because you don't know the Scriptures or the power of God/Yahweh.**

Will people be married on the new earth?

Luke 20: 27-40

27 Then came to him certain of the Sadducees, **which deny that there is any resurrection;** and they asked him,

28 Saying, Master, Moses wrote unto us, If any man's brother die, having a wife, and he die without children, that his brother should take his wife, and raise up seed unto his brother.

29 There were therefore seven brethren: and the first took a wife, and died without children.

30 And the second took her to wife, and he died childless.

31 And the third took her; and in like manner the seven also: and they left no children, and died.

32 Last of all the woman died also.

33 Therefore in the resurrection whose wife of them is she? for seven had her to wife.

34 And Immanuel answering said unto them, the children of this world marry, and are given in marriage:

35 But they which shall be accounted worthy to obtain that world, and the resurrection from the dead, neither marry, nor are given in marriage:

36 Neither can they die any more: for they are equal unto the Messengers; and **are the children of Yahweh,** being <u>**the children of the resurrection**</u>.

37 Now that the dead are raised, even Moses shewed at the bush, when he calleth the Lord/**Yahweh** the God/**MIGHTY ONE** of Abraham, and the God/**MIGHTY ONE** of Isaac, and the God/**MIGHTY ONE** of Jacob.

38 For he is not a God/**MIGHTY ONE** of the dead, but of the living: for all live unto him.

39 Then certain of the scribes answering said, Master, thou hast well said.

40 And after that they durst not ask him any question at all.

Matthew 22: 30 For in the resurrection <u>they neither marry, nor are given in marriage,</u> **but are as the angels/ Messengers of God/Yahweh in heaven.**

CHAPTER 5

THE SHROUD OF TURAN IS A FAKE!

A.   THE DESCRIPTION OF IMMANUEL:

Isaiah 53: 2

For He shall grow up before Him as a tender plant, and as a root out of a dry ground. **He hath no form nor comeliness**, and <u>**when we shall see Him, there is no beauty that we should desire Him.**</u>

I Corinthians 11: 14

Doth not even nature itself teach you, that, <u>**if a man have long hair, it is a shame unto him?**</u>

<u>**The Roman spearend was almost 2 feet long and over**</u> 7mm = almost 9/32 inch (= **a bit over 1/4 inch)**

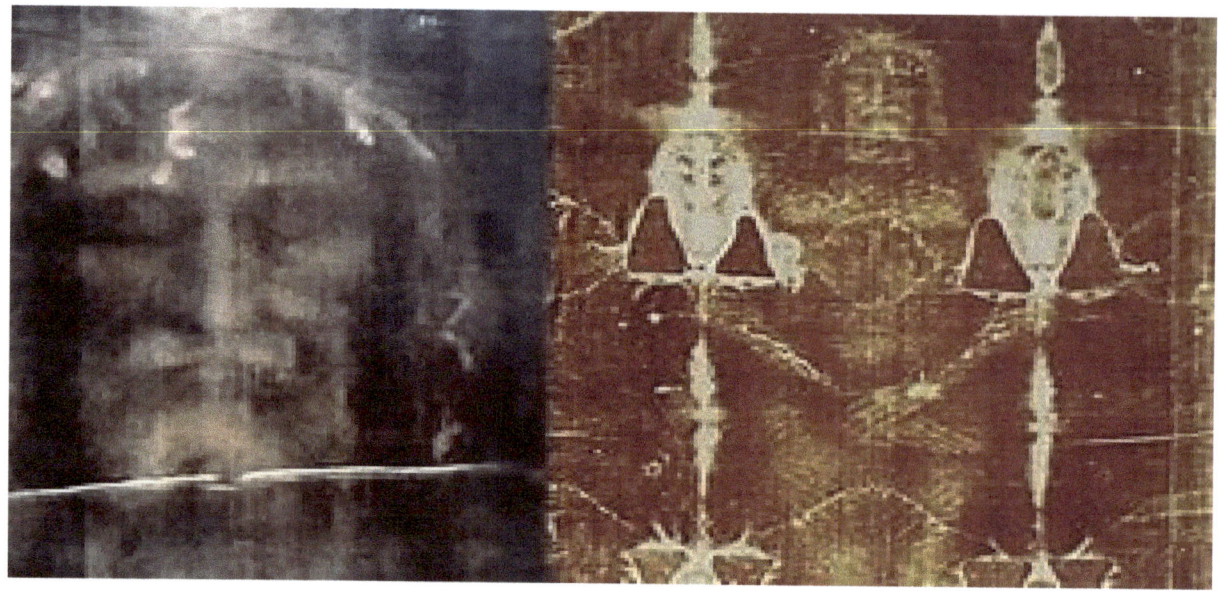

The image of the face has long hair and a beard. The body has curvatures as being muscular. Compare the picture of Zeus/Jupiter to the shroud. Like below:

Isaiah 50: 6

I gave My back to those who struck *Me*, **And My cheeks to those who plucked out the beard;** I did not hide My face from shame and spitting. Looks like the same physic.

IMMANUEL DIED ON A REAL TREE: NO NAILS WERE USED, SO NO NAIL HOLES IN HANDS, OR IN THE FEET, how did they get on the shroud when none ever existed? **THIS PROVES THE SHROUD IS A SATANIC LIE. SPEAR WOUND YES.**

Yet they say the shroud shows the nail holes in the hands and feet.

King James Version

ISAIAH 52: 14 14 As many were astonished at thee; **his visage was so marred more than any man, and his form more than the sons of men:**

New International Version

14 Just as there were many who were appalled at him — **his appearance was so disfigured beyond that of any human being and his form marred beyond human likeness—**

New Living Translation

14 But many were amazed when they saw him. His face was so disfigured he seemed hardly human, and from his appearance, one would scarcely know he was a man.

Good News Translation

14 **Many people were shocked when they saw him; he was so disfigured that he hardly looked human.**

Isaiah 50: 6

I gave my back to the smiters, and my cheeks to them that plucked off the hair: I hid not my face from shame and spitting.

Isaiah 53: 2 For he shall grow up before him as a tender plant, and as a root out of a dry ground: **he hath no form nor comeliness;** and when we shall see him, there is no beauty that we should desire him.

The shroud image is muscular. Immanuel was skinny without form, which again proves that the shroud is a fake.

THE SHROUD LOOKS LIKE A HUMAN, SO ANOTHER PROOF OF THE SHROUD BEING FAKE.

Deuteronomy 21: 22-23

22 And if a man have committed a sin/**TRANSGRESSION** worthy of death, and he be to be put to death, and thou **hang him on a tree:**

23 His body shall not remain all night upon the tree, but thou shalt in any wise bury him that day; for he that is hanged is accursed of Yahweh; that thy land be not defiled, which Yahweh giveth thee for an inheritance.

Acts 5: 30

Yahweh of our fathers raised up Immanuel, whom ye slew and hanged on a tree.

Acts 10: 39

And we are witnesses of all things which he did both in the land of the Jews, and in Zion; whom they slew and **hanged on a tree.**

Acts 13: 30

And **when they had fulfilled all that was written of him, they took him down from the tree**, and laid him in a sepulcher.

1 Peter 2: 24

Who his own self bare our transgressions in his own body on the tree, that we, being dead to transgressions, should live unto righteousness: by whose stripes ye were healed.

Galatians 3: 13

Yahweh hath redeemed us from the curse of the law, being made a curse for us: for it is written, **Cursed is every one that hangeth on a tree.**

John 19: 31-33

31. Then the Jews, because it was the day of preparation, so **THAT THE BODIES WOULD NOT REMAIN ON THE TREE** on the Sabbath (for that Sabbath was a high [SPECIAL] day), asked Pilate that their legs might be broken, and that they might be taken away.

Notice the bodies, plural; would not remain on the tree, singular. Now notice, it would be which way the soldiers went around the tree with who would have been next in line........to have the leg broken.

32. So the soldiers came, and broke the legs of the **first man and of the other who was killed with him**;

33. but coming to Immanuel, when they saw that he was already dead, they did not break his legs....

John 19: 18

Where **they killed him, and two others with him**, one on either side, and **Immanuel in the midst**.

Why didn't the soldiers go right down the line? If there were 3 different trees, or by Christian standards, Crosses. Because there was only one tree.

Mark 15: 27

And **with him they killed two thieves**; the **one on his right hand, and the other on his left**.

Luke 23: 29

29. For, behold, the days are coming, in the which they shall say, Blessed are the barren, and the wombs that never bare, and the paps which never gave suck.

[This is what's being said today.]

30. Then shall they begin to say to the mountains, Fall on us; and to the hills, Cover us.

[What people will say at Yahweh's return.]

31. For if they do these things in a green tree, what shall be done in the dry?

[Notice how he used a GREEN TREE when talking about the present back then and a dry when there would be no salvation. In other words, he was saying if they are doing this with him there and the coming of salvation, what will people do when there is no salvation given. We are seeing what's happening in the world today without salvation, and it's only going to get worse.]

32. And there were also two other, malefactors, led with him to be put to death.

They killed him and the malefactors, one on the right hand and the other on the left.

NOTE: All 3 were hung by their wrists from the same tree. There were not 3 different ones, but the same tree. Otherwise, the above scripture would have said, **"That the BODIES should not remain upon THE TREE."** It would have been plural TREES if they all were hung on different trees, but they were all on the same tree.

In verse 32 of the above verses, it says the soldiers came and **break the legs of the first and the other, which was KILLED WITH HIM**.

Matthew 27: 38

Then were there two thieves KILLED WITH HIM, one on the right hand, and another on the left.

NOTE: Nails in hands and feet are a lie.

THIS HAPPENED ON A REAL LIVE OLIVE TREE.

With the pagan word CROSS put into the scriptures, it makes it look like the scriptures teach that they all died on 3 different crosses, and the Messiah would have been on the middle one. Yet the centurion, instead of going down the line from left to right or right to left, breaking the legs, goes and breaks the legs of one of the thieves, then passes the middle cross that the Messiah was supposedly to be on and breaks the legs of the second thief, then returns to the middle cross and the Messiah was already dead, and did not break his legs. When you put the true word TREE, then it makes sense how that it was just one tree and not 3 of them. It would depend on what direction around the tree the centurion went for him to come to the Messiah, who did not have his leg broken. He was already dead, which proves that his beating was more severe than theirs.

X X X

USE THESE X'S TO REPRESENT EACH ONE OF THEM, HANGING ON THE SAME TREE. THE MIDDLE X IS THE MESSIAH SINCE ONE WAS ON HIS LEFT AND ONE ON HIS RIGHT, SO IMAGINE A TREE THEY ARE HANGING FROM, FROM THE WRISTS TIED WITH ROPE. DO YOU SEE HOW HE COULD HAVE ENDED UP WITH THE MESSIAH AS THE LAST ONE, NO MATTER WHICH DIRECTION HE WENT AROUND THE TREE? THE WAY HE WENT TO THE LEFT OR RIGHT AS LONG AS HE STARTED WITH ONE OF THE THIEVES ON EACH SIDE OF HIM TO END UP WITH THE MESSIAH AS THE LAST ONE. IF HE HAD STARTED WITH THE THIEF ON THE LEFT SIDE, HE WOULD HAVE GONE

TO HIS LEFT. IF HE HAD STARTED WITH THE ONE ON HIS RIGHT SIDE, HE WOULD HAVE GONE TO HIS RIGHT. BECAUSE HE STARTED FROM ONE OF HIS SIDES, HE HAD TO WALK BEHIND WHERE THE MESSIAH HUNG ON THE TREE.

Note: The Messiah was killed on the Mount of Olives, so there must have been plenty of Olive trees for the Mount of Olives to be named that. Josephus relates that Titus cut down all the trees in the besiege of Jerusalem in 70 A.D.

IT IS SAID that a Roman CROSS weighed 300 plus pounds. Which one person could never have dragged through the streets of Zion, as so many Christian pictures depict. Then others say it was the cross beam to the CROSS. IT IS SAID, weighed 100 to 145 pounds. Only a physically fit person could carry that for any length of time. You must remember he was severely beaten, and other things were done to him which would make it physically impossible for him to carry a cross beam. Even with his physical stature, he would not be able to carry it. He was beaten within an inch of his life and then hung by his wrists to finish the job. What was used, though, was some type of wood piece, a yoke that would have kept them from running off. and their arms were probably tied to it so a person could not escape, and it would wear a person out so that by the time they got to Golgotha they would be too worn out to even put up a fight. As scriptures show someone had to carry it for Immanuel because he was too weak and battered to even carry it very far.

Verses below where they exchanged the true word with Cross to show the deceit.

Galatians 5: 11

And I, brethren, if I yet preach/teach circumcision, why do I yet suffer persecution? then is the offence of the cross/ **LAW ceased.**

Colossians 2: 14

Blotting out the handwriting of ordinances that was against us, which was contrary to us, and took it out of the way, nailing it to his cross / **TREE;**

Colossians 1: 20

And, having made peace through the blood of his cross / **FLESH**, by him to reconcile all things unto himself; by him, I say, whether they be things in earth, or things in heaven.

KILLED ON AN OLIVE TREE....

PSALMS 52: 8

But I am like a green olive tree in the 'House of YAHWEH': I trust in the mercy and faithfulness of YAHWEH forever and ever.

...was not nailed, SO NO NAIL HOLES IN the HANDS OR FEET.used rope and strips of cloth were used, and the only piercing that he had was from the spear. Just another Roman lie.

Zechariah-12:10

And I will pour upon the house of **David**, and upon the inhabitants of Jerusalem/**Zion**, the spirit of grace/**PRAYER** and of supplications: and **they shall look upon me whom they have pierced**, and they shall mourn for him, as one mourneth for his only son, and shall be in bitterness for him, as one that is in bitterness for his firstborn.

Luke 23: 53

"And he took it down, and wrapped it in linen, and laid it in a sepulcher that was hewn in stone, wherein never man before was laid."

John 20: 3-8

3 Peter therefore went forth, and that other disciple, and came to the sepulchre.

4 So they ran both together: and the other disciple did outrun Peter, and came first to the sepulchre.

5 And he stooping down, *and looking in,* saw the linen clothes lying; yet went he not in.

6 Then cometh Simon Peter following him, and went into the sepulchre, and seeth the linen clothes lie,

7 And the napkin, that was about his head, not lying with the linen clothes, but wrapped together in a place by itself.

8 Then went in also that other disciple, which came first to the sepulcher, and he saw, and believed.

A facecloth was placed over Immanuel's' face before the other linen cloths would have been wrapped over the outside.

On a comparison with the account of Immanuel raising Lazarus from the dead. People had to unwrap Lazarus.

John 11: 43-44

43 **And when he thus had spoken, he cried with a loud voice,** Lazarus, come forth.

44 And **he that was dead came forth, bound hand and foot with graveclothes: and his face was bound about with a napkin. Immanuel said saith unto them, loose him, and let him go.**

CHAPTER 6

PROPER WAY THEY BAPTIZED:

Baptism does a person no good today since this is fully Satan's world and with no salvation.

*He was baptized and **went up straightway out of the water**:*

And straightway coming up out of the water,

They go down into the water deep enough that when the person goes down into the fetal position, the person will be completely covered with water. The one who baptizes holds one hand of the one being baptized for balance and the other on the back between shoulder blades. Then, as the baptism is started, the hand on the back goes to the top of the head, so when the person is baptized, they will know when they are completely under the water. The baptized person goes down into the fetal position and is then baptized in the name of Yahweh, since He is the Father, Son and Spirit. The one who did the baptism then took his hand and slid it off the head to the back between shoulder blades for support, and the person being baptized then knew to come up straightway out of the water. They used to bury people in the fetal position.

The way Christianity does baptism by laying the person back into the water and submersing them is wrong anyway. One person could not baptize another person that was a lot bigger than the baptizer. That is when they in Christianity use two people to do a baptism. Can you imagine one or even two people baptizing a Sumo wrestler? No wonder Catholics came up with sprinkling. When it was done the right way, it did not matter how big a person was because they go under and back up, with their own power. One person only was needed to baptize a person, like John the Baptist did all those that he had done by himself.

Matthew 3: 13-17

*Then cometh Immanuel from Galilee to Jordan unto John, to be baptized of him. But John forbade him, saying, I have need to be baptized of thee, and comest thou to me? And Immanuel answering said unto him, Suffer it to be so now: for thus it becometh us to fulfill all righteousness. Then he suffered him. And Immanuel, when he was baptized, **went up straightway out of the water**: and, lo, the heavens were opened unto him, and **he saw the Spirit of Yahweh descending like a dove, and lighting upon him**: And lo a voice from heaven, saying, This is my beloved Son, in whom I am well pleased.*

Mark 1: 9-11

*And it came to pass in those days, that **Immanuel came from Nazareth of Galilee,** and was baptized of John in Jordan. **And straightway coming up out of the water**, he saw the heavens opened, and **the Spirit like a dove descending upon him**: And there came a voice from heaven, saying, Thou art my beloved Son, in whom I am well pleased."*

Luke 3: 21, 22

*Now when all the people were baptized, it came to pass, that **Immanuel also being baptized, and praying**, the heaven was opened, And **the Spirit descended in a bodily shape like a dove upon him**, and a voice came from heaven, which said, Thou art my beloved Son; in thee I am well pleased.*

John 1: 29-33

The next day John seeth Immanuel coming unto him, and saith, **Behold the Lamb of Yahweh, which taketh away the transgressions of the world.** *This is he of whom I said, After me cometh a man which is preferred before me: for he was before me. And I knew him not: but that he should be made manifest to Judaea, therefore am I come baptizing with water. And John bare record, saying,* **I saw the Spirit descending from heaven like a dove, and it abode upon him. And I knew him not: but he that sent me to baptize with water, the same said unto me, Upon whom thou shalt see the Spirit descending, and remaining on him, the same is he which baptizeth with the Spirit.**

Mark 1: 4, 5

John did baptize in the wilderness, and taught **the baptism of repentance for the remission of transgressions**. *And there went out unto him all the land of Judaea, and they of Zion, and were all* **baptized of him in the river of Jordan**, **confessing their transgressions**.

Mark 16: 16

He that believeth and is baptized shall be saved; but he that believeth not shall be damned.

Water baptism does not save you, but the baptism of the Spirit infilling does. No one today is Spirit-filled.

Acts 2: 33

Therefore being exalted to the right hand of Yahweh, and having received from the Father the promise of the Spirit, He poured out this which you now see and hear.

Acts 2: 38

Then Peter said unto them, **_Repent, and be baptized every one of you in the name of Yahweh Messiah for the remission of transgressions, and ye shall receive the gift of the Spirit._**

Acts 8: 35-38

Then Philip opened his mouth, and began at the same scripture, and preached unto him Yahweh. And as they went on their way, they came unto a certain water: and the **_eunuch said, See, here is water; what doth hinder me to be baptized? And Philip said, If thou believest with all thine heart, thou mayest._** *And he answered and said,* **_I believe that Yahweh Messiah is the Son of Yahweh_**. *And he commanded the chariot to stand still: and* **_they went down both into the water, both Philip and the eunuch; and he baptized him_**.

Acts 16: 31, 33

And they said, **_Believe on Yahweh, and thou shalt be saved, and thy house_**. *And* **_he took them the same hour of the night, and washed their stripes; and was baptized, he and all his, straightway._**

The meaning of Baptism to the believer.

Romans 6: 3-6

Know ye not, that so many of us as were baptized into Yahweh Messiah were baptized into his death? Therefore we are buried with him by baptism into death: that like as Yahweh was raised up from the dead by the Spirit of the Father, even so we also should walk in newness of life. For if we have been planted together in the likeness of his death, we shall be also in the likeness of his resurrection: *Knowing this,* **_that our old man is killed with him, that the body of transgression might be destroyed, that henceforth we should not serve transgression._**

1 Corinthians 12: 13

For by one Spirit are we all baptized into one body, whether we be Jews or Gentiles, whether we be bond or free; and have been all made to drink into one Spirit. (Spirit Infilling)

Galatians 3: 27

For as many of you as have been baptized into the Messiah have put on the Messiah.

1 Peter 3: 21

The like figure whereunto even baptism doth also now save us (not the putting away of the filth of the flesh, but the answer of a good conscience toward Yahweh,) by the resurrection of Yahweh Messiah.

Water baptism does not save a person. The baptism of the Spirit infilling is what saves you for your redemption. It is Yahweh's Seal.

Matthew 3: 16

And Immanuel, when he was baptized, went up straightway out of the water: and, lo, the heavens were opened unto him, and he saw the Spirit of Yahweh descending like a dove, and lighting upon him:

NOTE: By Christian standards, the one they call Jesus in their belief system, they have to believe he was baptized in his own birth-given name. But scriptures teach everything was done in the Father's name, even baptisms, and why the son inherited the Father's name, and why He became Yahweh in the Flesh. So, no matter what you think the birth-given name was, it has nothing to do with salvation or baptisms.

Matthew 28: 19

Go ye therefore, and teach all nations, **baptizing them in the name of the Father, and of the Son, and of the Spirit:**

Note: (Yahweh is the name)

Acts 2: 38

Peter replied, "**Repent and be baptized, every one of you, in the name of Yahweh** for the forgiveness of your transgressions. And you will receive the gift of the Spirit.

Acts 8: 16

(For as yet he was fallen upon none of them: only **they were baptized in the name of Yahweh**.)

Acts 10: 48

So **he ordered that they be baptized in the name of Yahweh**. Then they asked Peter to stay with them for a few days.

Acts 19: 5

On hearing this, **they were baptized in the name of the Yahweh**.

Romans 6: 3

Or don't you know that all of us **who were baptized into Yahweh** were baptized into his death?

CHAPTER 7
TITHING IS NOT FOR TODAY

Yahweh not only did away with the Levite priesthood, animal offerings, and what we call Judaism but also tithing.

When did tithing start? It was paid by Abraham to Melchizedek.

Genesis 14: 18-20

18: And Melchizedek king of Salem brought forth bread and wine: and he was the priest of the most high Yahweh.

19: And he blessed him, and said, Blessed be Abram of the most high Yahweh, possessor of heaven and earth:

20: And blessed be the most high Yahweh, which hath delivered thine enemies into thy hand. And he gave him tithes of all.

Jacob vows a tenth of all his property to Yahweh.

Genesis 28: 20-22

20: And Jacob vowed a vow, saying, If Yahweh will be with me, and will keep me in this way that I go, and will give me bread to eat, and raiment to put on,

21: So that I come again to my father's house in peace; then shall Yahweh be my Mighty One.

22: And this stone, which I have set for a pillar, shall be Yahweh's house: and of all that thou shalt give me I will surely give the tenth unto thee.

Yahweh made tithing a law and commandment for the children of Judaea. You can see this in the following chapters and verses.

Leviticus 26: 46

46: These are the statutes and judgments and laws, which Yahweh made between him and the children of Israel in mount Sinai by the hand of Moses.

Lev. 27: 1, 30-34

1: And Yahweh spake unto Moses, saying,

30: And all the tithe of the land, whether of the seed of the land, or of the fruit of the tree, is Yahweh's: it is holy unto Yahweh.

31: And if a man will at all redeem ought of his tithes, he shall add thereto the fifth part thereof.

32: And concerning the tithe of the herd, or of the flock, even of whatsoever passeth under the rod, the tenth shall be set apart unto Yahweh.

33: He shall not search whether it be good or bad, neither shall he change it: and if he change it at all, then both it and the change thereof shall be set apart; it shall not be redeemed.

34: These are the commandments, which Yahweh commanded Moses for the children of Israel in mount Sinai.

Tithes given to Levites for inheritance.

Num. 18: 21-26

21: And, behold, I have given the children of Levi all the tenth in Israel for an inheritance, for their service which they serve, even the service of the tabernacle of the congregation.

22: Neither must the children of Israel henceforth come nigh the tabernacle of the congregation, lest they bear transgression, and die.

23: But the Levites shall do the service of the tabernacle of the congregation, and they shall bear their iniquity: it shall be a statute forever throughout your generations, that among the children of Israel they have no inheritance.

24: But the tithes of the children of Judaea, which they offer as a heave offering unto Yahweh, I have given to the Levites to inherit therefore, I have said unto them, Among the children of Judaea they shall have no inheritance.

25: And Yahweh spake unto Moses, saying,

26: Thus speak unto the Levites, and say unto them, When ye take of the children of Israel the tithes which I have given you from them for your inheritance, then ye shall offer up an heave offering of it for Yahweh, even a tenth part of the tithe.

Deut. 12: 5-6

5: But unto the place which Yahweh shall choose out of all your tribes to put his name there, even unto his habitation shall ye seek, and thither thou shalt come.

6: And thither ye shall bring your burnt offerings, and your sacrifices, and your tithes, and heave offerings of your hand, and your vows, and your freewill offerings, and the firstlings of your herds and of your flocks.

Deut. 14: 22-29

22: Thou shalt truly tithe all the increase of thy seed, that the field bringeth forth year by year.

23: And thou shalt eat before Yahweh, in the place which he shall choose to place his name there, the tithe of thy corn, of thy wine, and of thine oil, and the firstlings of thy herds and of thy flocks; that thou mayest learn to fear Yahweh always.

24: And if the way be too long for thee, so that thou art not able to carry it; or if the place be too far from thee, which Yahweh shall choose to set his name there, when Yahweh hath blessed thee:

25: Then shalt thou turn it into money, and bind up the money in thine hand, and shalt go unto the place which Yahweh thy Almighty shall choose:

26: And thou shalt bestow that money for whatsoever thy soul lusteth after, for oxen or for sheep, or for wine, or for strong drink, or for whatsoever thy soul desireth: and thou shalt eat there before Yahweh thy Almighty, and thou shalt rejoice, thou, and thine household,

27: And the Levite that is within thy gates; thou shalt not forsake him; for he hath no part nor inheritance with thee.

28: At the end of three years thou shalt bring forth all the tithe of thine increase the same year, and shalt lay it up within thy gates:

29: And the Levite, (because he hath no part nor inheritance with thee,) and the stranger, and the fatherless, and the widow, which are within thy gates, shall come, and shall eat and be satisfied; that Yahweh thy Almighty may bless thee in all the work of thine hand which thou doest.

Deut. 26: 12-14

12: When thou hast made an end of tithing all the tithes of thine increase the third year, which is the year of tithing, and hast given it unto the Levite, the stranger, the fatherless, and the widow, that they may eat within thy gates, and be filled;

13: Then thou shalt say before Yahweh, I have brought away the hallowed things out of mine house, and also have given them unto the Levite, and unto the stranger, to the fatherless, and to the widow, according to all thy commandments which thou hast commanded me: I have not transgressed thy commandments, neither have I forgotten them:

14: I have not eaten thereof in my mourning, neither have I taken away ought thereof for any unclean use, nor given ought thereof for the dead: but I have hearkened to the voice of Yahweh, and have done according to all that thou hast commanded me.

Neh. 10: 34-39

34: And we cast the lots among the priests, the Levites, and the people, for the wood offering, to bring it into the house of Yahweh, after the houses of our fathers, at times appointed year by year, to burn upon the table of Yahweh, as it is written in the law:

35: And to bring the firstfruits of our ground, and the firstfruits of all fruit of all trees, year by year, unto the House of Yahweh:

36: Also the firstborn of our sons, and of our cattle, as it is written in the law, and the firstlings of our herds and of our flocks to bring to the House of Yahweh, unto the priests that minister in the House of Yahweh.

37: And that we should bring the firstfruits of our dough, and our offerings, and the fruit of all manner of trees, of wine and of oil, unto the priests, to the chambers of the house of Yahweh; and the tithes of our ground unto the Levites, that the same Levites might have the tithes in all the cities of our tillage.

38: And the priest the son of Aaron shall be with the Levites, when the Levites take tithes: and the Levites shall bring up the tithe of the tithes unto the House of Yahweh, to the chambers, into the treasure house.

39: For the children of Judaea and the children of Levi shall bring the offering of the corn, of the new wine, and the oil, unto the chambers, where are the vessels of the sanctuary, and the priests that teach, and the porters, and the singers: and we will not forsake the House of Yahweh.

Notice here in the next verses, that Yahweh is speaking to the children of Judaea.

Malachi 3: 6-7

6: For I am Yahweh, I change not; therefore ye sons of Jacob are not consumed.

7: Even from the days of your fathers ye are gone away from mine ordinances, and have not kept them. Return unto me, and I will return unto you, saith Yahweh of hosts. But ye said, Wherein shall we return?

You will find many preachers quoting the following scriptures to make you think tithing is for today. These are the most favorite scriptures they use from the Old Covenant. In the name of Lord and God though not Yahweh's name.

Malachi 3: 8-10

8: Will a man rob Yahweh? Yet ye have robbed me. But ye say, Wherein have we robbed thee? In tithes and offerings.

9: Ye are cursed with a curse: for ye have robbed me, even this whole nation.

10: Bring ye all the tithes into the storehouse, that there may be meat in mine house, and prove me now herewith, saith Yahweh of hosts, if I will not open you the windows of heaven, and pour you out a blessing, that there shall not be room enough to receive it.

You see, if you miss just one tithe, then you are a thief and a robber. The Messiah came to give a better way in the New Covenant.

Let us now go to the New Covenant.

Matt. 23: 23

23: Woe unto you, scribes and Pharisees, hypocrites! For ye pay tithe of mint and anise and cummin, and have omitted the weightier matters of the law, judgment, mercy, and faith: these ought ye to have done, and not to leave the other undone.

Luke 11: 42

42: But woe unto you, Pharisees! For ye tithe mint and rue and all manner of herbs, and pass over judgment and the love of Yahweh: these ought ye to have done, and not to leave the other undone.

Luke 18: 9-14

9: And he spake this parable unto certain which trusted in themselves that they were righteous, and despised others:

10: Two men went up into the temple to pray; the one a Pharisee, and the other a publican.

11: The Pharisee stood and prayed thus with himself, Yahweh, I thank thee, that I am not as other men are, extortioners, unjust, adulterers, or even as this publican.

12: I fast twice in the week, I give tithes of all that I possess.

13: And the publican, standing afar off, would not lift up so much as his eyes unto heaven, but smote upon his breast, saying, Yahweh be merciful to me a transgressor.

14: I tell you, this man went down to his house justified rather than the other: for everyone that exalteth himself shall be abased; and he that humbleth himself shall be exalted.

In this chapter of Hebrews, it speaks of the law of tithes. The Levites were the only ones allowed to collect tithes. After the destruction of the House of Yahweh there was no more need for the Levites. The Levites will be reinstituted during the Millennium.

Hebrews 7: 1-28

1: For this Melchisedec, king of Salem, priest of the most high Yahweh, who met Abraham returning from the slaughter of the kings, and blessed him;

2: To whom also Abraham gave a tenth part of all; first being by interpretation King of righteousness, and after that also King of Salem, which is King of peace;

3: Without father, without mother, without descent, having neither beginning of days, nor end of life; but made like unto the Son of Yahweh; abideth a priest continually.

4: Now consider how great this man was, unto whom even the patriarch Abraham gave the tenth of the spoils.

5: And verily they that are of the sons of Levi, who receive the office of the priesthood, have a commandment to take tithes of the people according to the law, that is, of their brethren, though they come out of the loins of Abraham:

6: But he whose descent is not counted from them received tithes of Abraham, and blessed him that had the promises.

7: And without all contradiction the less is blessed of the better.

8: And here men that die receive tithes; but there he receiveth them, of whom it is witnessed that he liveth.

9: And as I may so say, Levi also, who receiveth tithes, paid tithes in Abraham.

10: For he was yet in the loins of his father, when Melchisedec met him.

11: If therefore perfection were by the Levitical priesthood, (for under it the people received the law,) what further need was there that another priest should rise after the order of Melchisedec, and not be called after the order of Aaron?

12: For the priesthood being changed, there is made of necessity a change also of the law.

13: For he of whom these things are spoken pertaineth to another tribe, of which no man gave attendance of the table.

14: For it is evident that Yahweh sprang out of Juda; of which tribe Moses spake nothing concerning priesthood.

15: And it is yet far more evident: for that after the similitude of Melchisedec there ariseth another priest,

16: Who is made, not after the law of a carnal commandment, but after the power of an endless life.

17: For he testifieth, Thou art a priest forever after the order of Melchisedec.

18: For there is verily a disannulling of the commandment going before for the weakness and unprofitableness thereof.

19: For the law made nothing perfect, but the bringing in of a better hope did; by the which we draw nigh unto Yahweh.

20: And inasmuch as not without an oath he was made priest:

21: (For those priests were made without an oath; but this with an oath by him that said unto him, Yahweh swear and will not repent, thou art a priest forever after the order of Melchisedec: 0

22: By so much was Immanuel made a surety of a better convenant.

23: And they truly were many priests, because they were not suffered to continue by reason of death:

24: But this man, because he continueth ever, hath and unchangeable priesthood.

25: Wherefore he is able also to save them to the uttermost that come unto Yahweh by him, seeing he ever liveth to make intercession for them.

26: For such an high priest became us, who is righteous, harmless, undefiled, separate from transgressors, and made higher than the heavens;

27: Who needeth not daily,as those high priests, to offer up sacrifice, first for his own transgressions, and then for the people's: for this he did once, when he offered up himself.

28: For the law maketh men high priests which have infirmity; but the word of the oath, which was since the law, maketh the Son, who is consecrated forevermore.

Another scripture that preachers use for tithing has nothing to do with tithing. I'll prove how it fits in with its own context of scriptures.

This is the scripture they use:

1 Cor. 16: 1-2

1: Now concerning the collection for the elect, as I have given order to the assemblies of Galatia, even so do ye.

2: Upon the first day of the week let every one of you lay by him in store, as Yahweh hath prospered him, that there be no gatherings when I come.

Let's see what Paul is actually talking about here and also putting the above scripture in the context where it rightfully belongs.

Acts 11: 27-30

27: And in these days came prophets from Zion unto Antioch.

28: And there stood up one of them named Agabus, and signified by the Spirit that there should be great dearth throughout all the world: which came to pass in the days of Claudius Caesar.

29: Then the disciples, every man according to his ability, determined to send relief unto the brethren which dwelt in Judaea:

30: Which also they did, and sent it to the elders<<assemblies by the hands of Barnabas and Saul.

1 Cor. 16: 1-5

1: Now concerning the collection for the elect, as I have given order to the assemblies of Galatia, even so do ye.

2: Upon the first day of the week let every one of you lay by him in store, as Yahweh hath prospered him, that there be no gatherings when I come.

3: And when I come, whomsoever ye shall approve by your letters, them will I send to bring your liberality unto Zion.

4: And if it be meet that I go also, they shall go with me.

5: Now I will come unto you, when I shall pass through Macedonia: for I do pass through Macedonia.

2 Cor. 8: 1-24

1: Moreover, brethren, we do you to wit of the grace<<riches of Yahweh bestowed on the assemblies of Macedonia;

2: How that in a great trial of affliction the abundance of their joy and their deep poverty abounded unto the riches of the liberality.

3: For to their power, I bear record, yea, and beyond their power they were willing of themselves;

4: Praying us with much entreaty that we would receive the gift, and take upon us the fellowship of the ministering to the saints<<Elect.

5: And this they did, not as we hoped, but first gave their own selves to Yahweh, and unto us by the will of Yahweh.

6: Insomuch that we desired Titus, that as he had begun so he would also finish in you the same grace<<riches also.

7: Therefore, as ye abound in everything, in faith, and utterance, and knowledge, and in all diligence, and in your love to us, see that ye abound in this grace also.

8: I speak not by commandment, but by occasion of the forwardness of others, and to prove the sincerity of your love.

9: For ye know the grace of our Master, Yahweh the Messiah, that, though he was rich, yet for your sakes he became poor, that ye through his poverty might be rich.

10: And herein I give my advice: for this is expedient for you, who have begun before, not only to do, but also to be forward a year ago.

11: Now therefore perform the doing of it; that as there was a readiness to will, so there may be a performance also out of that which ye have.

12: For if there be first a willing mind, it is accepted according to that a man hath, and not according to that he hath not.

13: For I mean not that other men be eased, and ye burdened:

14: But by an equality, that now at this time your abundance may be a supply for their want, that their abundance also may be a supply for your want: that there may be equality:

15: As it is written, He that had gathered much had nothing over; and he that had gathered little had no lack.

16: But thanks be to Yahweh, which put the same earnest care into the heart of Titus for you.

17: For indeed he accepted the exhortation; but being more forward, of his own accord he went unto you.

18: And we have sent with him the brother, whose praise is in the word throughout all the assemblies;

19: And not that only, but who was also chosen of the assemblies to travel with us with this grace<<gift, which is administered by us to the esteem of Yahweh, and declaration of your ready mind:

20: Avoiding this, that no man should blame us in this abundance which is administered by us:

21: Providing for honest things, not only in the sight of Yahweh, but also in the sight of men.

22: And we have sent with them our brother, whom we have oftentimes proved diligent in many things, but now much more diligent, upon the great confidence which I have in you.

23: Whether any do enquire of Titus, he is my partner and fellow helper concerning you: or our brethren be enquired of, they are the messengers of the assemblies, and the esteem of Yahweh.

24: Wherefore show ye to them, and before the assemblies, the proof of your love, and of our boasting on your behalf.

You should be able to see by now that the scriptures prove tithing was for the children of Judaea. It is not for the New Covenant. <<Yahweh<< gave people a better way, which will be proven also by scripture.

If tithing was really for today like preachers say, why aren't people giving a tenth of ALL their first fruits like the law of tithing says? By the law only, the Levites were allowed to accept tithes from the people. That being the law, then these pastors who teach tithing must be Levites because they accept tithes from the people. Why don't they all have farms to store all the first fruits? They tell you today it is all money. The Levites lost their job with the destruction of the House of Yahweh.

Let us go back to the scriptures and find what the Messiah taught instead of tithing from his people.

1 John 3: 17-18

17: But whoso hath this world's good, and seeth his brother have need, and shutteth up his bowels of compassion from him, how dwelleth the love of Yahweh in him?

18: My little children, let us not love in word, neither in tongue; but in deed and in truth.

Matt. 6: 1-4

1: Take heed that ye do not your alms before men, to be seen of them: otherwise ye have no reward of your Father which is in heaven.

2: Therefore when thou doest thine alms, do not sound a trumpet before thee, as the hypocrites do in the synagogues and in the streets, that they may have praise of men. Verily I say unto you, They have their reward.

3: But when thou doest alms, let not thy left hand know what thy right hand doeth:

4: That thin alms may be in secret: and thy Father which seeth in secret himself shall reward thee openly.

Romans 12: 8

8: Or he that exhorteth, on exhortation: he that giveth, let him do it with simplicity, he that ruleth, with diligence; he that showeth mercy, with cheerfulness.

2 Cor. 9: 6-15

6: But this I say, He which soweth sparingly shall reap also sparingly; and he which soweth bountifully shall reap also bountifully.

7: Every man according as he purposeth in his heart, so let him give; not grudgingly, or of necessity: for Yahweh loveth a cheerful giver.

8: And Yahweh is able to make all bountifulness abound toward you; that ye, always having all sufficiency in all things, may abound to every good work:

9: (As it is written, He hath dispersed abroad; he hath given to the poor: His righteousness remaineth forever.

10: Now he that ministereth seed to the sower both minister bread for your food, and multiply your seed sown, and increase the fruits of your righteousness;)

11: Being enriched in everything to all bountifulness, which causeth through us thanksgiving to Yahweh.

12: For the administration of this service not only supplieth the want of the elect, but is abundant also by many thanksgivings unto Yahweh;

13: While by the experiment of this ministration they praise Yahweh for your professed subjection unto the Word of Yahweh, and for your liberal distribution unto them, and unto all men;

14: And by their prayer for you, which long after you for the exceeding Spirit of Yahweh in you.

15: Thanks be unto Yahweh for his unspeakable gift.

Matt. 25: 34-40

34: Then shall the King say unto them on his right hand, come, ye blessed of my Father, inherit the kingdom prepared for you from the foundation of the world:

35: For I was an hungered, and ye gave me meat: I was thirsty, and ye gave me drink: I was a stranger, and ye took me in:

36: Naked, and ye clothed me: I was sick, and ye visited me: I was in prison, and ye came unto me.

37: Then shall the righteous answer him, saying, Master, when saw we thee an hungered, and fed thee? Or thirsty, and gave thee drink?

38: When saw we thee a stranger, and took thee in? Or naked, and clothed thee?

39: Or when saw we thee sick, or in prison and came unto thee?

40: And the King shall answer and say unto them, Verily I say unto you, inasmuch as ye have done it unto one of the least of these my brethren, ye have done it unto me.

Matt. 19: 21

21: Immanuel said unto him, If thou wilt be perfect, go and sell that thou hast, and give to the poor, and thou shalt have treasure in heaven: and come and follow me.

Luke 3: 10-11

10: And the people asked him, saying, what shall we do then?

11: He answereth and saith unto them, He that hath two coats, let him impart to him that hath none; and he that hath meat, let him do likewise.

Luke 6: 38

38: Give, and it shall be given unto you, good measure, pressed down, and shaken together, and running over, shall men given into your bosom. For with the same measure that ye meet withal it shall be measured to you again.

Luke 11: 41

41: But rather give alms of such things as ye have; and, behold, all things are clean unto you.

Luke 12: 33-34

33: Sell that ye have, and give alms; provide yourselves bags which wax not old, a treasure in the heavens that faileth not, where no thief approacheth, neither moth corrupteth.

34: For where your treasure is there will your heart be also.

Acts 20: 35

35: I have showed you all things, how that so laboring ye ought to support the weak, and to remember the words of Yahweh, how he said, It is more blessed to give than to receive.

1 Cor. 13: 33

And though I bestow all my goods to feed the poor, and though I give my body to be burned, and have not charity, it profiteth me nothing.

Ephesians 4: 28

28: Let him that stole steal no more: but rather let him labor, working with his hands the thing which is good, that he may have to give to him that needeth.

1 Timothy 5: 16

16: If any man or woman that believeth have widows, let them relieve them, and let not the assemblies be charged; that it may relieve them that are widows indeed.

Romans 15: 26-27

26: For it hath pleased them of Macedonia and Achaia to make a certain contribution for the poor saints<<Elect which are at Jerusalem<<Zion.

27: It hath pleased them verily; and their debtors they are. For if the Gentiles have been made partakers of their spiritual things, their duty is also to minister unto them in carnal things.

Matt. 5: 42

42: Give to him that asketh thee, and from him that would borrow of thee turn not thou away.

Galations 2: 10

10: Only they would that we should remember the poor; the same which I also was forward to do.

Notice in the following four verses that the people were not paying tithes but giving from their abundance.

Mark 12: 41-44

41: And Immanuel sat over against the treasury, and beheld how the people cast money into the treasury: and many that were rich cast in much.

42: And there came a certain poor widow, and she threw in two mites, which make a farthing.

43: And he called unto him his disciples, and saith unto them, Verily I say unto you, That this poor widow hath cast more in, than all they which have cast into the treasury:

44: For all they did cast in of their abundance; but she of her want did cast in all that she had, even all her living.

Mark 14: 77

For ye have the poor with you always, and whensoever ye will ye may do them good: but me ye have not always.

Luke 6: 30-35

30: Give to every man that asketh of thee; and of him that taketh away thy goods ask them not again.

31: And as ye would that men should do to you, do ye also to them likewise.

32: For if ye love them which love you, what thank have ye? For transgressors also love those that love them.

33: And if ye do good to them which do good to you, what thank have ye? For transgressors also do even the same.

34: And if ye lend to them of whom ye hope to receive, what thank have ye? For transgressors also lend to transgressors, to receive as much again.

Luke 14: 12-14

12: Then said he also to him that bade him, When thou makest a dinner or a supper, call not thy friends, nor thy brethren, neither thy kinsmen, nor thy rich neighbors; lest they also bid thee again, and a recompense be made thee.

13: But when thou makest a feast call the poor, the maimed, the lame, the blind:

14: And thou shalt be blessed; for they cannot recompense thee; for thou shalt be recompensed at the resurrection of the just.

1 Tim. 6: 17-19

17: Charge them that are rich in this world, that they be not highminded, nor trust in uncertain riches, but in the living Yahweh, who giveth us richly all things to enjoy;

18: That they do good, that they be rich in good works, ready to distribute, willing to communicate;

19: Laying up in store for themselves a good foundation against the time to come, that they may lay hold on eternal life.

James 2: 13-18

13: For he shall have judgment without mercy, that hath showed no mercy; and mercy rejoiceth against judgment.

14: What doth it profit, my brethren, though a man say he hath faith, and have not works? Can faith save him?

15: If a brother or sister be naked, and destitute of daily food,

16: And one of you say unto them, Depart in peace, be ye warmed and filled; not withstanding ye give them not those things which are needful to the body; what doth it profit?

17: Even so faith, if it hath not works, is dead, being alone.

18: Yea, a man may say, Thou hast faith, and I have works: show me thy faith without thy works, and I will show thee my faith by my works.

CONCLUSION: Tithing is not for today. They gave from their abundance.

You are in Christianity that goes against Yahweh's truth and makes it a lie for your greedy preachers, or what have you, to put people under bondage.

Most of all, if it came not from the heart, he did not want it. Just more proof that Christians are taken in by lies, but it is Satan's world of deceit.

I would like to add this bit of information: The U.S. government gave religious organizations tax exemptions because they were to take care of the poor in this country. But you see who ended up doing it, the government. While they build these million-dollar churches and even now buying multi-million-dollar stadiums to use. A money-making racket. No wonder a lot of these foreigners become preachers when they come here. I have seen people that start going to these churches and, in their minds, get saved, and the next thing you know they start preaching, really knowing nothing.

CHAPTER 8
THE FIRST 5 SEALS

The 6th and 7th Seals, I do not want to teach until I know they are true to what they represent along with the Trumpets. All the Vials are poured out during the Tribulation Period on those who take the Mark of the Beast. I believe when something is to be opened for understanding that it will be revealed at that time. So many different things are involved to get a complete understanding of the last two Seals. We know his imminent return happens during them. I want to do one more book to put them in when finished doing a study on everything involved with them, along with other findings on other subjects.

Daniel 12:9-10

9 And he said, Go thy way, Daniel: for **the words are closed up and sealed till the time of the end.**

10 **Many shall be purified, and made white, and tried; but the wicked shall do wickedly: and none of the wicked shall understand; but the wise shall understand**

Revelation 1:19 - Remember what John was told in this verse.

"**Write the (1)** things which thou hast seen, **and (2)** the things which are, **and the things (3)** which shall be hereafter."

Revelation 6:

1. And I saw when the Lamb opened one of the seals, and I heard, as it were the noise of thunder, one of the four beasts saying, Come and see.

A.   BABYLONIAN EMPIRE:

2. And I saw, and behold a white horse: and he that sat on him had a bow; and a crown was given unto him: and he went forth conquering, and to conquer.

3. And when he had opened the second seal, I heard the second beast say, Come and see.

B.   MEDEO-PERSIA EMPIRE:

4. And there went out another horse *that was* red: and *power* was given to him that sat thereon to take peace from the earth, and that they should kill one another: and there was given unto him a great sword.

C.   GRECIAN EMPIRE:

5. And when he had opened the third seal, I heard the third beast say, Come and see. And I beheld, and lo a black horse; and he that sat on him had a pair of balances in his hand.

6. And I heard a voice in the midst of the four beasts say, A measure of wheat for a penny, and three measures of barley for a penny; and *see* thou hurt not the oil and the wine.

7. And when he had opened the fourth seal, I heard the voice of the fourth beast say, Come and see.

D.   ROMAN EMPIRE:

8. And I looked, and behold a pale horse: and his name that sat on him was Death, and Hell followed with him. And power was given unto them over the fourth

part of the earth, to kill with sword, and with hunger, and with death, and with the beasts of the earth.

E.   PAPACY RULE:

9. And when he had opened the fifth seal, I saw under the altar the souls of them that were slain for the Word of Yahweh, and for the testimony which they held:

10. And they cried with a loud voice, saying, How long, O Yahweh, righteous and true, dost thou not judge and avenge our blood on them that dwell on the earth?

11. And white robes were given unto every one of them; and it was said unto them, that they should rest yet for a little season, until their fellow servants repeated word also and their brethren, that should be killed as they *were*, should be fulfilled.

They are waiting for the 7-Year Peace Plan Elect to be killed as they were.

F. YAHWEH'S COMING AND WRATH POURED OUT:

12. And I beheld when he had opened the sixth seal, and, lo, there was a great earthquake; and the sun became black as sackcloth of hair, and the moon became as blood;

13. And the stars of heaven fell unto the earth, even as a fig tree casted her untimely figs, when she is shaken of a mighty wind.

14. And the heaven departed as a scroll when it is rolled together; and every mountain and island were moved out of their places.

15. And the kings of the earth, and the great men, and the rich men, and the chief captains, and the mighty men, and every bondman, and every free man, hid themselves in the dens and in the rocks of the mountains;

16. And said to the mountains and rocks, Fall on us, and hide us from the face of him that sits on the throne, and from the wrath of the Lamb:

17. For the great day of his wrath is come; and who shall be able to stand?

G.   FIRST SEAL - BABYLONIAN EMPIRE - WHITE HORSE

The following all represent the Babylonian Empire

1. **Head of Gold = Babylonian Empire - Daniel 2:38**
2. **Lion with wings = Babylonian Empire - Daniel 7:4**
3. **Mouth of a Lion - Babylonian Empire Revelation 13:2 RIDER ON WHITE HORSE- BABYLONIAN EMPIRE - Revelation 6:2**

H.   THIS WHITE HORSE REPRESENTS: FALSE MESSIAH

Nimrod is the White Horse rider with the crown and bow. Nimrod the Assyrian.

He represents the Babylonian Empire, which I will prove. He, by conquest, was given the first kingdom on earth. The first false messiah by paganism, he gave birth.

77

Nimrod came in his own name, and the world received him.

John 5:43

I am come in my Father's name, and ye receive me not: if another shall come in his own name, him ye will receive.

John 5:44

How can you believe, who receive righteousness from one another, and do not seek the righteousness that *cometh* from Yahweh only?

The Church of God is now teaching that it is Nimrod who is the rider on this White Horse. Their video is no longer on YouTube, which they did not teach before. They are teaching, though, that the White Horse represents a counterfeit Christianity, but all Christianity is a lie and farce. Yet they teach the other horses that Christianity has always taught them to be, like when I was growing up, which is not true.

Who does this represent?

Genesis 10:8

And Cush begat Nimrod: he began to be a mighty one in the earth.

1 Chronicles 1:10

Cush begot Nimrod; he began to be a mighty one on the earth.

I. THE TWO BABYLONS BY ALEXANDER HISLOP

Kronos was the first king of Babylon, or Nimrod; consequently, the first centaur was the same.

Now, the way in which the centaur was represented on the Babylonian coins...

Fig. 16.

... and in the Zodiac... is very striking the centaur was the same as the sign Sagittarius, or "The Archer."

If the founder of Babylon's glory was "The Mighty Hunter," whose name, even in the days of Moses, was a Proverb...

Genesis 10:9

He was a mighty hunter before Yahweh: wherefore it is said, Even as Nimrod, the mighty hunter before Yahweh.

When we find the "Archer" with his bow and arrow as a symbol of the Supreme Babylonian Divinity...

...and the "Archer" among the signs of the Zodiac that originated in Babylon, I think we may safely conclude that this Man-horse or Horse-man archer primarily referred to him {Nimrod}...

... and was intended to perpetuate the memory at once of his fame as a huntsman and his skill as a horse breaker.

Nimrod was Noah's great-grandson, son of Cush, and he is being the son of Ham.

The word "HUNTER" was translated from the original Hebrew word "TZUD," which has the meaning of hunter of men, to ensnare to beguile.

Nimrod's birthday was December 25, and how they produced the birth of the Christian sun deity Jesus. December 25 is the rebirth of all sun deities. Jesus, Christ, Lord, God, Sacred, Amen, Adonai, and Angel are a few sun deity names that were put into the Word of Yahweh to propagandize it by Constantine.

Yahweh's name was in the scriptures over 6000 times. Yet anywhere a pagan deity name is spoken of, they got it right every time.

There were no kingdoms back then, only cities, and he WENT FORTH, CONQUERING these cities and lands until he built the first kingdom on Earth. Nimrod was the king of the first kingdom on earth, which was the beginning of and became the Babylonian Empire. This is why Nimrod represents the Babylonian Empire in verse 2 of Revelation Chapter 6.

As Genesis 10:8 states: "He began to be <u>a mighty one on the earth</u>."

He defied Yahweh by building the "Tower of Babel," so Yahweh confounded the languages of the people and scattered them abroad.

Genesis 11:8-9

8 So Yahweh scattered them abroad from thence upon the face of all the earth: and they left off to build the city.

9 Therefore is the name of it called Babel; because Yahweh did there confound the language of all the earth: and from thence did Yahweh scatter them abroad upon the face of all the earth.

At the time of Constantine, the Roman Empire engulfed the whole of humanity. So, from the Tower of Babel to when Constantine ruled, that is the area where these people with new languages settled and moved to different lands because of wars or persecutions throughout history. This is how the United States was founded; today, citizens speak over 400 + languages from many diverse cultures. Add on page 8

This is how many pagan cultures were made and why there are so many sun deity names from all these diverse cultures that worshiped Nimrod as the sun under all these different names.

J. TOWER OF BABEL

Genesis 11: 1-9

1. And the whole earth was of one language, and of one speech.

2. And it came to pass, as they journeyed from the East, that they found a plain in the land of Shinar; and they dwelt there.

3. And they said one to another, Go to, let us make brick, and burn them thoroughly. And they had brick for stone, and slime had they for mortar.

4. And they said, Go to, let us build us a city and a tower, whose top may reach unto heaven; and let us make us a name, lest we be scattered abroad upon the face of the whole earth.

5. And YAHWEH CAME DOWN TO SEE the city and the tower, which the children of men built.

6. And Yahweh said, Behold, the people is one, and they have all one language; and this they begin to do: and now nothing will be restrained from them, which they have imagined to do.

7. Go to, LET US GO DOWN, and there confound their language, that they may not understand one another's speech.

8. So Yahweh scattered them abroad from thence upon the face of all the earth: and they left off to build the city.

9. Therefore is the name of it called Babel; because Yahweh did there confound the language of all the earth: and from thence did Yahweh scatter them abroad upon the face of all the earth.

The People's Bible Encyclopedia page 791, copyright 1924:

NIMROD - the name of a person mentioned in the Old (Covenant) as the son of Cush (Genesis 10:8 and 1 Chronicles 1:10). Who was celebrated as a great hunter. To him is ascribed the foundation of the great Babylonian empire and the building of the cities, which were afterward combined together under the general name of Nineveh. He, therefore becomes also the founder of Assyria, and this country is therefore called by the prophet Micah (5:6) the land of Assyria.

So, Nimrod is the rider on the WHITE HORSE, he brought false paganism into existence, and he was the first FALSE MESSIAH. Christianity will be the last day of religion in this Mystery Babylon religious system. Nimrod was the first Pontifex Maximus and the Pope who holds the title of Pontifex Maximus, and why he is called Pope is traced back to Nimrod and the same Babylonian Religious Government System that is being pushed today. Constantine was the last Emperor of the Roman Empire, and he started pagan Christianity. He changed the Roman Empire government from secular over religious to religious over secular government and became the first Pontifex Maximus over this Christianity and the Papacy government system that took the place of the emperors and secular over religious government. Constantine was the one who covered up the truth of Yahweh and made it a lie after all the elects were killed off during the 11 Roman

Emperor Persecutions. History of the cover-up of what Constantine had done teaches that there were only 10 Persecutions. This Babylonian religious system is what Yahweh will destroy at His coming, and it all started with Nimrod and Constantine helped to carry it forward to the end times and its destruction by Yahweh Messiah.

NIMROD'S KINGDOM was GIVEN TO HIM, or HIS CROWN. He had the first kingdom on this earth.

The BOW represents a conqueror, a great hunter, and the HUNTER of the SOULS OF MEN with his false worship or paganism. When reading the scriptures where the word Gentile is, you can exchange it for pagan or heathen.

Pontifex Maximus, that title was handed down through the empires, and today, the Pope holds that title. The throne of this Babylonian religious system will end up in Zion since the Pope has that title now and why he is called Pope, the last one will move to Zion a few years before Yahweh returns. Christianity will become the last day of Mystery Babylonian religion when it becomes the religion of the world under the Papacy.

<u>Nimrod was the first king, the first false messiah, and the first Pontifex Maximus</u>. He was the first person after the flood that Satan influenced to rebel and to lead others to rebel against Yahweh. Nimrod and his wife Semiramis were worshipped as deities, and from here is where this mother and son worship had started.

The Pope is traced back to Nimrod, not Peter, and why the Popes want to worship themselves as a deity, the reason the last Pope (that I believe will be Nimrod himself) will rule the world from Zion.

The two-horned MITRE, which the Pope wears when he sits on the high altar at Rome and receives the adoration of the Cardinals, is the very Mitre worn by the priests of Dagon, the fish-deity of the Philistines and Babylonians.

- The Two Babylons by Alexander Hislop; p. 215, copyright 1903

The Mystery religion of ancient Babylon / Assyria was noted for the priestly class of Dagon in much the same way that the "Mystery" religion of Rome has copied it.

...there are strong evidences that Dagon was Nimrod.... All scholars agree that the name and worship of Dagon were imported from Babylonia.

| The Religious "Mitre" Hat From Babylon | The Priest of Ancient "Dagon" Fish Worship |

- The Two Babylons, Hislop, p. 215, copyright 1903

"In their veneration and worship of Dagon, the high priest of paganism would put on a garment that had been created from a huge fish! The head of the fish formed a Mitre above that of the old man, while its scaly, fan-like tail fell as a cloak behind, leaving the human limbs and feet exposed."

Definition - "Ichthyic" - "of, pertaining to, or characteristic of fishes; the fish world in all its orders."- Oxford English Dictionary (C. E.)

ICHTHYS, GREEK FOR FISH
PHILISTINE FISH-GOD DAGON

We know Babylon is where false worship and religions came from. Christianity Absorbs all pagan religions with the Pontifex Maximus (Pope) over it.

Revelation 17:5 And upon her forehead **(Zion)** was a name written, Mystery, Babylon the Great, The Mother of Harlots and Abominations of The Earth.

K. SECOND SEAL - MEDO-PERSIA EMPIRE - RED HORSE

IMAGE OF A MAN

Daniel 2:32 & 39

Breast and Arms of Silver = Medio-Persia Empire 4 BEASTS

Daniel 7:5

2nd Beast

Bear with 3 ribs in mouth = Medio-Persia Empire

4 BEASTS IN ONE

Revelations 13:2

Feet of a Bear = Medo-Persia Empire

Daniel 8:3:

Ram with two horns = Medio-Persia Empire

7 Seals

Revelation 6:4

SECOND SEAL - Medio-Persia Empire (539 BCE - 330 BCE) Red Horse

Revelation 6:4 And there went out another horse that was red: and power was given to him that sat thereon to take peace from the earth, and that they should kill one another: and there was given unto him a great sword.

RED HORSE represents the Medio-Persian Empire, and it is Cyrus the Great who sits on the horse.

The World Story - 1963, page 78:

Cyrus the Great united the Medes and Persians and then attacked Lydia, a kingdom in western Asia Minor. The Lydians sought help from Babylonia and Egypt, but Cyrus defeated them in 546 B.C. After organizing his conquests, Cyrus marched on Babylon, which yielded to him without a struggle.

The Ancient World - 1979, page 42:

In 553, one of the minor Indo-European tribes of Iran, the Persians, successfully challenged the overlordship of the Medes, and Cyrus the Aachaemenian established a new ruling dynasty that became one power. This fulfills, THEY SHOULD KILL ONE ANOTHER.

Christianity and Civilization - 1947, page 39:

The Persians, a people akin to the Medes, exploded in a great burst of military activity (to take peace from the earth) to create the greatest empire up to that time. Led by such capable men as Cyrus the Great and Darius, they united all the people of the Near East in an empire that extended from India to the Aegean and from the Black Sea to Nubia. Greece alone finally checked the spread of this Oriental power.

Daniel 7:5, this BEAR represents the Medio-Persian Empire:

Daniel 7:5 And behold another beast, a second like to a bear, and it raised up itself on one side, and it had three ribs in the mouth of it between the teeth of it: and they said thus unto it, Arise, devour much flesh.

"a bear and it raised up itself on one side." The Persians were stronger than the Medes and why it raised up on one side.

The 3 RIBS in the bear's mouth are the 3 empires Medio-Persia destroyed in its conquests to become one of the greatest empires on earth. This is the great sword he was given.

The bear with three ribs in its mouth symbolizes Medo-Persia

The RIBS represents:

1. **Lydian Empire**

2. **Egyptian Empire**

3. **Babylonian Empire**

Isaiah, 45:1 <u>Thus saith the LORD/YAHWEH</u> to his anointed, to Cyrus, whose right hand I have holden, to subdue nations before him; and I will loose the loins of kings, to open before him the two leaved gates; and the gates shall not be shut;

1. a. (He was given a great sword). b. (to take peace from the earth)

The following fulfills the above (a) and (b):

A. **Cyrus conquered the Medes first,**
   a. **They were akin to one another: This fulfills that they should kill one another.**

2. **Together, the Medes and Persians conquered 3 Empires: Lydian, Babylonian, and Egyptian.**

The end of the Medio-Persia Empire:

Daniel 8:3-7

3. Then I lifted up mine eyes, and saw, and, behold, there stood before the river a ram which had two horns: and the two horns were high; but one was higher than the other, and the higher came up last.

Note: Two horns represent the Medes and Persians. The higher horn that came up last was the Persians because the Medes and Persians were kin and the Persians defeated the Medes first, then in unity they became a great power.

4. I saw the ram pushing westward, and northward, and southward; so that no beasts might stand before him, neither was there any that could deliver out of his hand; but he did according to his will, and became great.

5. And as I was considering, behold, an he goat came from the west on the face of the whole earth, and touched not the ground: and the goat had a notable horn between his eyes.

6. And he came to the ram that had two horns, which I had seen standing before the river, and ran unto him in the fury of his power.

7. And I saw him come close unto the ram, and he was moved with choler against him, and smote the ram, and brake his two horns: and there was no power in the ram to stand before him, but he cast him down to the ground, and stamped upon him: and there was none that could deliver the ram out of his hand.

Daniel 8:20 The ram which thou sawest having two horns are the kings of Media and Persia. Daniel 8:21 And the rough goat is the king of Grecia: and the great horn that is between his eyes is the first king. Note: Alexander the Great

As you can see, this is proven perfectly by Scripture and history.

L. "Cyrus the Great" (2nd Seal - Red Horse)

There went out another horse. This horse was red. This one took peace from the earth, with many people dead. Three empires fell by his great sword. Medo-Persia became the Great Ram with two horns with one accord.

"The ram pushing westward, and northward, and southward; so that no beasts might stand, neither was there any that could deliver out of his hand; but he did accordingly to his will, and became great." This notorious man took his stand.

The Medo-Persian Empire is also known as the bear, which had the three ribs in its mouth to show how it faired. The Medes and Persians became a powerful clan, death, and destruction to many a different man.

Cyrus the Great united the Medes and Persians, and they then defeated the Lydian, Babylonian, and Egyptian Empires, who all yielded to him. So, this bear did rise and devoured much flesh which to the world looked mighty grim.

By Gary W. Stanfield

M. THIRD SEAL - GRECIAN EMPIRE - BLACK HORSE

THE IMAGE OF A MAN

Daniel 2:32-33

Belly and Thighs of Brass = Grecian Empire

THE 4 BEASTS

Daniel 7:5

3rd Beast

Leopard = Grecian Empire

4 BEASTS IN ONE

Revelation 13:2

Like a leopard = Grecian Empire

Daniel 8:21

He-Goat with horn = Grecian Empire

7 SEALS

Revelation 6:5-6

Third Seal

Black Horse = Greek Empire (330 BCE - 63 BCE)

Revelation 6:5-6

5. And when he had opened the third seal, I heard the third beast say, Come and see. And I beheld, and lo a black horse; and he that sat on him had <u>a pair of balances</u> in his hand.

6. And I heard a voice in the midst of the four beasts say, <u>A choenix of wheat for a denarius</u>, and <u>three choenikes of barley for a denarius</u>; and <u>do not harm the oil and the wine</u>.

The <u>BLACK HORSE</u> represents <u>Trade.</u>

Then the Black Horse rider who is "Alexander the Great," Also had balances in his hand to put food on their plate. The Greeks traded Oil and Wine to get their barley and wheat. This represents the Grecian Empire after Medo-Persia's defeat.

(A denarius was a common wage for a day's work during that time in Greek history, and a choenix was a Greek dry measurement which was about a quart by our measurement today of wheat or three choenikes which is about 3 quarts of barley are basically subsistence diets).

Wheat BALANCES

This represents the Grecian Empire, which became a great world trading power, and is why it says, " I heard a <u>voice in the midst of the four beasts say</u>, a measure of wheat for a penny, three measures of barley for a penny," because it covered all the old empire territory and the new one to come, the Roman Empire.

<u>Christianity and Civilization - 1947, page 49</u>:

Since the soil of Greece was not good for grain and other staple foods. The Greeks sought these products through trade and thus developed into a seafaring, venturesome people.

A History of Civilization - 1960, page 50:

In ancient times, therefore, little could be grown in summer except drought-resistant fruit like <u>olives and grapes</u>. For the rest, the farmers produced barley and other grains that could be harvested in the early summer, wine, honey, and very little else.

Olives into Olive Oil

Grapes into Wine

A History of Civilization - 1960, page 51:

The Greeks quite early carried on an active maritime trade; they exchanged the olive oil and wine of the Aegean world for the metals, grains, and slaves needed in the homeland.

<u>A Survey of European Civilization - 1939, page 37</u>:

Wheat from Egypt, wine and olive oil from Greece, spices from Arabia, or tin from Britain providing ready cargoes for the ships as they moved back and forth like shuttles weaving a vast web irresistibly into a single complex economic and cultural pattern.

<u>A Survey of European Civilization - 1939, page 41</u>:

Greeks had, at first, little to offer until they increased their production of wine and olive oil and began to manufacture products for sale.

<u>Exploring The Old World - 1965, pages 93 and 94</u>:

As more Greek tribes moved into the valleys, the people found that they could not grow enough food there. They began to plant figs, grapes, and olives on the hillsides. From the olives, they made olive oil. This was a precious product. The Greeks used it for cooking, as butter, as a body lotion, and as oil for their lamps. In the valleys and on the coastal plains, they raised WHEAT, BARLEY, and vegetables. Because there was so little good land in Greece, they used every bit they could to give them food and materials for their clothing. The farmers produced more of some foods than they could use at home. They traded these foods, such as olive oil and wine, with Egyptian and Phoenician merchants for much-needed grain. The ancient Greeks raised olive trees on their hillsides. From the olives, they pressed olive oil which was a rich food product and also valuable for trade. Today it is still an important product of Greece and one of her chief exports.

<u>Wisdom of The West - 1959, page 33</u>:

The soil of Greece is not suitable for cultivation on a large scale. As the population grew it thus became necessary to import grain from everywhere.

We have learned the balances in the hand represent the great trading empire of Greece and why it speaks of wheat and barley being measured. It was needed in Greece because they could not grow much of it. They were not to hurt the oil or wine, for they were their greatest trading products.

History proves what the Scriptures are talking about.

N.   "Alexander the Great" (3rd Seal - Black Horse)

He rides in on the Black horse, Alexander the Great,

With balances in his hand along with the weight.

But first the goat with the notable horn had to break,

the horns of the ram to deliver its fate.

The Grecian Empire became the third beast,

When they conquered Medo-Persia from the East.

"I heard a voice in the midst of the four beasts say,

A choenix of wheat for a denarius,

And three choenikes of barley for a denarius;

and do not harm the oil and the wine."

Greece traded the oil and the wine

For grains like barley and wheat.

So those in Greece, could eat.

Olives and grapes were about all Greece could grow.

Very little barley and wheat could they sow.

They made the oil and the wine,

one from a tree the other a vine.

The barley and wheat they had to buy,

only through trade for them a supply.

By Gary Wendell Stanfield

O.   The Downfall of the Grecian Empire:

Daniel 8:2

Now that being broken, whereas four stood up for it, four kingdoms shall stand up out of the nation, but not in his power.

People Become Civilized by Trevor Cairns, page 92, copyright 1974.

Alexander the Great died, and four of his generals split the Greek Empire amongst themselves.

1. Egypt: General Ptolemy

2. Syria: General Seleucus

3. Thrace: General Lysimachus

4. Macedonia: General Cassander

P. FOURTH SEAL - ROMAN EMPIRE - PALE HORSE

The <u>PALE HORSE</u> represents <u>Death /Emperor</u>

The Pale Horse rider is Death / Emperor. (THEM) The Emperors of Rome. Today, that is the Pope who sits under Saint Peter's Dome. The Roman Empire killed Yahweh's people in many a way. The believers all died for their savior, Messiah Yahweh.

Revelation 6:8 : Seals

Fourth Seal / Pale Horse = Roman Empire (63 BCE - WE ARE STILL LIVING IN THE ROMAN EMPIRE TODAY, THE POPES TOOK THE PLACE OF THE EMPERORS

Daniel 2:33 & 40:

The Image of a Man

Legs of Iron = Roman Empire

Daniel 7:7:

The 4 Beasts

4th Beast

Beast with Iron Teeth = Roman Empire

Revelation 13:2

Beast - PAPACY BEAST - 1 And I stood upon the sand of the sea and saw a beast rise up out of the sea, having seven heads and ten horns, and upon his horns ten crowns, and upon his heads the name of blasphemy.

And the beast (PAPACY)which I saw was like unto a leopard (GRECIAN EMPIRE and his feet were as the feet of a bear (MEDIO PERSIAN EMPIRE), and his mouth as the mouth of a lion (BABYLONIAN EMPIRE): and the dragon (SATAN) gave him his power, and his seat, and great authority.

You must remember that the POPES TOOK THE PLACE OF THE EMPERORS THAT ALSO HELD THE TITLE OF PONTIFEX MAXIMUS.

LUKE 4:5-7

⁵ And the devil, taking him up on a high mountain, shewed unto him all the kingdoms of the world in a moment of time.

⁶ And <u>the devil said unto him, All this power will I give thee, and the glory of them: for that is delivered unto me; and to whomsoever I will I give it.</u>

<u>SO, WHO DID SATAN GIVE IT TO? HE GAVE IT TO THE EMPERORS, AND CONSTANTINE WAS THE FIRST PONTIFEX MAXIMUS THAT NOT ONLY STARTED THE PAPACY BUT WAS ALSO THE FIRST POPE OVER HIS PAGAN CHRISTIANITY. WE ARE STILL LIVING IN THE ERA OF THE ROMAN EMPIRE, WHICH NEVER FELL BUT WAS CHANGED FROM AN EMPEROR SECULAR GOVERNMENT TO A PAPACY RELIGIOUS GOVERNMENT..</u>

⁷ If thou therefore wilt worship me, all shall be thine.

⁸ And Immanuel answered and said unto him, Get thee behind me, Satan: for it is written, Thou shalt worship Yahweh thy Mighty One, and him only shalt thou serve.

Revelation 6:8 <u>And I looked, and behold a pale horse</u>: and his name that sat on him was Death, and the grave followed with him (EMPEROR). And power was given unto them (Emperors) over the fourth part of the earth, to kill with sword, and with hunger, and with death, and with the beasts of the earth.

Daniel 7:20-21 - THE LITTLE HORN IS Constantine WHO WAS THE FIRST POPE OVER CHRISTIANITY AND HE STARTED THE PAPACY.

²⁰ <u>And of the ten horns that were in his head, and of the other which came up, and before whom three fell; even of that horn that had eyes, and a mouth that spake very great things, whose look was more stout than his fellows.</u>

²¹ I beheld, and <u>the same horn/ Constantine made war with the saints / ELECT, and prevailed against them</u>;

Revelation 12:11

¹¹ And they overcame him by the blood of the Lamb, and by the word of their testimony; and they loved not their lives unto the death.

The last of the Spirit filled Elect were all killed off by Constantine with his 11th Roman Emperor Persecution and Yahweh took his Spirit of salvation away and why there is no salvation available since that time and even upto today.

Daniel 8:

²³ And <u>in the latter time of their kingdom, when the transgressors are come to the full, a king of fierce countenance, and understanding dark sentences, shall stand up.</u>

²⁴ And <u>his power shall be mighty, but not by his own power: and he shall destroy wonderfully, and shall prosper, and practice, and shall destroy the mighty and the RIGHTEOUS people.</u>

²⁵ And <u>through his policy also he shall cause craft to prosper in his hand; and he shall magnify himself in his heart, and by peace shall destroy many: he shall also stand up against the K[ng of Kings; but he shall be broken without hand.</u>

Revelation 2:10-12

¹⁰ Fear none of those things which thou shalt suffer: behold, Satan shall cast some of you into prison, that ye may be tried; and ye shall have TRIBULATION ten days: be thou faithful unto death, and I will give thee a crown of life.

¹¹ He that hath an ear, let him hear what the Spirit saith unto the assemblies; He that overcometh shall not be hurt of the second death.

101

Revelation 12:11 And they overcame him by the blood of the Lamb, and by the word of their testimony; and they loved not their lives unto the death.

2 Thessalonians 2:8-12

8. And then shall that Wicked be revealed, whom Yahweh shall consume with the spirit of his mouth, and shall destroy with the brightness of his coming:

9. Even him, whose coming is after the working of Satan with all power and signs and lying wonders,

10. And with all deceivableness of unrighteousness in them that perish; because they received not the love of the truth, that they might be saved.

11. And <u>for this cause Yahweh shall send them strong delusion, that they should believe a lie:</u>

12. <u>That they all might be damned who believed not the truth, but had pleasure in unrighteousness.</u>

<u>Story of Nations - 1956, page 152</u>:

Emperor Nero murdered thousands of Chr//tians/(the Elect) whom he falsely accused of setting fire to the city. Many (of the) devout Chr//tians/(Elect) were thrown to hungry wild beasts in the arenas to provide the Romans entertainment, as well as to discourage the spread of (the) Chr//tianity (FAITH IN YAHWEH MESSIAH).

<u>Exploring The Old World - 1965, page 131</u>:

TO STAMP OUT Christianity (the FAITH in Yahweh Messiah), Christians (the Elect) were thrown to lions, crucified, burned alive, or killed by gladiators.

Revelation 6:8 **<u>And I looked, and behold a pale horse</u>: and his name that sat on him was Death, and the grave followed with him (EMPEROR). And power was given** unto them (Emperors) over the fourth part of the earth, to kill with sword, and with hunger, and with death, and with the beasts of the earth.

NOTICE: the crucifixion is not mentioned in the above verse, nor being burned alive yet, yet history has added both because the Papacy changed history to support their lies.

And this was not the religion of Christianity that they wanted to stamp out. This was the very reason why Christianity was created so that it could absorb all other religions.

One thing that is missing about Nero is that he couldn't possibly have persecuted Christians since Christianity did not exist until the 4th century. THERE WAS A PAGAN RELIGION BY THE SAME NAME, BUT THEY WERE NOT KILLED DURING THE PERSECUTIONS.

Matthew 24:34 Verily I say unto you, This generation shall not pass, till all these things be fulfilled.

There were ten periods of persecution from Emperor Nero being the first in 64 C.E., to Emperor Diocletian in 303 C.E., varying in length. These are the 4th Seal.

History will teach you that there were only Ten Roman Persecutions when there were Eleven.

These are the 4th Seal:

Emperor

Emperor/Date (A.D.)

1. Nero 54-68

2. Domitian 81-96

3. Trajan 98-117

4. Marcus Aurelius 161-180

5. Septimius Severus 193-211

6. Maximinus the Thracian 235-238

7. Decius Trajan 249-251

8. Valerian 253-260

9. Lucius Aurelian 270-275

10. Diocletian 284-305

11. Constantine ruled from 306 -337

Constantine ruled from 306 to 337

Roman Empire was changed to a religious government under Constantine.

Diocletian died in 305, and Constantine took over in 306, so Constantine continued Diocletian's Persecution as his own.

Constantine ruled from 306 to 337

The last (the 11th) persecution (of Constantine's) ended in 313.

311 CE – The Edict of Toleration by Galerius was issued in 311 by the Roman Tetrarchy of Galerius, Constantine, and Licinius, officially ending the Diocletian persecution of Christianity; this is not true Constantine was covering up his own Persecution.

Daniel 7:21 I beheld, and the same horn made war with the Elect, and prevailed against them;

The Little Horn of Daniel is Constantine, and he killed off the last of Yahweh's Elect with the 11th Roman Emperor Persecution. See how they covered up what Constantine did by acting like Constantine was ending Diocletian's Persecution and not his own.?

313 – Roman Emperors Constantine I and Licinius issued the Edict of Milan that legalized Christianity across the whole Empire.

The Little Horn of Daniel is Constantine, and he killed off the last of Yahweh's Elect.

Edict of Milan, a proclamation that permanently established religious toleration for Christianity within the Roman Empire. It was the outcome of a political agreement concluded in Mediolanum (modern Milan) between the Roman emperors Constantine I and Licinius in February 313. WHO issued the Edict of Toleration?

CONSTANTINE KILLING OFF THE LAST OF YAHWEH'S ELECT WITH THE 11TH PERSECUTION.

Back to Daniel 7:21.

21. I beheld, and the same horn made war with the elect, and prevailed against them;

THE EMPEROR WHO BECAME POPE CONSTANTINE KILLED OFF THE LAST OF YAHWEH'S ELECT BACK THEN.

After Nero came the persecutions from Emperor Domitian, then Emperor Decius in 250 C.E., after him came Emperor Valerian in 257 to 258 C.E., and finally, the last of the 10 and worst under Emperor Diocletian, who began his rule in 284 C.E., and his persecutions started in 303 C.E. and his rule ended in 305 C.E., while Maximian was Emperor of the West. Constantine finished them off with the 11th Roman Emperor Persecution.

All books, records, and writings were confiscated and burned, like in other persecutions. Every person, including children suspected of being of the faith in Yahweh, was killed without recourse to laws or by any other means. Horsemen rode across the empire with a public proclamation of extermination.

Constantine ruled from 306 to 337 C.E. in 312 C.E., he was proclaimed Emperor by the Senate, and *he made Christianity in 313 (Edict of Milan), the official state religion of the Roman Empire.*

Q. The Roman Empire (4th Seal - Pale Horse)

"And I looked, and behold a pale horse: and his name that sat on him was Death, and the grave followed with him. And power was given unto THEM {EMPERORS} over the fourth part of the earth, to kill with sword, and with hunger, and with death, and with the beasts of the earth."

"And they overcame him {Satan} by the blood of the Lamb, and by the word of their testimony; for they loved not their lives even unto their death." This was done by the eleven Roman persecutions until the last one took their last breath. They all were laid to rest, and each and everyone was surely blessed.

The Council of Trent was brought about to counter the Reformation.

What was done?

1. They started the Catholic denomination in Christianity in 1559.

2. They started the Jesuit Order.

The Jesuits helped carry out two major objectives of the Counter-Reformation: The Jesuits established numerous schools and universities throughout Europe and pushed the supremacy of the Pope and Catholic church. WE STILL LIVE IN THE ERA OF THE COUNTER-REFORMATION.

3. The Roman Catholic Church had its Latin Vulgate, which was done by Jerome, put into the English LANGUAGE AND CALLED IT THE Douay-Rheims.

Matthew 24:34

Verily I say unto you, This generation shall not pass, till all these things be fulfilled.

Many died horrible deaths, thrown to lions, impaled,

killed by gladiators, alive were they burned.

Their souls with everlasting life was for what they yearned.

So, for their testimony to prove that Yahweh was true,

they had to die and this they knew.

By the Spirit they were brave, now they are all in the grave.

These are those under the table that Yahweh told, "to rest,"

Till those like them will be killed and will also pass the test.

His future tribulation people the Anti-Messiah will not deceive.

Then after this they shall all be redeemed

and Yahweh's wrath on those that did not in Him believe.

By Gary Wendell Stanfield

R. FIRST FOUR HORSEMEN SEALS

Nimrod the White Horse rider with the crown and bow.
Represents the Babylonian Empire and that I will show.
He by conquest was given the first kingdom on earth.
The first false messiah by paganism he gave birth.

"Cyrus the Great" the Red Horse rider with the "Great Sword."
Persia fought their kin the Medes then with one accord,
Became the ram and bear which took peace from the earth.
Medo-Persian Empire with war expanded their empires girth.

Then the Black Horse rider who is "Alexander the Great,"
Had balances in his hand to put food on their plates.
The Greeks traded Oil and Wine to get their barley and wheat.

This represents the Grecian Empire after Medo-Persia's defeat.

The Pale Horse rider is Death, the Emperors of Rome.
Today that is the Pope who sits under Saint Peter's Dome.
The Roman Empire killed Yahweh's people in many a way.
The believers all died for their savior, Messiah Yahweh.

S. By Gary Wendell Stanfield

T.5TH SEAL - PAPACY RULE

THE 3 BEASTS OF REVELATION:

- The first beast is called "the Dragon/Satan" (Revelation 12:3).
- The second beast is called "the Beast" (Revelation 13:1-4). PAPACY
- The third beast is called "the False Prophet" (Revelation 13:11-15; Revelation 16:13). POPE

The number or name of the beast is 666, which is "a man's number."

WHEN YOU SPEAK ABOUT THE PAPACY, YOU SPEAK ABOUT THE POPE AND WHEN YOU SPEAK ABOUT THE POPE YOU SPEAK ABOUT THE PAPACY AND WHY THE POPE IS THE IMAGE OF THE PAPACY; JUST LIKE YAHWEH MESSIAH IS THE

VERY IMAGE OF THE FATHER, SO WHEN YOU SPEAK OF THE FATHER YOU ARE ALSO SPEAKING OF THE SON AND VISE VERSA.

Daniel 2:33,34

33. its legs of iron, its feet partly of iron and partly of clay.

34. "You continued looking until a stone was cut out without hands, and it struck the statue on its feet of iron and clay and crushed them....

The "legs of iron" was the Roman Empire. The feet, partly of iron and partly of clay, represent the Papacy. The 10 toes of the Roman Empire in its last form represent the One World Empire and why the stone / Yahweh Messiah crushes the feet at His return.

Constantine ruled from 306 to 337 C.E. in 312 C.E., he was proclaimed Emperor by the Senate, and he made Christianity in 313 (Edict of Milan) the official state religion of the Roman Empire. Constantine was the last Emperor of the Roman Empire who killed off the last of Yahweh's elect. At that time is when he started Christianity and the Papacy, he became the first Pontifex Maximus {Pope} over Christianity.

Christianity was created to absorb all pagan religions, since only pagans were left in the Roman Empire at that time, to bring them all under one heading and one authority: Christianity and the Pope. It was also created to send people to the Lake of Fire, not to save them from it! We inherited the lies of our pagan or heathen forefathers, whichever word you prefer to use.

U.   NIMROD AND CONSTANTINE

It was Emperor Constantine who started Christianity.

He had changed Yahweh's Word, which was insanity.

Just so he could deceive the world and all humanity.

This was done for control and for his own self-vanity.

Nimrod and Constantine are two of the same,

To deceive humanity was their whole game.

This is why both of them are fully to blame

And why they both will burn in the flame.

Constantine's vision of the Cross he would sell,

So, in Nimrod's paganism, humanity would dwell.

If Christians knew the truth, surely they would yell,

Because, in their beliefs, they would all go to hell.

This Babylonian religion will be destroyed by the King,

Yahweh Messiah to Him believers will securely cling.

That's when His people, a new song they will sing,

When Yahweh ends this Babylonian religious thing.

111

By Gary Wendell Stanfield

Revelation chapter 6, verses 10 and 11, the 5th Seal, tells us that the true believers were all killed and they were to wait till their fellow brethren in the future end time tribulation period would be killed too. Then Yahweh would avenge their blood and judge the world.

Revelation 6:9

9: And when he had opened the fifth seal, I saw under the table the souls of them that were slain for the Word of Yahweh, and for the testimony which they held:

Amos 8:11,12

Behold, the days come, saith Yahweh, that I will send a famine in the land, not a famine of bread, nor a thirst for water, but of hearing the Words of Yahweh: and they shall wander from sea to sea, and from the north even to the east, they shall run to and fro *to seek the Word of Yahweh, and shall not find it.*

Daniel 12:4

But thou, O Daniel, shut up the words, and seal the book, even to the time of the end: many shall run to and fro, and knowledge shall be increased.

Revelation 14:6-7.

"And I saw another Messenger fly, in the midst of heaven, having the "Everlasting Truth" ...to preach<<<teach unto them that dwell on the earth, and to every nation,

NOTE: As you should be able to see, the truth was made a lie, or this Messenger would not have the Everlasting Truth to be preached to every nation. You should see now the scriptures prove the truth was made a lie.

Romans 10:14

How then shall they call on Him in whom they have not believed? and how shall they believe in Him of whom they have not heard? and how shall they hear without a teacher?

THE FIFTH SEAL IS THE TIME OF PAPACY RULE. WE ARE STILL LIVING IN THE ERA ROMAN EMPIRE EVEN THOUGH THE POPE SUFFERED HIS DEADLY WOUND AND LOST HIS POWER WHEN NAPOLEAN CAPTURED HIM AND TOOK HIS POWER AWAY, "THE DEADLY WOUND." WE ARE NOW SEEING THE COME BACK TO POWER OF THE POPE. WE ARE LIVING AT THE VERY END OF THE FIFTH SEAL WHEN THE PAPACY IS ABOUT TO TAKE AND RULE THE WORLD FROM ZION. HE WAS, HE IS NOT, BUT YET IS.

Daniel 7:8 I considered the horns, and, behold, there came up among them another little horn, before whom there were three of the first horns plucked up by the roots: and, behold, in this horn *were* eyes like the eyes of man, and a mouth speaking great things.

Revelation 6:9-11

9: And when he had opened the fifth seal, I saw under the table the souls of them that were slain for the Word of Yahweh, and for the testimony which they held:

Notice these believers were killed during the Fourth Seal of the Roman Empire for the testimony which they held. Which was that Yahweh was true.

10: And they cried with a loud voice, saying, How long, O Yahweh, righteous and true, doest thou not judge and avenge our blood on them that dwell on the earth?

11: And white robes were given unto every one of them: and it was said unto them, that they should rest yet for a little season until their fellow servants also and their brethren,

113

This is fulfilled in Chapter 19 of Revelation. Revelation 19:2 For true and righteous are His judgments: for He hath JUDGED the great whore, which did corrupt the earth with her fornication, and hath AVENGED the blood of His servants at her hand.

Notice the space between those who are told to rest for a little season and the fellow brethren who are to be murdered as they were should be fulfilled. These fellow brethren are those who are killed during the last Tribulation Period, the last part of the 7-Year Peace Plan, the time when Yahweh pours out the Latter Rain of His Spirit. Why is this?

Luke 24:47-48

47. And that repentance and remission of transgressions should be TAUGHT IN HIS NAME among all nations, beginning at Zion.

48. Ye are witnesses of these things.

This all happened back then. The whole Roman Empire heard the truth and had the choice to believe or not to believe, and those back then were witnesses to this. The true believers were all killed off back then. Now, we are waiting for the latter-day believers to be killed as they were. After the truth once again is taught to every person this time being every nation on earth IN HIS NAME, YAHWEH MESSIAH. You will have the choice to believe or not to believe before the Mark of the Beast is enforced.

This truth is to be taught again during the Peace Plan, which is at the very end of the 5th Seal. It will be the fulfillment of Matt. 24:14, where it says: "This truth of 'THE KINGDOM' shall be taught in all the world for a WITNESS unto all nations: and then shall the end come." This has NO reference to Christianity that is now being preached. The truth will be as a WITNESS, that is. It is the announcement that the time has come for Yahweh's Kingdom to be.

Revelation 14:6-7.

"And I saw another Messenger fly, in the midst of heaven, having the "Everlasting Truth" ...to teach unto them that dwell on the earth, and to every nation, It will be taught first by Eliyah and Moses the two Witnesses (Mal. 4:5-6): and by those that believe at that time to tell people of salvation and the coming of the Messiah to sit on Throne of David, and for the purpose of gathering His people for the Millennial Kingdom on this earth and not in heaven. "Where I am, there ye shall be also."

Jeremiah 25:33

And the slain of Yahweh shall be at that day from one end of the earth even unto the other end of the earth: they shall not be lamented, neither gathered, nor buried; they shall be dung upon the ground.

Luke 17:26-27

26. And as it was in the days of Noah, so shall it be also in the days of the Son of man.

27. They did eat, they drank, they married wives, they were given in marriage, until the day of Noah entered into the ark, and the flood came, <u>AND DESTROYED THEM ALL.</u>

Matthew 24:37-39

37. But as the days of Noah *were,* so also will the coming of the Son of Man be.

38. For as in the days before the flood, they were eating and drinking, marrying and giving in marriage, until the day that Noah entered the ark,

39. and did not know until the flood came and took them all away, so also will the coming of the Son of Man be.

<u>Yahweh will kill not only all the armies that will go against Zion from all nations but will kill every human left on earth because they were not believers, JUST LIKE IN THE DAYS OF NOAH.</u>

During this space of the Fifth Seal, when this Mystery Babylon religion, the Apostate and Harlot religion (Christianity) came into existence.

2 Thess. 2:3-7

3: Let no man deceive you by any means: for that day shall not come except there comes a falling away first, and that man of transgression be revealed, the son of perdition;

He was revealed as the Little Horn of Daniel 7 – Constantine. Who was the first Pope and started the religious form of government, The Papacy.

CHAPTER 9

THE 10 HORNS – GLOBAL GOVERNMENT – THE LAST FORM OF THE ROMAN EMPIRE AS A GLOBAL EMPIRE – 10 WORLD UNIONS:

Revelation 17: 16

16. And the <u>ten horns which thou sawest upon the beast (Papacy)</u>, these shall hate the whore (Zion) and shall make her desolate and naked and shall eat her flesh, and burn her with fire.

These kings ARE NOT the European Community.

NOTICE: these kings have no kingdom, but they receive POWER AS KINGS (they receive their kingdoms when the beast comes to power.) for <u>one hour with the beast.</u> (A VERY SHORT TIME, THE SAME AMOUNT OF TIME IT WILL TAKE TO DESTROY JERUSALEM) They give their power and strength unto the beast. THIS IS A WORLD ORDER!!!!! The world will be split into 10 Unions, and someone will be given power over each Union. Remember, this is a peace plan for the whole world. The Pope will want people who he can trust to go along with what he says.

Revelation 17:13 says THESE SHALL HAVE ONE MIND. (I'm wondering if Jesuits won't be put over each one of them this time around, so the Papacy knows it has full control.

Revelation 12:9

9. <u>And the great dragon was cast out, that old serpent, called the Devil, and Satan, which deceiveth the whole world: he was cast out into the earth, and his angels were cast out with him.</u>

Revelation 19:11-21

11. And I saw heaven opened, and behold a white horse, and he that sat upon him was called Faithful and True, and in righteousness he doth judge and make war.

12. His eyes were as a flame of fire, and on his head were many crowns; and he had a name written, that no man knew, but he himself.

13. And he was clothed with a vesture dipped in blood: and his name is called The Word of Yahweh.

14. And the armies which were in heaven followed him upon white horses (Spacecraft), clothed in fine linen, white and clean.

15. And out of his mouth goeth a sharp sword, that with it he should smite the nations: and he shall rule them with a rod of iron: and he treadeth the winepress of the fierceness and wrath of Yahweh.

16. And he hath on his vesture and on his thigh a name written, KING OF KINGS.

17. And I saw a Messenger standing in the sun; and he cried with a loud voice, saying to all the fowls that fly in the midst of heaven, Come and gather yourselves together unto the supper of the great Yahweh;

18. That ye may eat the flesh of kings, and the flesh of captains, and the flesh of mighty men, and the flesh of horses, and of them that sit on them, and the flesh of all men, both free and bond, both small and great.

19. And I saw the beast, and the kings of the earth, and their armies, gathered together to make war against him that sat on the horse, and against his army.

20. And the beast was taken, and with him the false prophet that wrought miracles before him, with which he deceived them that had received the mark of the beast, and them that worshipped his image. These both were cast alive into a lake of fire burning with brimstone.

21. And the remnant was slain with the sword of him that sat upon the horse, which sword proceeded out of his mouth: and all the fowls were filled with their flesh. Revelation 11:18 And the nations were angry, and thy wrath has come, and the time of the dead, that they should be judged, and that thou shouldest give reward unto thy servants the prophets, and to the saints, and them that FEAR THY NAME (Yahweh), small and great; and shouldest destroy them which destroy the earth.

"The Club of Rome had its beginnings in April of 1968 when leaders from ten different countries gathered in Rome...The organization claims to have the solutions for world peace and prosperity...The Club of Rome has been charged with the task of overseeing the regionalizaton and unification of the entire world...

"The Club's findings and recommendations are published from time to time in special, highly confidential reports, which are sent to the power-elite to be implemented. The Club released one such report, entitled Regionalized and Adaptive Model of the Global World System. The document reveals that the Club has divided the world into TEN POLITICAL/ECONOMIC REGIONS, which it refers to as KINGDOMS."

The Club of Rome is using environmental policies and the unified protection of the worldwide environment as a force moving towards a new world order. This group has divided the world into 10 regions and has placed Mikhail Gorbachev as chairman of the World Environmental Movement from his base in San Francisco.

What is going on while they put together each Union? They are also working on expanding each Union with other Unions till they have a complete One World Union or Order.

"Capitalists" and the Communist Dimension

The ultimate object of the parties of the Socialist International is nothing less than world government. As a first step towards it, they seek to strengthen the United Nations....

— Declaration of the Socialist International 1962 Conference, Oslo, Norway

The conflict between the two great superpowers ... <u>will be replaced by the USDR</u> (<u>a union of socialist democratic republics</u>). This will be the penultimate <u>stage of progress toward a truly global world federal union...</u>

This is what these 10 <u>ten</u> political/ economic regions, unions, or kingdoms are starting to look like.

WILL UPDATE AS THEY GET THEIR FLAG AND MONETARY SYSTEM.

1. Western - European Union - Euro -

A.   THE BEGINNINGS OF THE EUROPEAN UNION AND ONE WORLD GOVERNMENT:

Richard Nikolaus Eijiro, Count of Coudenhove-Kalergi (November 16, 1894 – July 27, 1972) was an Austrian-Japanese politician, philosopher, and count of Coudenhove-Kalergi. The pioneer of European integration, he served as the founding president of the Paneuropean Union for 49 years which would be the preliminary ideological foundation of the European Union.

Coudenhove-Kalergi was the first recipient of the Charlemagne Prize in 1950.

Some of the Recipients of the Charlemagne Prize.

1956 United Kingdom Sir Winston S. Churchill

1987 United States Henry Kissinger

1999 United Kingdom Tony Blair

2000 United States Bill Clinton

2004 Vatican City / Poland John Paul II (extraordinary prize)
2008 Germany Angela Merkel

Coudenhove-Kalergi is recognized as the founder of the first popular movement for a united Europe. His intellectual influences ranged from Immanuel Kant, Rudolf Kjellen, and Oswald Spengler to Arthur Schopenhauer and Friedrich Nietzsche in politics. He was an enthusiastic supporter of the "fourteen points" made by Woodrow Wilson on 8 January 1918 and the pacifist initiatives of Kurt Hiller. In December 1921, he joined the Masonic lodge "Humanitas" in Vienna. In 1922, he co-founded the Pan-European Union (PEU) with Archduke Otto von Habsburg as "the only way of guarding against an eventual world hegemony by Russia."

European integration would be the first step in creating a world government. With the rise of Fascism in Europe, the project was abandoned, and the "Pan-European" movement was forced to dissolve, but after the Second World War, Kalergi, thanks to frantic and tireless activity and the support of Winston Churchill, the Jewish Masonic Lodge B'nai B'rith and major newspapers like the New York Times, the plan manages to be accepted by the United States Government. The CIA [Jesuit controlled] later undertakes the completion of the project.

In his book «Praktischer Idealismus," Kalergi indicates that the residents of the future "United States of Europe" will not be the People of the Old Continent but a kind of sub-humans, products of miscegenation. He clearly states that the peoples

of Europe should interbreed with Asians and colored races, thus creating a multinational flock with no quality and easily controlled by the ruling elite.

Although no textbook mentions Kalergi, his ideas are the guiding principles of the European Union. The belief that the peoples of Europe should be mixed with Africans and Asians to destroy our identity and create a single mestizo race is the basis of all community policies that aim to protect minorities, not for humanitarian reasons but because of the directives issued by the ruthless Regime that machinates the greatest genocide in history. The Coudenhove-Kalergi European Prize is awarded every two years to Europeans who have excelled in promoting this criminal plan. Among those awarded with such a prize are Angela Merkel and Herman Van Rompuy.

1946 - Winston Churchill spoke of the need to form a 'European Family' or a 'United States of Europe' to ensure peace and prosperity for Europe.

The EU has its origins in the European Movement (1947), which was founded by Knight of Malta Joseph Retinger, who also founded the Bilderberg Group (1954).

1951 - "The Treaty of Paris," which was signed by Belgium, France, West Germany, Italy, the Netherlands, and Luxembourg. Which established the following ECSC.

1951 - "The European Coal and Steel Community" (ECSC) was an international organization serving to unify certain Continental European countries after World War II. The ECSC was the first international organization to be based on the principles of supranationalism.

1955 - The European flag of 12 gold stars on a blue background was created. The flag Heitz designed was adopted by the Council of Europe on December 8, 1955. December 8 being the date that the Roman Catholic Church celebrates its belief in the Immaculate Conception of Mary.

"Most people don't think about it, but the EU symbol was thought up by a Roman Catholic in honor of Mary," says P. H. Op't Hof (Chairman of The National Foundation for the Preservation of the Political Reformed Principles). The Vatican newspaper, L'Osservatore Romano, stated that the designer of the symbol, Arsène Heitz, said he had been inspired by reported visions of the Virgin Mary in 19th-century Paris.

David N. Samuel, author of European Union and the Roman Catholic Influence in Britain, wrote, "There is a natural affinity between the powerful state and the Roman Catholic theocratic ideal. The Church of Rome makes no bones about calling on its members to vote in a particular way, as it did in the Italian elections of 1992."

1957 - The ECSC was joined by two other similar communities, the European Economic Community and the European Atomic Energy Community.

1957 - The Treaty of Rome establishing the "European Economic Community" (EEC) was signed by 'The Original Six'. The formation of the EEC was the first step toward the common market and had two main goals: firstly, to transform trade, industry, and manufacturing in the Community; secondly, to take a step closer to a unified Europe.

European Community (EC), previously (from 1957 until Nov. 1, 1993) European Economic Community (EEC), by the name Common Market, designed to integrate the economies of Europe.

1967 - All its institutions were merged with that of the European Economic Community, but it retained its own independent legal personality.

The building was designed by Jacques Cuisinier and constructed in 1967 at the same time as the Berlaymont Building to group together more scattered departments of the European Commission. However, with the Commission refusing to share the Berlaymont with the Council of the European Union, Charlemagne was given to the Council's secretariat in 1971. This had previously been in the city center.

1987 - The Single European Act, EEC members committed themselves to remove all remaining barriers to a common market by 1992. The act also gave the EEC formal control of community policies on the environment, research and technology, education, health, consumer protection, and other areas.

1991 - "Treaty On European Union."

1993 - European Community (EC), previously (from 1957 until Nov. 1, 1993) European Economic Community (EEC), by name Common Market, designed to integrate the economies of Europe.

By the "Maastricht Treaty" (formally known as the Treaty on European Union; 1991), the European Economic Community was renamed the European Community and was embedded into the EU as the first of its three "pillars" (the second being a common foreign and security policy and the third being police and judicial cooperation in criminal matters). The treaty also provided the foundation for an economic and monetary union, which included the creation of a single currency, the EURO. The three communities were subsumed under the European Union (EU). The EC, or Common Market, then became the principal component of the EU.

2002 - The "European Community" came about when The Treaty of Paris expired, and all the ECSC activities and resources were absorbed by the European Community.

United States of Europe, European states, European federation, and Federal Europe are names used to refer to several similar hypothetical scenarios of the unification of Europe.

2002 - Vatican-issued Euro coins have the Pope's image with twelve stars.

Around 2003 - Pope John Paul II told Western Europe to come together under their Christian Heritage and move over to Socialism.

B.   PAPAL PRONOUNCEMENTS ON EUROPE

On August 31st, 2003, Pope John Paul II entrusted the future of the new Europe to the Virgin Mary. In the words of the Catholic news agency Zenit,

"He placed Europe in Mary's hands so that it would 'become a symphony of nations committed to building together the civilization of love and peace.' Last

Sunday, the Holy Father urged that the final draft of the European Constitution should recognize explicitly the Christian roots of the continent, as they constitute a 'guarantee of a future.'"

2004 - European Union Constitution signed on Romes Capitoline Hill

2009 - The European Union legally replaced the European Community. It took 42 years to make the European Union and the Papacy is over it.

2012 - Peter Sutherland, the non-executive chairman of Goldman Sachs International and the UN's special representative for migration, urged the European Union to "do its best to undermine" the "homogeneity" of its member states and create "multicultural states" in Europe. More Papacy Agendas for the world.

2015 - With nuns and priests in the Middle East refugee camps telling the Muslims to migrate to other countries, Pope Francis floods the E.U. with Muslims.

European Union Flag
Established: 11 / 01 / 1993

Vatican-issued Euro coins have the Pope's image with twelve stars.

A. The Pope told Western Europe to come together under their Christian roots and to come over to Socialism

B. "Most people don't think about it, but the EU symbol was thought up by a Roman Catholic in honor of Mary," says P. H. Op't Hof (Chairman of The National Foundation for the Preservation of the Political Reformed Principles). The Vatican newspaper, L'Osservatore Romano, stated that the designer of the symbol, Arsène Heitz, said he had been inspired by reported visions of the Virgin Mary in 19th-century Paris.

The flag Heitz designed was adopted by the Council of Europe on December 8, 1955. December 8 being the date that the Roman Catholic Church celebrates its belief in the Immaculate Conception of Mary C. David N. Samuel, author of *European Union and the Roman Catholic Influence in Britain*, wrote, "There is a natural affinity between the powerful state and the Roman Catholic theocratic ideal. The Church of Rome makes no bones about calling on its members to vote in a particular way, as it did in the Italian elections of 1992."

European Union Constitution was signed on 10-29-04 in Romes Capitoline Hill.

Where it is all heading: <u>The servants of globalization are trying to convince us that to deny our identity is a progressive and humanitarian act and that "racism" is wrong because they want us all to be blind consumers. It is necessary, now more than ever, to counter the lies of the System to awaken the revolutionary spirit of the Europeans. Everyone must see the truth that European Integration amounts to genocide. We have no other option, and the alternative is national suicide.</u>

2. Eurasian Union

Eurasian Union Flag

http://www.boston.com/news/world/europe/2014/03/06/putin-uses-carrot-and-stick-dominate-neighbors/56F8UoYDfvb7cXNCWgaQTP/story.html

A. We Will Strive to Ensure a New World Order: Vladimir Putin Outlines Plans for the EU

Posted on February 28, 2012 at 8:13 pm by Becket Adams In an article published just before Russia's upcoming election, Russian Prime Minister Vladimir Putin calls on eurozone leaders to consider the idea of creating what he calls a "Union of Europe."

That's right, writes Business Insider Adam Taylor, a Union of Europe, not a European Union, a free trade zone (and perhaps more) stretching from Lisbon to Vladivostok.

3. North American Union - Amero

THE BEGINNINGS OF A NORTH AMERICAN UNION / NEW WORLD ORDER IN THE UNITED STATES:

C. RONALD REAGAN:

NOTE: Watch how Reagan puts forth the ideas, and starts it, then... each President after pushes the same agendas and even magnifies them.

When Reagan was Governor of California, he was against Socialized Medicine, but after becoming President, he passed a bill for Socialized healthcare.

1979 - Proposed a North American agreement to produce a North American Continent where goods and people would cross boundaries more freely; this is the start of NAFTA.

"NAFTA is a major stepping stone to the New World Order." Henry Kissinger when campaigning for the passage of NAFTA.

1981 - Presented the idea of a North American Common Market.

B. The CIA was granted legal authority to spy on U.S. citizens with Executive Order 12333.

1983 - INTERPOL as a public international organization. Reagan had extended "appropriate privileges, exemptions, and immunities" but kept it subject to searches and seizures under appropriate legal circumstances. Reagan's order carried certain exemptions requiring that INTERPOL operations be subject to several U.S. laws, such as the Freedom of Information Act. Obama, however, removed those restrictions in his Dec. 16 amendment to Executive Order 12425. Executive Order -- Amending Executive Order 12425

1984 - Announced that full diplomatic relations between the United States and the Vatican had been established. The President did this over the opposition of the office of the Secretary of State. Done against our laws.

1985 - Notified Congress to begin negotiations with a Canada Free Trade Agreement. Gave 90 days to approve it.

1986 - Reagan, when Governor of California, was against Socialized Medicine. But after becoming President he passed a bill called the Emergency Medical

Treatment and Active Labor Act, or EMTALA. Thus socializing medicine and giving Illegal Aliens emergency healthcare.

1987 - Makes speech at U.N. for the world to come together in case we are attacked by aliens from another world. (One World Government)

"In this new world economy, national boundaries are increasingly becoming obsolete." - Ronald Reagan.

Pope John Paul II was the first Pope in history that has called for a "New World Order" outwardly, and it took place over 25 years after becoming Pope.

B. U.S. / Canada Free Trade Agreement finalized.

1988 - The Vatican condemned the Declaration of Independence as wickedness and called the Constitution of the United States a Satanic Document. — Avro Manhattan, The Dollar, and the Vatican, Ozark Book Publishers, p. 26.

D.   Death To A Nation And "Old Glory"

In 1776, Betsy Ross was commissioned to sew the first Colonial Flag.

The 13 red and white stripes represent the first original 13 colonies.

The flag's beginning had 13 stars, where since 1960 it has had 50 stars.

Through the many years, it had its ups and downs but kept its wag.

It has flown through many battles and wars and never has quit flying.

Has waved for freedom to all the immigrants who come to our shores.

Some had harder times than others for their freedom of this new life.

They also came to love "Old Glory" and fought for her with their dying.

"Old Glory" has been done a lot to, soiled, torn, walked on and burned.

Draped over the caskets of the honored dead who served for this country.

An emblem for people to stand in unity with and to serve honorably under.

A piece of cloth, it is what she stands for and the respect she has earned.

Today there is an agenda to get rid of the U.S. flag and to replace it.

Also getting rid of our heritage and pride of our country and its people.

People need to wake-up to the fact the U.S. is being destroyed from within.

This government is full of deceitful demonic traitors, and they won't quit.

They want this country and its flag to become just a memory to the old.

They are out for a North American Union, not States, but countries as one.

Canada and Mexico along with the U.S. will form one of 10 world unions.

So, the very young will never know or the freedoms that flag had showed.

So those with American pride, when you see her now, shed a tear for her.

It won't be too long before you will see the last "Old Glory" coming down.

For this country will no longer be known for freedom or its flag a waving.

Just a country living its end, losing our flag and freedoms that once were.

By Gary W. Stanfield

E.   GEORGE H. W. BUSH:

1991 - Bush speaks about a One World Order.

1992 - Mexico / Canada / U.S., North Atlantic Free Trade Agreement / NAFTA.

GARY WENDELL STANFIELD SR.

F. BILL CLINTON:

1993 - North American Development Bank And Border Cooperation Commission.

B. NAFTA - The U.S. Senate approved it by 60 to 38 on November 20, three days later. It was signed into law by President Bill Clinton on December 8, 1993, and entered force on January 1, 1994. Although it was signed by President Bush, it was a priority of President Clinton's.

1995 - TRANSATLANTIC COMMON MARKET can be traced back to the Clinton administration's decision to join the 1995 New Transatlantic Agenda with the European Commission.

G.   GEORGE W. BUSH:

2002 - Bush administration is working on a Social Security accord that would put tens of thousands of Mexicans [in Mexico] onto the Social Security roster and send hundreds of millions of dollars in benefits south of the border.

2005 - Security and Prosperity Partnership Of North America between Mexico / U.S. / Canada, without Congress approval.

Open Border Policy - Bush pursued a globalist agenda to create a North American Union, effectively erasing our borders with both Mexico and Canada. This was the hidden agenda behind the Bush administration's true open borders policy. The Bush administration truly wants the free, unimpeded movement of people across open borders with Mexico and Canada.

Texas NAFTA Highway; I-35, from Mexico to Canada.

2006 - VATICAN CITY, OCT. 24, 2006 (Zenit.org).- Bishops in the New World are doing what they can to promote Pope John Paul II's concept of the Americas as one continent, reports the Vatican.

132

A Vatican communiqué issued Saturday reported that the Special Council for America of the Secretariat of the Synod of Bishops has proposed including U.S. and Canadian bishops as delegates to the 5th General Conference of the Latin American Episcopate, which Benedict XVI plans to attend in Aparecida, Brazil, next May.

The final communiqué of the 11th meeting of the council, held in the Vatican on Oct. 2-3, confirmed the "hope" breathed in Rome about preparations for that meeting.

"It is hoped that delegations of the episcopate of the United States and of Canada will also participate to keep alive what has been called 'John Paul II's geography' of an America considered as one united continent," stated the communiqué.

The theme of the meeting will be "Disciples and Missionaries of Jesus Christ so That Our Peoples Will Have Life in Him." ZE06102405

North American Competitive Council. The council is part of the Security and Prosperity Partnership (SPP) that was established by the American, Canadian, and Mexican governments at the Trilateral meeting in Cancun, Mexico. As you will see from the attached article, "Sellout of America," the SPP plan is spelled out in detail in the CFR"s 59-page document entitled "Building a North American Community." It describes a five-year plan for the establishment by 2010 of an economic and security community with a common outer security perimeter, i.e., no borders between the three countries.

2007 - The Transatlantic Economic Council appears to be following a plan written in 1939 by a world government advocate who sought to create a Transatlantic Union as an international governing body. Transatlantic Economic Council by the U.S. and the EU through an agreement signed by President Bush and German Chancellor Angela Merkel. This council was started to achieve the creation of the Transatlantic Common Market by 2015

The Streit Council is named after Clarence K. Streit, whose 1939 book "Union Now" called for the creation of a Transatlantic Union as a step toward world government.

President Bush intends to abrogate U.S. sovereignty to the North American Union, a new economic and political entity that the President is quietly forming, much as the European Union has formed. { The beginnings of the European Union will be next after the North American Union beginnings.}

H. BARACK OBAMA:

2009 - Executive Order 13524 -- Amending Executive Order 12425 (Reagan) - to extend the appropriate privileges, exemptions, and immunities to the International Criminal Police Organization (INTERPOL)

2010 - Mexico to Build Southern Border Fence

The United States gave Mexico several millions of dollars to help build this fence.

2011 - "Beyond The Border," Canada and U.S., without Congress approval. National security vision is defined not by U.S. national borders but by a continental view of a "North American perimeter." The move toward a North American Union received another big boost.

After economic integration and homogenization of Mexico, the U.S. and Canada have been completed, at exchange rates that represent the lowered standard of living of the Americans and the Canadians.

Barack Obama and Canadian Prime Minister Stephen Harper met in Washington, D.C., to hammer out a deal on creating a common "perimeter" around the two countries while diminishing the role of the nations' shared border and developing a biometric system to track North Americans. This is a continuation of the Bush administration.

Mexico's President Fox said there will be a North American Union in 2023.

CREATING AMERICA'S FIRST DICTATOR THROUGH SENATE LEGISLATION S.679

Presidential Appointment Efficiency and Streamlining Act of 2011 President WILL HAVE the sole power to appoint people to positions of his choosing within our government, sped through the Senate and then made its way into the House and then to the President to sign. Yes, the other hand is quickly forming into a dictatorial fist that is about to smash our Constitution.

As you will recall, the beginning of the end of liberty in Rome commenced with Augustus Caesar, who compromised the authority of the Senate through the force of arms, and basically, the Senate became a facade {Like the U.S. Senate is today}.

America is poised with this bill, to morph immediately from a Republic into an empire with the privileged eunuchs of the Senate as window dressing and a dictator – the first American Caesar – at the country's helm.

"We will implement a National Civilian Security Force as large as the military." "Our police will be just as strong and have the same weapons as the military."

This One World Government is sometimes referred to as the New World Order. The Council on Foreign Relations has openly stated that its intentions are to bring about the surrender of the sovereignty of the national independence of the U.S. with the aim of creating a One World Government. The Council referred to as CFR, has influence in all vital areas of American life and around the world. Members have run or are running the major media outlets, including NBC, CBS, The New York Times, the Washington Post, and many other publications.

This most recent attack on the U.S. dollar's global reserve status comes on the heels of a report about a secret plot against the dollar involving Gulf Arab states, Russia, China, France, and Japan. According to the U.K.'s Independent, the Gulf countries are planning to create their own regional currency and stop pricing oil in dollars. The United Nations recently called for an end to the dollar's position as well. When this happens, oil will skyrocket. I've read where they have it planned in 2012 for the dollar to collapse, which will cause an uprising, most likely right around election time, so there won't be an election.

The Pope at the time wanted the One World Government up and running by the year 2000. As you can see, they are about 16 years behind their agenda and have to catch up. They are now saying 2025 for a One World Government.

This will be the North American Union Flag.

United States/Mexico/Canada

A. The NAFTA Agreement, as well as many other agreements, are solidifying North America as 1 of 10 world regions.

B. VATICAN CITY, _OCT. 24, 2006_ (Zenit.org).- Bishops in the New World are doing what they can to promote Pope John Paul II's concept of the Americas as one continent, reports the Vatican.

A Vatican communiqué issued Saturday reported that the Special Council for America of the Secretariat of the Synod of Bishops has proposed including U.S. and Canadian bishops as delegates to the 5th General Conference of the Latin American Episcopate, which Benedict XVI plans to attend in Aparecida, Brazil, next May.

The final communiqué of the 11th meeting of the council, held in theVatican on Oct. 2-3, confirmed the "hope" breathed in Rome about preparations for that meeting.

"It is hoped that delegations of the episcopate of the United States and of Canada will also participate to keep alive what has been called 'John Paul II's geography' of an America considered as one united continent," stated the communiqué.

The theme of the meeting will be "Disciples and Missionaries of Jesus Christ so That Our Peoples Will Have Life in Him." ZE06102405

C. In 2005, President Bush signed an agreement with Canada and Mexico without the approval of Congress or the people. To erase all borders and ignore the enforcement of Immigration Laws with this Union. The American Constitution will become obsolete when this happens.

The Vatican condemned the Declaration of Independence as wickedness and called the Constitution of the United States a Satanic Document. — Avro Manhattan, The Dollar, and the Vatican, Ozark Book Publishers, 1988, p. 26.

When the North American Union comes about, the Constitution, Bill of Rights, and State's Rights will all become void.

D. Carrol Quigley (deceased Bill Clinton mentor, Professor of History at Georgetown University, member of the CFR): In his book "Hope & Tragedy," he stated: "The C.F.R. is the American Branch of a society which originated in England and believes national boundaries should be obliterated and one world role

137

established." In other words, the CFR's activities are treasonous to the U.S. Constitution. They mean to put an end to the United States and make the U.S. part of their global government scheme. One only has to read their own publication, "Foreign Affairs Magazine," to get a first hand lesson in their treachery.

E. "Beyond the Border Declaration" by signing the declaration, the Obama administration has implemented without congressional approval a key initiative President Bush began under the Security and Prosperity Partnership of North America, moving the United States and Canada beyond the North American Free Trade Agreement, commonly known as NAFTA, toward a developing North American Union regional government.

WND has reported since 2006 that a blueprint published in 2005 by the Council on Foreign Relations titled "Building a North America Community" called for the establishment of a common security perimeter around North America by 2010 to facilitate the free movement of people, trade, and capital between the three nations of North America.

North American Competitive Council. The council is part of the Security and Prosperity Partnership (SPP) that was established by the American, Canadian, and Mexican governments at the June 2006 Trilateral meeting in Cancun, Mexico. As you will see from the attached article, "Sellout of America," the SPP plan is spelled out in detail in the CFR"s 59-page document entitled "Building a North American Community." It describes a five-year plan for the establishment by 2010 of an economic and security community with a common outer security perimeter, i.e., no borders between the three countries.

F. This One World Government is sometimes referred to as the New World Order. The Council on Foreign Relations has openly stated that its intentions are to bring about the surrender of the sovereignty of the national independence of the U.S. with the aim of creating a One World Government. The Council referred to as CFR, has influence in all vital areas of American life and around the world. Members have run or are running the major media outlets, including NBC, CBS, The New York Times, the Washington Post, and many other publications.

G. This most recent attack on the U.S. dollar's global reserve status comes on the heels of a report about a secret plot against the dollar involving Gulf Arab states, Russia, China, France, and Japan. According to the U.K.'s Independent, the Gulf countries are planning to create their own regional currency and stop pricing oil in dollars. The United Nations recently called for an end called for an end to the dollar's position as well. When this happens, oil will skyrocket. I've read where they have it planned in 2012 for the dollar to collapse, which will cause an uprising, most likely right around election time, so there won't be an election.

H. After economic integration and homogenization of Mexico, the U.S. and Canada have been completed at exchange rates that represent the lowered standard of living of the Americans and the Canadians.

4. South American Union - Sucre

South American Union Flag

Established: 12 / 08 / 2004A. Critics of the Union of South American Nation's efforts to establish a common currency see it as playing right into the hands of the world banking cartel. The clustering and assimilation of currencies facilitates the eventual merger into a one-world currency promoted by the Council on Foreign Relations and its political puppets. They see the move toward the South American Union with its single currency as easily fitting with the European Union and current efforts to establish the North American Union.

5. African Union -

Established: 12 / 08 / 2004

A. Critics of the Union of South American Nations's efforts to establish a common currency see it as playing right into the hands of the world banking cartel. The clustering and assimilation of currencies facilitates the eventual merger into a one-world currency promoted by the Council on Foreign Relations and its political puppets. They see the move toward the South American Union with its single currency as easily fitting with the European Union and current efforts to establish the North American Union.

5. African Union - Afro

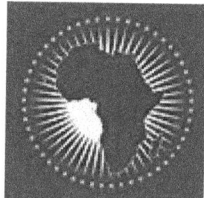

African Union Flag

Established: 07 / 09 / 2002

Afro-African Union Flag Established: 07 / 09 / 2002

6. Mediterranean Union - All Muslim countries. Mediterranean Union Flag

The Muslim Brotherhood is to bring all Muslim countries into a Muslim Union/Caliphate, and why all the problems in the Middle East? The fact that the upper hierarchy of the Muslim Brotherhood is Illuminati. So it goes right to Rome and the Papacy. The Muslim Brotherhood fought with Hitler during WW2.

The Muslim Brotherhood is suggesting that they can step in and transform the Egyptian government into a stable country under a form of Islamic Socialism, and

TRUTH REVEALED

they are providing support to the student protestors and youths that are filling the streets.

Obama is supplying the Muslim Brotherhood and Egypt with F16 Jets and 220 Abram Tanks.

7. Asian Pacific Union

The union, if formed, would have a common charter, institutions, and currency. Although John Howard, the former Prime Minister of Australia, spoke of a Pacific Union whilst in office, his government's emphasis was focused on bilateral relations and agreements with the individual states of the Forum.

Established: 12 / 08 / 2004

A. Critics of the Union of South American Nations's efforts to establish a common currency see it as playing right into the hands of the world banking cartel. The clustering and assimilation of currencies facilitates the eventual merger into a one-world currency promoted by the Council on Foreign Relations and its political puppets. They see the move toward the South American Union with its single currency as easily fitting with the European Union and current efforts to establish the North American Union.

The APU was organized in Tokyo in 1965 by the initiative of parliamentarians from five nations in Asia - the Republic of China (Taiwan), Japan, the Republic of Korea, the Republic of the Philippines, and the Kingdom of Thailand.

The establishment and purpose of the APU, unprecedented in Asian history, received an enthusiastic response from the Asian nations. Year after year, Indonesia, the Khmer Republic, Malaysia, Laos, and the Republic of Vietnam joined the APU. In 1973 and 1974, however, some nations ceased to be members due to the unavoidable circumstances of their own countries or from a political change befallen their region. At the 24th Council Meeting of the APU held in Seoul from

141

June 13 to 15, 1978, the Republic of Nauru in the Central Pacific was admitted as a full member. At the 17th General Assembly held in Tokyo in 1981, the Territory of Guam, the Republic of Vanuatu, the Republic of Palau, and the Federated States of Micronesia joined the Union as associate members. At the 18th General Assembly held in Agana, Guam, the Republic of the Marshall Islands and the Commonwealth of the Northern Mariana Islands joined the Union as associate members. At the 18th General Assembly, the Charter of the Union was amended, above all, in Art. 8 (voting) and Art. 12 (Steering Committee). So far as the membership is concerned, the Republic of Vanuatu and Fiji were admitted to the Union in 1983, and Solomon Islands joined as a full member in 1986. In 1987, the Federated States of Micronesia and the Republic of the Marshall Islands became a full member, respectively, because of their acquisition of independent sovereign status. In 1988, the Republic of the Philippines reentered the Union and regained the former position of founding member. In the same year, the Independent State of Papua New Guinea, the Kingdom of Tonga, and Western Samoa joined as a full member, respectively. In 1989, the Republic of Kiribati, in 1990 Cook Islands, and in 1991 Tuvalu were admitted to the Union, respectively. In 1992 Republic of Fiji returned to her membership in the Union. In 1993, Vietnam and the Lao People's Democratic Republic were granted admission to the Union, but Vietnam is participating in APPU conferences as an observer because her internal procedure is not completed yet. In 1994, the Republic of Palau became a full member because she gained her independence. Then, in 2000, Mongolia was admitted to the Union, including not only Japan, South Korea, Australia, New Zealand, Indonesia, Malaysia, the Philippines, Singapore, and Thailand.

Asian-Pacific Postal Union

The Asian-Pacific Postal Union (APPU) was formed (in its current form) by an International treaty through an Asian-Pacific Postal Convention signed in Yogyakarta on 27 March 1981. The organization has origins dating back to 1961.

The purpose of the union is to extend, facilitate, and improve postal relations and promote cooperation in the field of postal services between the member countries;

Is there such a thing as a Pacific Union?

Harmonizing both the CER and the Pacific Regional Trade Agreement (PARTA) is one possibility for moving towards this goal. The idea's future has become somewhat confused with the Rudd Government's call for an Asia-Pacific Community, which would have a wider membership than a Pacific Union. "Beyond Cooperation: Towards an Oceanic Community."

8. Asian Union - Asian Union Flag

9. Caribbean Union - Caribbean Union Flag

10. Australian or South Africa Union -

1. Once the formation of these major trading blocks is completed, the next step would be the unification of the blocks into a one-world government. This one-world government is sometimes referred to as the New World Order.

2. With the acceptance of South America's Union accepting the "Sucre" then the North American Union will push for the "Amero." (That's the US/Canada/Mexico single fiat currency that has been in the planning stages for decades.) By gradually having fewer and fewer fiat currencies in the world, eventually, our One World Government planners will claim that we might as well have a global fiat currency to really facilitate global trade.

Medvedev Shows Off Sample Coin of New 'World Currency' at G-8 By Lyubov Pronina

July 10 (Bloomberg) -- Russian President Dmitry Medvedev illustrated his call for a supranational currency to replace the dollar by pulling from his pocket a sample coin of a "united future world currency."

143

"Here it is," Medvedev told reporters today in L'Aquila, Italy, after a summit of the Group of Eight nations. "You can see it and touch it."

The coin, which bears the words "unity in diversity," was minted in Belgium and presented to the heads of G-8 delegations, Medvedev said.

The question of a supranational currency "concerns everyone now, even the mints," Medvedev said. The test coin "means they're getting ready. I think it's a good sign that we understand how interdependent we are."

Medvedev has repeatedly called for creating a mix of regional reserve currencies as part of the drive to address the global financial crisis while questioning the U.S. dollar's future as a global reserve currency. Russia's proposals for the G-20 meeting in London in April included the creation of a supranational currency.

3. Regional governments. This council would resolve regional conflicts, promote military cooperation, and allow for the regional coordination of weapons production.

4. Each will have its own Union flag.

"He Who Does Not Remember History Is Condemned To Repeat It" - Georges Santayana

Revelations 13:1-3

1. And I stood upon the sand of the sea, and saw a beast rise up out of the sea, having seven heads and ten horns, and upon his horns ten crowns, and upon his heads the name of blasphemy.

2. And the beast which I saw was like unto a leopard (Grecian Empire), and his feet were as the feet of a bear (Medo-Persia Empire), and his mouth as the mouth of a lion (Babylonian Empire): and the dragon gave him his power, and his seat, and great authority.

144

3. _And I saw one of his heads as it were wounded to death; and his deadly wound was healed: and all the world wondered after the beast._

Napolean took the Pope's power away and now he is regaining it back and just about there for the 10 World Unions then over to his One World Order.

�_The will of the Pope is the supreme law of all lands._� � Archbishop John Ireland, St. Paul, Minn.

Why is it the Pope has such tremendous power? Why, the Pope is the ruler of the world. All the emperors, all the kings, all the princes, all the presidents of the world are as these altar boys of mine. The Pope is the ruler of the world. Priest Phelan in _Western Watchman_, June 27, 1912.

From Pope Leo XIII

Encyclical Letter June 20, 1894 :

"We hold upon this earth the place of God Almighty."1825, Pope Leo XII issued a papal coin with the writings "SEDET SUPER UNIVERSUM," which means the " Universal seat of authority over the entire world." Satan's seat is in Rome right now but will be moved to ZION when the Papacy regains its power and will rule the world from Jerusalem, which will become the World Capital at that time.

This should prove the Pope is over the United Nations and one day will step forward and claim his authority.

The Vatican Agenda:

The reason no country has said Jerusalem is the capital of Israel is because the Papacy has been trying to get control of ZION for centuries. This was preplanned back in 1948 when Israel became a nation.

When the peace talks with Israel started the Vatican stepped forward and said they wanted to be part of the peace talks too.

The Papacy wants ZION to be split among the Christian, Jewish, and Islam, and the Pope will be the overseer.

I. ONE WORLD ORDER

DANIEL 2:40-43

40 And the fourth kingdom shall be strong as iron: forasmuch as iron breaketh in pieces and subdueth all *things*: and as iron that breaketh all these, shall it break in pieces and bruise.

41 And whereas thou sawest the feet and toes, part of potters' clay, and part of iron, the kingdom shall be divided; but there shall be in it of the strength of the iron, forasmuch as thou sawest the iron mixed with miry clay.

42 And *as* the toes of the feet *were* part of iron, and part of clay, *so* the kingdom shall be partly strong, and partly brittle.

The Papacy cannot rely on its own power, and why it must have strong country armies to back it up. Since it is a religious government, it must have a secular army's backing to do its fighting.

[source--AAP December 27, 2005]

Pope Benedict, in his first Christmas address on Sunday, urged humanity to unite against terrorism, poverty, and environmental blight and called for a "New World Order" to correct economic imbalances.

Revelations 13:1-3

1 And I stood upon the sand of the sea and saw a beast rise up out of the sea, having seven heads and ten horns, and upon his horns ten crowns, and upon his heads the name of blasphemy.

2 And the beast which I saw was like unto a leopard, and his feet were as the feet of a bear, and his mouth as the mouth of a lion: and the dragon gave him his power, and his seat, and great authority.

3 And I saw one of his heads as it were wounded to death; and his deadly wound was healed: and all the world wondered after the beast.

"By the end of this decade we will live under the first One World Government that has ever existed in the society of nations ... a government with absolute authority to decide the basic issues of human survival. One world government is inevitable." - Pope John Paul II.

Pope calls for a new world order

Barney Zwartz

July 9, 2009

POPE Benedict XVI has proposed a new world political authority "with real teeth," possibly in place of the United Nations, to enforce an ethical financial order and end the global financial crisis.

Calling for more aid, a bigger role for trade unions, and an economic system aimed at the common good as well as profit, the Pope said only a moral market could end the crisis and solve world poverty.

His suggested political authority would manage globalization, revive economies, stop the crisis deepening, protect the environment, and regulate worldwide migration. It would need to be universally recognized and given power to ensure compliance from all countries.

The world's wealth was growing, but so was inequality. Aid to developing countries also provided economic benefits to donors, he said.

One was that people should be allowed to decide how to allocate a portion of their taxes that would help welfare and aid. Another was that trade unions should also work for non-members, particularly workers in developing countries.

"As society becomes ever more globalized, it makes us neighbors but does not make us brothers," he said.

Pope Calls For A New World Order: The San Francisco Chronicle had a front-page story with the title, "Pope Calls for a New World Order He endorses capitalism with a social conscience." This article stated that the pope has a vision of a post-Communist world of economic and social justice, leaving room for capitalism, with a moral core but no place for "consumer societies."

I always figured they were about 15 years behind their goal date. The goal date was the year 2000, not it's 2025.

Daniel 7:26 But the court will sit, and his power will be taken away and completely destroyed forever. Then the sovereignty, power, and greatness of the kingdoms under the whole heaven will be handed over to the elect, the people of the Most High. His kingdom will be an everlasting kingdom, and all rulers will worship and obey Him."

REVELATION CHAPTER 18

THIS WHOLE CHAPTER IS SPEAKING ABOUT ZION:

18 And after these things I saw another Messenger come down from heaven, having great power; and the earth was lightened with his righteousness.

2 And he cried mightily with a strong voice, saying, Babylon the great is fallen, is fallen, and is become the habitation of devils, and the hold of every foul spirit, and a cage of every unclean and hateful bird.

3 For all nations have drunk of the wine of the wrath of her fornication, and the kings of the earth have committed fornication with her, and the merchants of the earth are waxed rich through the abundance of her delicacies.

4 And I heard another voice from heaven, saying, Come out of her, my people, that ye be not partakers of her transgressions, and that ye receive not of her plagues.

5 For her transgressions have reached unto heaven, and Yahweh hath remembered her iniquities.

6 Reward her even as she rewarded you, and double unto her double according to her works: in the cup which she hath filled fill to her double.

7 How much she hath glorified herself, and lived deliciously, so much torment and sorrow give her: for she saith in her heart, I sit a queen, and am no widow, and shall see no sorrow.

8 Therefore shall her plagues come in one day, death, and mourning, and famine; and she shall be utterly burned with fire: for strong is Yahweh who judgeth her.

9 And the kings of the earth, who have committed fornication and lived deliciously with her, shall bewail her, and lament for her, when they shall see the smoke of her burning,

10 Standing afar off for the fear of her torment, saying, Alas, alas that great city Babylon, that mighty city! for in one hour is thy judgment come.

11 And the merchants of the earth shall weep and mourn over her; for no man buyeth their merchandise any more:

¹² The merchandise of gold, and silver, and precious stones, and of pearls, and fine linen, and purple, and silk, and scarlet, and all thyine wood, and all manner vessels of ivory, and all manner vessels of most precious wood, and of brass, and iron, and marble,

¹³ And cinnamon, and odors, and ointments, and frankincense, and wine, and oil, and fine flour, and wheat, and beasts, and sheep, and horses, and chariots, and slaves, and souls of men.

¹⁴ And the fruits that thy soul lusted after are departed from thee, and all things which were dainty and goodly are departed from thee, and thou shalt find them no more at all.

¹⁵ The merchants of these things, which were made rich by her, shall stand afar off for the fear of her torment, weeping and wailing,

¹⁶ And saying, Alas, alas that great city, that was clothed in fine linen, and purple, and scarlet, and decked with gold, and precious stones, and pearls!

¹⁷ For in one hour so great riches is come to naught. And every shipmaster, and all the company in ships, and sailors, and as many as trade by sea, stood afar off,

¹⁸ And cried when they saw the smoke of her burning, saying, What city is like unto this great city!

¹⁹ And they cast dust on their heads, and cried, weeping and wailing, saying, Alas, alas that great city, wherein were made rich all that had ships in the sea by reason of her costliness! for in one hour is she made desolate.

²⁰ Rejoice over her, thou heaven, and ye apostles and prophets; for Yahweh hath avenged you on her.

²¹ And a mighty Messenger took up a stone like a great millstone, and cast it into the sea, saying, Thus with violence shall that great city Babylon be thrown down, and shall be found no more at all.

22 And the voice of harpers, and musicians, and of pipers, and trumpeters, shall be heard no more at all in thee; and no craftsman, of whatsoever craft he be, shall be found any more in thee; and the sound of a millstone shall be heard no more at all in thee;

23 And the light of a candle shall shine no more at all in thee; and the voice of the bridegroom and of the bride shall be heard no more at all in thee: for thy merchants were the great men of the earth; for by thy sorceries were all nations deceived.

24 And in her was found the blood of prophets, and of elect, and of all that were slain upon the earth.

REVELATION CHAPTER 19

Revelation 19:

1 And after these things I heard a great voice of much people in heaven, saying, Halleluyah; Salvation, and honor, and power, unto Yahweh our Mighty One:

2 For true and righteous are his judgments: for He hath judged the great whore, which did corrupt the earth with her fornication, and hath avenged the blood of His servants at her hand.

3 And again they said, Halleluyah. <u>And her smoke rose up for ever and ever.</u>

4 And the four and twenty elders and the four beasts fell down and worshipped Yahweh that sat on the throne, saying, Halleluyah.

5 And a voice came out of the throne, saying, Praise our Yahweh, all ye His servants, and ye that fear him, both small and great.

6 And I heard as it were the voice of a great multitude, and as the voice of many waters, and as the voice of mighty thunderings, saying, Halleluyah: for Yahweh Almighty omnipotent reigned.

7 Let us be glad and rejoice, and give honor to Him: for the marriage of the Lamb is come, and his wife hath made herself ready.

8 And to her was granted that she should be arrayed in fine linen, clean and white: for the fine linen is the righteousness of believers.

9 And he saith unto me, Write, Blessed are they which are called unto the marriage supper of the Lamb. And he saith unto me, These are the true sayings of Yahweh.

10 And I fell at his feet to worship him. And he said unto me, See thou do it not: I am thy fellow servant, and of thy brethren that have the testimony of Yahweh: worship Yahweh: for the testimony of Yahweh is the spirit of prophecy.

11 And I saw heaven opened, and behold a white horse; and he that sat upon him was called Faithful and True, and in righteousness He doth judge and make war.

12 His eyes were as a flame of fire, and on his head were many crowns; and He had a name written, that no man knew, but he Himself.

13 And He was clothed with a vesture dipped in blood: and His name is called The Word of Yahweh.

14 And the armies which were in heaven followed Him upon white horses {spacecraft}, clothed in fine linen, white and clean.

15 And out of His mouth goeth a sharp sword, that with it He should smite the nations: and He shall rule them with a rod of iron: and He treadeth the winepress of the fierceness and wrath of Almighty Yahweh.

16 And He hath on his vesture and on his thigh a name written, King of kings.

17 And I saw an Messenger standing in the sun; and he cried with a loud voice, saying to all the fowls that fly in the midst of heaven, Come and gather yourselves together unto the supper of the great Yahweh;

18 That ye may eat the flesh of kings, and the flesh of captains, and the flesh of mighty men, and the flesh of horses, and of them that sit on them, and the flesh of all men, both free and bond, both small and great.

19 And I saw the beast, and the kings of the earth, and their armies, gathered together to make war against Him that sat on the horse, and against his army.

20 And the beast was taken, and with him the false prophet that wrought miracles before him, with which he deceived them that had received the mark of the beast, and them that worshipped his image. These both were cast alive into a lake of fire burning with brimstone.

21 And the remnant were slain with the sword of Him that sat upon the horse, which sword proceeded out of his mouth: and all the fowls were filled with their flesh.

The Seven Last Plagues are referred to as the Wrath of Yahweh!

Let no one foolishly imagine that they will not occur; because the Scriptures must be fulfilled.

Yahweh's people will be saved from His wrath when it is poured out.

1 Thessalonians 5:8–9

8. But since we belong to the day, let us be self-controlled, putting on faith and love as a breastplate, and the hope of salvation as a helmet.

9. For <u>Yahweh did not appoint us to suffer wrath</u> {HIS WRATH} but to receive salvation through our Master, Yahweh Messiah.

Ephesians 5:1-7

1. Be ye therefore followers of Yahweh, as dear children;

2. And walk in love, as the Messiah also hath loved us, and hath given himself for us an offering and a sacrifice to Yahweh for a sweet smelling savour.

3. But fornication, and all uncleanness, or covetousness, let it not be once named among you, as becometh believers;

4. Neither filthiness, nor foolish talking, nor jesting, which are not convenient: but rather giving of thanks.

5. For this ye know, that no whoremonger, nor unclean person, nor covetous man, who is an idolater, hath any inheritance in the kingdom of the Messiah and of Yahweh.

6. Let no man deceive you with vain words: for because of these things cometh the wrath of Yahweh upon the children of disobedience.

7. Be not ye therefore partakers with them.

Romans 13:4

For he is the minister of Yahweh to thee for good. But if thou do that which is evil, be afraid; for he beareth not the sword in vain: for he is the minister of Yahweh, a revenger to execute wrath upon him that doeth evil.

Jeremiah 4:23-27

"I beheld the earth, and, lo, it was without form, and void; and the heavens, and they had no light. I beheld the mountains, and, lo, they trembled, and all the hills moved lightly. I beheld, and, lo, there was no man, and all the birds of the heavens were fled. I beheld, and, lo, the fruitful place was a wilderness, and all the cities thereof were broken down at the presence of Yahweh, and by His fierce anger. For thus hath Yahweh said, The whole land shall be desolate; yet will I not make a full end."

Revelation 11:15

And the seventh Messenger sounded; and there were great voices in heaven, saying, The kingdoms of this world are become the kingdoms of our Yahweh, and of his Messiah; and He shall reign for ever and ever.

Isaiah 34:8,9

8 For it is the day of the Yahweh's vengeance, and the year of recompenses for the controversy of Zion.

9 And the streams thereof shall be turned into pitch, and the dust thereof into brimstone, and the land thereof shall become burning pitch.

10 It shall not be quenched night nor day; the smoke thereof shall go up for ever: from generation to generation it shall lie waste; none shall pass through it for ever and ever.

Revelation 14:10,11

10 The same shall drink of the wine of the wrath of Yahweh, which is poured out without mixture into the cup of his indignation; and he shall be tormented with fire and brimstone in the presence of the righteous Messengers, and in the presence of the Lamb:

11 And the smoke of their torment ascendeth up for ever and ever: and they have no rest day nor night, who worship the beast and his image, and whosoever receiveth the mark of his name.

Revelation 19:2,3

2 For true and righteous are his judgments: for He hath judged the great whore (ZION), which did corrupt the earth with her fornication, and hath avenged the blood of His servants at her hand.

3 And again they said, Halleluyah. And her smoke rose up for ever and ever.

When scriptures speak of smoke rising forever and ever, it just means, that whatever scriptures is speaking of when that is said, that whatever it is will not ever exist again.

REVELATION CHAPTER 20

[1] And I saw a Messenger come down from heaven, having the key to the bottomless pit and a great chain in his hand.

[2] And he laid hold on the dragon, that old serpent, which is the Devil, and Satan, and bound him a thousand years,

[3] And cast him into the bottomless pit (Grave), and shut him up, and set a seal upon him, that he should deceive the nations no more, till the thousand years should be fulfilled: and after that he must be loosed a little season.

[4] And I saw thrones, and they sat upon them, and judgment was given unto them:

12 heads of the 12 tribes and the 12 disciples, will sit on the thrones.

Ruben, Simeon, Levi, Judah, Zebulun, Issachar, Dan, Gad, Asher, Naphtali, Joseph, Benjamin

Luke 22:30

That ye may eat and drink at my table in my kingdom and sit on thrones judging the twelve tribes of Judaea.

Matthew 19:28

And Immanuel said unto them, Verily I say unto you, that ye which have followed me, (the 12 disciples) in the regeneration when the Son of man shall sit in the throne of his glory/righteousness, ye also shall sit upon twelve thrones, judging the twelve tribes of Judaea.

And I saw the souls of them that were beheaded for the witness of Yahweh Messiah, and for the word of Yahweh, and which had not worshipped the beast, neither his image, neither had received his mark upon their foreheads, nor in their hands; and they lived and reigned with Yahweh Messiah a thousand years.

5 But the rest of the dead lived not again until the thousand years were finished. This is the first resurrection.

6 Blessed and righteous is he that hath part in the first resurrection: on such the second death hath no power, but they shall be priests of Yahweh and of Messiah and shall reign with him a thousand years.

7 And when the thousand years are expired, Satan shall be loosed out of his prison (the Grave),

8 And shall go out to deceive the nations which are in the four quarters of the earth, Gog, and Magog, to gather them together to battle: the number of whom is as the sand of the sea.

9 And they went up on the breadth of the earth, and compassed the camp of the saints about, and the beloved city: and fire came down from Yahweh out of heaven and devoured them.

10 And the devil that deceived them was cast into the lake of fire and brimstone, where the beast and the false prophet are, and shall be tormented day and night for ever and ever.

[11] And I saw a great white throne, and him that sat on it, from whose face the earth and the heaven fled away; and there was found no place for them.

[12] And I saw the dead, small and great, stand before Yahweh; and the books were opened: and another book was opened, which is the book of life: and the dead were

judged out of those things which were written in the books, according to their works.

[13] And the sea gave up the dead which were in it; and death and the grave delivered up the dead which were in them: and they were judged every man according to their works.

CHAPTER 10
THE SON OF PERDITION:

4: Who opposeth and exalteth himself above all that is called a deity, or that is worshipped; so that he as a deity sitteth in the temple of God / a deity, shewing himself that he is a deity.

5: Remember ye not, that, when I was yet with you, I told you these things?

6: And now ye know what witholdeth that he might be revealed in his time.

7: For the mystery of iniquity doth already work: only he who now letteth will let, until he be taken out of the way. [Yahweh's Spirit of salvation was taken from the earth]

The mystery of iniquity was already at work in the Roman Empire. The Roman Empire's government was changed from a secular to a religious government, and that is when the son of perdition was revealed which is the Pontifex Maximus (POPE).

The Emporers wanted to be worshiped as a deity. The Pope wants to be worshiped as a deity also, in that he puts himself in the place of Yahweh here on earth and has infallible powers.

2 Thess. 2:8-12

8: And then shall that Wicked be revealed, whom Yahweh shall consume with the spirit of his mouth and shall destroy with the brightness of his coming.

9: Even him, whose coming is after the working of Satan with all power and signs and lying wonders.

10: And with all deceivableness of unrighteousness in them that perish; because they received not the love of the truth, that they might be saved.

11: And for this cause Yahweh shall send them strong delusion, that they should believe a lie:

12: That they all might be damned who believed not the truth but had pleasure in unrighteousness.

We are living at the end of the Fifth Seal, which the end of the Fifth Seal is the Armageddon War and the return of Yahweh.

The following scriptures are the future brethren of those under the table in Revelation 6:11, who are waiting for those to be murdered as they were. Yahweh's Elect will not worship the image of the beast.

Revelation 13:15

And he had power to give life unto the image of the beast, that the image of the beast should both speak, and cause that as many as would not worship the image of the beast should be murdered.

A.   THE IMAGE OF THE BEAST/PAPACY IS THE POPE.

2 Thessalonians 2:4

Who opposeth and exalteth himself above all that is called a mighty one, or that is worshiped; so that he as a mighty one sitteth in the temple of a mighty one, shewing himself that he is a mighty one.

Revelation 13:7-8

The beast in Chapter 13 is the Pope.

7. And it was given unto him to make war with the elect, and to overcome them: and power was given him over all kindreds, and tongues, and nations.

8. And all that dwell upon the earth shall worship him, whose names are not written in the book of life of the Lamb slain from the foundation of the world.

Here is something else that proves the above SPACE between those under the table and the future ones, which is the FORMER and LATTER RAIN. The outpouring of Yahweh's Spirit. The Former Rain was poured out starting at Pentecost, and the Latter Rain was poured out before Yahweh's return and the last believers to be murdered as they were. The former Rain of Yahweh's Spirit was given, then Yahweh's Spirit of salvation was taken away - the Latter Rain of Yahweh's Spirit is when it will be given again.

Acts 2:1-21

1 And when the day of Pentecost was fully come, they were all with one accord in one place.

2 And suddenly there came a sound from heaven as of a rushing mighty wind, and it filled all the house where they were sitting.

3 And there appeared unto them cloven tongues like as of fire, and it sat upon each of them.

4 And they were all filled with the Spirit, and began to speak with other tongues, as the Spirit gave them utterance.

5 And there were dwelling at Zion Jews, devout men, out of every nation under heaven.

6 Now when this was noised abroad, the multitude came together, and were confounded, because that every man heard them speak in his own language.

7 And they were all amazed and marvelled, saying one to another, Behold, are not all these which speak Galilaeans?

8 And how hear we every man in our own tongue, wherein we were born?

9 Parthians, and Medes, and Elamites, and the dwellers in Mesopotamia, and in Judaea, and Cappadocia, in Pontus, and Asia,

10 Phrygia, and Pamphylia, in Egypt, and in the parts of Libya about Cyrene, and strangers of Rome, Jews and proselytes,

11 Cretes and Arabians, we do hear them speak in our tongues the wonderful works of Yahweh.

12 And they were all amazed, and were in doubt, saying one to another, What meaneth this?

13 Others mocking said, these men are full of new wine.

14 But Peter, standing up with the eleven, lifted up his voice, and said unto them, Ye men of Judaea, and all ye that dwell at Zion, be this known unto you, and hearken to my words:

15 For these are not drunken, as ye suppose, seeing it is but the third hour of the day.

16 But this is that which was spoken by the prophet Joel; Joel 2:23 - Be glad then, ye children of Zion, and rejoice in Yahweh: for he hath given you the former rain moderately, and he will cause to come down for you the rain, the former rain, and the latter rain in the first month.

17 And it shall come to pass in the last days, saith Yahweh, I will pour out of my Spirit upon all flesh: and your sons and your daughters shall prophesy, and your young men shall see visions, and your old men shall dream dreams:

18 And on my servants and on my handmaidens, I will pour out in those days of my Spirit; and they shall prophesy: AT THE TIME OF MOSES AND ELIYAH.

The Remaining 3 Verses are showing when the Latter Rain is poured out. Those at Pentecost were experiencing a glimpse, a taste of what would happen again by the Spirit just before Yahweh returns.

19 And I will shew wonders in heaven above, and signs in the earth beneath; blood, and fire, and vapor of smoke:

20 The sun shall be turned into darkness, and the moon into blood, before the great and notable day of Yahweh comes:

21 And it shall come to pass, that whosoever shall call on the name of Yahweh shall be saved.

Daniel 12:4

4 But thou, O Daniel, shut up the words, and seal the book, even to the time of the end: many shall run to and fro, and knowledge shall be increased.

THIS IS ALL ABOUT BRINGING ABOUT THE GLOBAL RELIGION DURING THE GLOBAL GOVERNMENT - WE ARE LIVING AT THE VERY END OF THE 5TH SEAL WHEN THE POPE IS GETTING BACK HIS POWER, RIGHT BEFORE YAHWEH'S RETURN.

Daniel 7:23 - *Thus, he said, the fourth beast shall be the fourth kingdom upon earth, which shall be diverse from all kingdoms, and shall devour the whole earth, and shall tread it down, and break it in pieces.*

B.   Christianity Made for a Purpose

No religion or church will change a nation.
They are all built on the wrong foundation.
Yes, religion is an all-man-made prevarication
They are found on every continent and nation

Christianity was created to deceive man,
Such a big part to Satan's deceitful plan.
To deliver the world and men into his hand,
Yahweh's plan of salvation is to save man.

Yahweh Messiah is a Faith, not a religion
One day you will have to make a decision.
This is what will cause the end time division.
When Christianity becomes the world religion.

Immanuel, born to become Yahweh in the flesh.
The real truth will be given to man all afresh,
Then wheat from the chaff will Yahweh thresh.
The elect will be taken, those left, burning flesh.

By Gary Wendell Stanfield

"Rome, when in minority, is as gentle as a lamb, when in equality, is as clever as a fox, and when in the majority, is as fierce as a tiger."

"The Pope is not only the representative of Jesus Christ, but he is Jesus Christ, Himself, hidden under the veil of human flesh." — Catholic National, July 1895.

Pope Boniface VIII, *Unam Sanctam*, Nov. 18, 1302: "Now, therefore, we declare, say, determine, and pronounce that for every human creature it is necessary for salvation to be subject to the Roman pontiff."

Papal Bull - Unam Sanctum: "Furthermore, we declare, we proclaim, we define that it is absolutely necessary for salvation that every human creature be subject to the Roman Pontiff." (Declaratio quod subesse Romano Pontifici est omni humanae creaturae de necessitate salutis) From Pope Leo XIII's Encyclical Letter June 20, 1894 :

"We hold upon this earth the place of God Almighty."

Pope St. Gregory the Great: "The holy universal Church teaches that it is not possible to worship God truly except in her and asserts that all who are outside of her will not be saved."

Pope Gregory "Presented himself as heir to the unlimited commission ... over all souls." Encyclopedia Britannica; 1990, vol. 26 - page 927.

"There is no higher authority ...." Pastor Actermus 1870.

"The Pope and God are the same, so he has all power in Heaven and earth." — Pope Pius V, quoted in Barclay, Chapter XXVII, p. 218, "Cities Petrus Bertanous."

Los Angeles Times December 12, 1984, quoted Pope John Paul II as saying, "Don't go to God for the forgiveness of sins. Come to me." And God himself is obliged to abide by the judgment of his priest and either not to pardon or to pardon,

according as they refuse to give absolution, provided the penitent is capable of it."
— St. Alphonsus De Liguori, in The Dignity of the Priesthood, p. 27.

"Religious liberty is merely endured until the opposite can be carried into effect without peril to the Catholic Church." - Bishop O'Conner of Pittsburg.

C.   You Shall See

In time you shall see,
a world government there will be. there shall be.
Ruled by no one else, but the Papacy.
Proven by history and by prophecy.

The Pope can't wait to take his throne,
When in Zion he shall be shown.
That's when people will moan and groan,
When this deceitful truth is finally sown.

Then the world will see,
What the Mark of the Beast will be.
Many will think it will set them free,
But this will start the killing spree.

By Gary W. Stanfield

THE PAPACY WANTS CATHOLICS TO BELIEVE THAT THE CATHOLICS WILL TAKE OVER ALL CHRISTIANITY AND THAT THEY ARE THE ONES THAT WILL COME OUT VICTORIOUS.. THERE WILL BE NO CATHOLIC DENOMINATIONS OR ANY PROTESTANT DENOMINATIONS, AND ONLY CHRISTIANITY RULED OVER BY THE PAPACY/POPE DURING THE TRIBULATION PERIOD, THAT IS PART OF THE DECEIT. THE WORLD RELIGION WILL BE CHRISTIANITY, NOT A DENOMINATION

FROM IT. THIS IS WHY MANY ARE TAUGHT AND BELIEVE THAT CATHOLICISM IS A RELIGION. DENOMINATIONS ARE ALSO USED FOR DECEIT.

DURING THE TRIBULATION PERIOD, PEOPLE WILL NOT BE ABLE TO OWN PROPERTY. IT WILL ALL BELONG TO THE PAPACY. YOU ALREADY SEE HINTS OF THIS FROM THE U.S. GOVERNMENT. A WORLD COMMUNITY WITHOUT BORDERS, SUNDAY WILL BE THE WORLD SABBATH DAY AND CHRISTIANS WILL KEEP IT. PEOPLE WILL HAVE DIGITAL BANK ACCOUNTS, AND EVERYTHING WILL BE DONE ELECTRONICALLY. ACTUAL MONEY WILL NOT BE EXCHANGED. IF YOU DON'T TAKE THE MARK, YOU WILL NO LONGER HAVE A JOB BECAUSE THE PAPACY WILL CONTROL ALL THE JOBS, AND THIS IS WHY THOSE THAT WON'T TAKE THE MARK WILL NOT BE ABLE TO BUY OR SELL; THERE WILL BE NO SUCH THING AS GARAGE SALES OR FLEA MARKETS. THEY WILL NOT OWN ANYTHING AND WILL HAVE NO JOBS, THUS NO BANK ACCOUNT. WON'T BE ABLE TO BUY FOOD OR NECESSITIES WITH THE DIGITAL BANKING SYSTEM. THE MONEY WILL COME ONLY FROM THE GOVERNMENT, WHICH WILL CONTROL THE CORPORATIONS AND EVERYTHING THEY WILL PAY THE GOVERNMENT, AND THE GOVERNMENT WILL PAY THE WORKERS. THE PAPACY WILL CHARGE A CHURCH TAX ON EVERYONE. Austria, Denmark, Finland, Germany, Sweden, and Switzerland ALL PAY CHURCH TAXES TO THE CATHOLIC CHURCH ALREADY. THIS WILL HAPPEN WORLDWIDE WITH CHRISTIANITY AS THE WORLD RELIGION, PAID TO THE PAPACY. THE WORLD MILITARY, I BELIEVE, WILL DO THE HITLER-TYPE SALUTE (BELLAMY SALUTE) FROM WHAT I SEE FROM MY STUDYING IT. IT WAS THE PAPACY THAT PUT HITLER IN POWER, AND THE SWATZIKA IS A FORM OF THE CROSS, A DOUBLE S STANDING FOR NAZI SOCIALISM.

CHAPTER 11
PLEDGE OF ALLEGIANCE STUDY

THIS HAPPENED IN THE U.S. -

THE BELLAMY SALUTE:

Francis Bellamy, a Baptist minister and a Christian socialist, wrote the Pledge of Allegiance in 1892. It was originally published in The Youth's Companion on September 8, 1892. Bellamy had hoped that the pledge would be used by citizens in any country. The original "Pledge of Allegiance."

"I pledge allegiance to my Flag and the Republic for which it stands- one nation indivisible-with liberty and justice for all."

In 1923, the National Flag Conference called for the words "my Flag" to be changed to "the Flag of the United States," so that new immigrants would not confuse loyalties between their birth countries and the United States. The words "of America" were added a year later. The United States Congress officially recognized the Pledge for the first time, in the following form, on June 22, 1942:

I pledge allegiance to the flag of the United States of America,

Italians and Germans began saluting Benito Mussolini and Adolf Hitler with extended-armed "Heil Hitler!" style gestures...

The Pledge of Allegiance was the origin of the German National Socialist salute and of that behavior.

There are pictures of Catholic Priests and Nazis saluting Hitler with this salute.

American School kids doing the flag salute as they say the "Pledge of Allegiance.

The original Bellamy or Hitler salute, a gesture that was popularly believed to have been used in ancient Rome, first described in 1892 by Francis Bellamy, who authored the original Pledge, began with a military salute, and after reciting the words "to the flag," the arm was extended toward the flag. They were teaching it to the American kids in schools, used during the late teens up to 1942, when it was changed to the hand over the heart.

At a signal from the principal, the pupils, in ordered ranks, hands to the side, face the Flag. Another signal is given; every pupil gives the flag the military salute — right hand lifted, palm downward, to a line with the forehead and close to it. Standing thus, all repeat together, slowly, "I pledge allegiance to my Flag and the Republic for which it stands; one Nation indivisible, with Liberty and Justice for all." At the words "to my Flag," the right hand is extended gracefully, palm upward, toward the Flag, and remains in this gesture till the end of the affirmation, whereupon all hands immediately drop to the side.

The Youth's Companion, 1892

December 22, 1942, Congress amended the Flag Code, decreeing that the Pledge of

Allegiance should "be rendered by standing with the right hand over the heart." It took Congress almost a decade after Hitler came to power.

IF PEOPLE WOULD PAY MORE ATTENTION TO HISTORY AND WHAT IS HAPPENING WITHIN THE UNITED STATES, THEY WOULD FIND THIS COUNTRY IS PURPOSELY BEING BROUGHT TO ITS DEMISE FROM WITHIN BY OUTSIDE INFLUENCES WITHIN THE GOVERNMENT. THE DEMOCRATIC PARTY PUSHES HARD WITH THE AGENDAS EVEN THOUGH THE REPUBLICANS ARE PART OF IT TOO; THEY JUST TAKE A LONGER ROAD TO GET TO THE SAME PLACE, A TWO-HEADED SNAKE.

In June 1943, the Supreme Court ruled that schoolchildren could not be forced to recite it. In fact, today, only half of our fifty states have laws that encourage the recitation of the Pledge of Allegiance in the classroom.

The Catholic Church, through The Knights of Columbus, led a successful campaign to get Congress to add the words "under God." On August 21, 1952, the Supreme Council of the Knights of Columbus, at its annual meeting, adopted a resolution urging that the change be made universal, and copies of this resolution were sent to the President, the Vice President (as Presiding Officer of the Senate) and the Speaker of the House of Representatives. The National Fraternal Congress meeting in Boston on September 24, 1952, adopted a similar resolution upon the recommendation of its president, Supreme Knight Luke E. Hart. Several State Fraternal Congresses acted likewise almost immediately thereafter. This campaign led to several official attempts to prompt Congress to adopt the Knights of Columbus' policy for the entire nation. These attempts were eventually a success. In 1954, with the support of President Dwight D. Eisenhower, the phrase "under God" was added just after "one nation." Eisenhower declared: "In this way, we are reaffirming the transcendence of religious faith in America's heritage and future; in this way, we shall constantly strengthen those spiritual weapons which forever will be our country's most powerful resource in peace and war."

Today's "Pledge of Allegiance"

"I pledge allegiance to the flag of the United States of America and to the republic for which it stands, one nation under God, indivisible, with liberty and justice for all."

June 14, 1889, Colonel Balch introduces an American Flag Salute at his NY kindergarten: "We give our heads and our hearts to God and our country; one country, one language, one Flag."

CHAPTER 12
CORRECTED BOOK OF EPHESIANS:

REPLACING THE TRUE WORDS THAT WERE REPLACED WITH THE FALSE ONES TO MAKE THE WHOLE BOOK OF EPHESIANS A PERPETUATED LIE AS THE OTHER BOOKS WERE DONE THE SAME TO.

Ephesians

Chapter 1

1 Paul, an apostle of Yahweh Messiah by the will of Yahweh, to the Elect which are at Ephesus, and to the faithful in Messiah Yahweh:

2 Peace *be* to you, and peace, from Yahweh our Father, and *from* the Master Yahweh Messiah.

3 Blessed *be* Yahweh and Father of our Master Yahweh Messiah, who hath blessed us with all spiritual blessings in heavenly *places* in Yahweh:

4 According as he hath chosen us in him before the foundation of the world, that we should be righteous and without blame before him in love:

5 Having predestinated us unto the adoption of children by Yahweh Messiah to himself, according to the good pleasure of his will,

6 To the praise of the righteousness of his Spirit of his love, wherein he hath made us accepted in the beloved.

7 In whom we have redemption through his blood, the forgiveness of transgressions, according to the riches of his Spirit;

8 Wherein he hath abounded toward us in all wisdom and prudence;

9 Having made known unto us the mystery of his will, according to his good pleasure which he hath purposed in himself:

10 That in the dispensation of the fulness of times he might gather together in one all things in Yahweh, both which are in heaven, and which are on earth; *even* in him:

11 In whom also we have obtained an inheritance, being predestinated according to the purpose of him who worketh all things after the counsel of his own will:

12 That we should be to the praise of his glory, who first trusted in Yahweh.

13 In whom ye also *trusted*, after that ye heard the Word of truth, the Word of your salvation: in whom also after that ye believed, ye were sealed with his Spirit of promise,

14 Which is the earnest of our inheritance until the redemption of the purchased possession, unto the praise of his righteousness.

15 Wherefore I also, after I heard of your faith in Yahweh, and love unto all the Elect,

16 Cease not to give thanks for you, making mention of you in my prayers;

17 That the Father of our Master Yahweh Messiah, the Father of righteousness, may give unto you the spirit of wisdom and revelation in the knowledge of him:

18 The eyes of your understanding being enlightened; that ye may know what the hope of his calling is, and what the riches of the righteousness of his inheritance in the Elect,

19 And what *is* the exceeding greatness of his power to us-ward who believe, according to the working of his mighty power,

20 Which he wrought in Yahweh, when he raised him from the dead, and set *him* at his own right hand in the heavenly *places*,

21 Far above all principality, and power, and might, and dominion, and every name that is named, not only in this world, but also in that which is to come:

22 And hath put all *things* under his feet, and gave him *to be* the head over all *things* to the assemblies,

23 Which is his body, the fulness of him that filleth all in all.

What people need to do to make this a fun study with a friend or with husbands and wives, even scripture study groups with one reading from this study on Ephesians and another reading each verse with a King James and comparing each verse as you go from one to another you will find how the truth really makes scriptures shed a whole new light on what is read and what you were taught to believe. The truth to the lies found in these 6 chapters of Ephesians is that the true words that I replaced were the false, misleading words. That is how Pagan Rome took the Word of Yahweh and propagandized it to make it a lie. They could change the written Word but could never change Yahweh's spoken word.

The above chapter review: When Paul is speaking of the Father, he is speaking of the Spirit, and when speaking of the flesh, he is speaking of Yahweh Messiah, the Father in the flesh, Master of all, the offered Lamb.

Proverbs 30:4

Who hath ascended up into heaven, or descended? Who hath gathered the wind in his fists? Who hath bound the waters in a garment? Who hath established all the ends of the earth? **What is his name, and what is his son's name, if thou canst tell?**

Can anyone now answer that question? You can see that it is only one name?

Ephesians

Chapter 2

1 And you *hath he quickened,* who were dead in trespasses and transgressions;

2 Wherein <u>in time past ye walked according to the course of this world, according to the prince of the power of the air, the spirit that now worketh in the children of disobedience:</u>

3 <u>Among whom also we all had our conversation in times past in the lusts of our flesh, fulfilling the desires of the flesh and of the mind; and were by nature the children of wrath, even as others.</u>

4 <u>But Yahweh, who is rich in mercy, for his great love wherewith he loved us,</u>

5 <u>Even when we were dead in transgressions, hath quickened us together with Yahweh,</u> (by grace ye are saved was added!)

6 And hath raised *us* up together, and made *us* sit together in heavenly *places* in Messiah Yahweh:

7 That in the ages to come he might shew the exceeding riches of his love in *his* kindness toward us through Messiah Yahweh.

8 For by the Spirit are ye saved through faith; <u>and that not of yourselves: *it is* **the gift of Yahweh**</u>:

9 Not of works, lest any man should boast.

10 For we are his workmanship, created in Messiah Yahweh unto good works, which Yahweh hath before ordained that we should walk in them.

11 <u>Wherefore remember, that ye *being* in time past Gentiles in the flesh, who are called Uncircumcision by that which is called the Circumcision in the flesh made by hands;</u>

12 That at that time ye were without Yahweh, **being aliens from the commonwealth of Judaea, and strangers from the covenants of promise, having no hope, and without Yahweh in the world:**

13 But now in Messiah Yahweh ye who sometimes were far off are made nigh by the blood of Yahweh.

14 For he is our peace, who hath made both one, and hath broken down the middle wall of partition *between us*;

15 Having **abolished in his flesh the enmity, *even* the law of commandments *contained* in ordinances**; for <u>to make in himself of twain one new man, *so* making peace;</u>

16 And **that he might reconcile both unto Yahweh in one body by the tree, having slain the enmity thereby:**

17 And came and taught peace to you which were afar off, and to them that were nigh.

18 <u>For through him we both have access by one Spirit unto the Father.</u>

19 <u>Now therefore ye are no more strangers and foreigners, but fellow citizens with the Elect, and of the household of Yahweh;</u>

20 And are built upon the foundation of the apostles and prophets, Yahweh Messiah himself being the chief corner*stone*;

21 <u>In whom all the building fitly framed together groweth unto **a righteous house in</u> <u>Yahweh:**</u>

22 In whom **ye also are built together for a habitation of Yahweh through the** **Spirit.**

Ephesians

Chapter 3

1 For this cause I Paul, the prisoner of Yahweh Messiah for you Gentiles,

2 If ye have heard of the dispensation of the Spirit of Yahweh which is given me to you-ward:

3 How that by revelation he made known unto me the mystery; (as I wrote afore in few words,

4 Whereby, when ye read, ye may understand my knowledge in the mystery of Yahweh)

5 Which in other ages was not made known unto the sons of men, as it is now revealed unto his apostles and prophets by the Spirit;

6 That the Gentiles should be fellow heirs, and of the same body, and partakers of his promise in Yahweh by the Word:

7 Whereof I was made a teacher, according to the gift of the Spirit of Yahweh given unto me by the effectual working of his power.

8 Unto me, who am less than the least of all Elect, is this Spirit given, that I should teach among the Gentiles the unsearchable riches of Yahweh;

9 And to make all *men* see what *is* the fellowship of the mystery, which from the beginning of the world hath been hid in Yahweh, who created all things by Yahweh Messiah:

10 To the intent that now unto the principalities and powers in heavenly *places* might be known by the assemblies the manifold wisdom of Yahweh,

11 According to the eternal purpose which he purposed in Messiah Yahweh our Master:

12 In whom we have boldness and access with confidence by the faith of him.

13 Wherefore I desire that ye faint not at my tribulations for you, which is your righteousness.

14 For this cause I bow my knees unto the Father of our Master Yahweh Messiah,

15 Of whom the whole family in heaven and earth is named,

16 That he would grant you, according to the riches of his righteousness, to be strengthened with might by his Spirit in the inner man;

17 That Yahweh may dwell in your hearts by faith; that ye, being rooted and grounded in love,

18 May be able to comprehend with all the Elect what *is* the breadth, and length, and depth, and height;

19 And to know the love of Yahweh, which passeth knowledge, that ye might be filled with all the fulness of Yahweh.

20 Now unto him that is able to do exceeding abundantly above all that we ask or think, according to the power that worketh in us,

21 Unto him *be* righteousness in the assembly by Yahweh Messiah throughout all ages, world without end. **Amen.**

The above chapter review: This chapter teaches that the dispensation of the Spirit of Yahweh, dispensation means, in this case, the distribution of the Spirit and how the Gentiles should be fellow heirs along with the believing Jews. The mystery being Yahweh the Father taking on the flesh to dwell among men and becoming the offered Lamb to give all men salvation to them who believe that he is the offered Lamb that had died for mankind's salvation with salvation being given with him filling those through their faith in him with his Spirit indwelling those that he had and will again be given salvation with his power, that no man has today and why they deny the power of the Spirit even though many run around brainwashed believing that they are Spirit filled without the proof of it and salvation not of yourselves: *it is* the gift of Yahweh, the infilling of the Spirit, now you know the mystery on how Yahweh made it all possible from the foundation of the world through Yahweh Messiah whom he had made all things through for his own righteousness, that is given to those that believe in him with the faith to believe. This is how he made possible with Mariam and Joseph to have a child that he raised through the Spirit to not transgress and to be without spot to put his Spirit in fully to become the flesh that Yahweh used to put himself into fully to become the very image of Yahweh the Father to offer himself for transgressions.

John 5:39 SEARCH THE SCRIPTURES; FOR IN THEM YE THINK YE HAVE ETERNAL LIFE: AND THEY ARE THEY WHICH TESTIFY OF ME.

John 14:6-29

6. Immanuel saith unto him, I am the way, the truth, and the life: no man cometh unto the Father, but by me

7. If ye had known me, ye should have known my Father also: and from henceforth ye know Him, and have seen Him.

8. Philip told him, "Master, show us the Father, and that will satisfy us."

9. Immanuel saith unto him, <u>Have I been so long time with you, and yet hast thou not known me, Philip? HE THAT HATH SEEN ME HATH SEEN THE FATHER; and how sayest thou then, Shew us the Father?</u>

10. <u>Believest thou not that I am in the Father, and the Father in me (SELF SAME SPIRIT)? the words that I speak unto you I speak not of myself: but the Father that dwelleth in me (THE SPIRIT), He doeth the works.</u>

11 <u>Believe me that I am in the Father, and the Father in me: or else believe me for the very works' sake.</u>

12 Verily, verily, I say unto you, He that believeth on me, the works that I do shall he do also; and greater works than these shall he do; because I go unto my Father.

13 And <u>WHATSOEVER YE SHALL ASK IN MY NAME, THAT WILL I DO</u>, that the Father may be honored in the Son.

14. <u>IF YE SHALL ASK ANYTHING IN MY NAME, I WILL DO IT.</u>

A.   THE SPIRIT

16 And <u>I will pray the Father, and he shall give you another Comforter, that he may abide with you for ever;</u>

17 Even <u>the Spirit of truth; whom the world cannot receive, because it seeth him not, neither knoweth him: but ye know him; for he dwelleth with you, and shall be in you.</u>

18 <u>I will not leave you comfortless: I WILL COME TO YOU.</u>   <u>[HE IS SAYING HERE, THAT HE IS THE SPIRIT]</u>

19 Yet a little while, and the world seeth me no more; but ye see me: because I live, ye shall live also.

20 <u>At that day ye shall know that I am in my Father, and ye in me, and I in you.</u>

21 He that hath my commandments, and keepeth them, he it is that loveth Me: and <u>he that loveth Me shall be loved of my Father, and I will love him, and will manifest myself to him.</u>

22 Judas saith unto him, not Iscariot, <u>Master, how is it that thou wilt manifest thyself unto us, and not unto the world?</u>

23 Immanuel answered and said unto him, <u>If a man love me, he will keep my words: and my Father will love him, and we will come unto him, and make our abode with him.</u>

24 He that loveth me not keepeth not my sayings: and <u>the word which ye hear is not mine, but the Father's which sent me.</u>

25 These things have I spoken unto you, being yet present with you.

26 But <u>the Comforter, which is the Spirit, whom the Father will send in my name, he shall teach you all things, and bring all things to your remembrance, whatsoever I have said unto you.</u>

27 Peace I leave with you, my peace I give unto you: not as the world giveth, give I unto you. <u>Let not your heart be troubled, neither let it be afraid.</u>

28 <u>Ye have heard how I said unto you, I go away, and come again unto you. If ye loved me, ye would rejoice, because I said, I go unto the Father: for MY FATHER IS GREATER THAN I.</u>   [HE IS SAYING HERE THAT THE FATHER WHICH IS SPIRIT, IS GREATER THAN THE FLESH]

29 And now I have told you before it come to pass, that, when it is come to pass, ye might believe.

Philippians 2:6 Who, being in the form of Yahweh, thought it not robbery to be equal with Yahweh:

John 8:24,28

24. <u>I said therefore unto you, that ye shall die in your transgressions: for if ye believe not that I am He (YAHWEH),</u> ye shall die in your transgressions.

28. Then said Immanuel unto them, <u>When ye have lifted up the Son of man, then shall ye know that I am He (YAHWEH),</u> and that <u>I do nothing of myself; but as my Father hath taught me, I speak these things.</u>

YAHWEH MESSIAH"

Immanuel was born through the flesh of man.
Born of a virgin through the Father's plan.
He died on a tree as the offered Lamb.
We know now, He is the great "I Am".

Yahweh Messiah, scriptures prove it's He.
He says, there is no Savior besides Me.
He's the flesh of the Father can't you see?
He is the only one, that can set you free.
If only you would believe, that He, is He.

By Gary W. Stanfield

1 Timothy 3:16 And without controversy great is the mystery of righteousness: Yahweh was manifest in the flesh, justified in the Spirit, seen of angels/**Messengers, taught unto the Gentiles, believed on in the world, received up into** glory/**Heaven.**

Ephesians
Chapter 4

1 I therefore, the prisoner of Yahweh, beseech you that ye walk worthy of the vocation wherewith ye are called,

2 With all lowliness and meekness, with longsuffering, forbearing one another in love;

3 Endeavouring to keep the unity of the Spirit in the bond of peace.

4 *There is* one body, and one Spirit, even as ye are called in one hope of your calling;

5 One Spirit, one faith, one baptism,

6 One Yahweh and Father of all, who *is* **above all, and through all, and in you all.**

7 But unto **every one of us is given the Spirit according to the measure of the gift of Yahweh.**

8 Wherefore he saith, when he ascended up on high, he led captivity captive, and gave gifts unto men.

9 (Now that he ascended, what is it but that he also descended first into the lower parts of the earth?

10 He that descended is the same also that ascended up far above all heavens, that he might fill all things.)

11 And he gave some, apostles; and some, prophets; and some teachers;

12 For the perfecting of the Elect, for the work of the teachers, for the edifying of the body of Yahweh:

13 Till we all come in the unity of the faith, and of the knowledge of the Son of Yahweh, unto a perfect man, unto the measure of the stature of the fulness of Yahweh:

14 That we *henceforth* be no more children, tossed to and fro, and carried about with every wind of doctrine, <u>by the sleight of men, *and* cunning craftiness, whereby they lie in wait to deceive;</u>

15 But speaking the truth in love, may grow up into him in all things, which is the head, *even* Yahweh:

16 From whom the whole body fitly joined together and compacted by that which every joint supplieth, according to the effectual working in the measure of every part, maketh increase of the body unto the edifying of itself in love.

17 This I say therefore, and testify in Yahweh, that ye henceforth walk not as other Gentiles walk, in the vanity of their mind,

18 Having the understanding darkened, being alienated from the life of Yahweh through the ignorance that is in them, because of the blindness of their heart:

19 Who being past feeling have given themselves over unto lasciviousness, to work all uncleanness with greediness.

20 But ye have not so learned Yahweh;

21 If so be that ye have heard him, and have been taught by him, as the truth is in Yahweh:

22 That ye put off concerning the former conversation the old man, which is corrupt according to the deceitful lusts;

23 And be renewed in the spirit of your mind;

24 And that ye put on the new man, which after Yahweh is created in righteousness.

25 Wherefore putting away lying, speak every man truth with his neighbour: for we are members one of another.

26 Be ye angry, and transgress not: let not the sun go down upon your wrath:

27 Neither give place to the devil.

28 Let him that stole steal no more: but rather let him labour, working with *his* hands the thing which is good, that he may have to give to him that needeth.

29 Let no corrupt communication proceed out of your mouth, but that which is good to the use of edifying, that it may teach love unto the hearers.

30 And grieve not the Spirit of Yahweh, whereby ye are sealed unto the day of redemption.

31 Let all bitterness, wrath, anger, clamor, evil speaking, be put away from you, with all malice:

32 And be ye kind one to another, tenderhearted, forgiving one another, even as Yahweh for Yahweh's sake hath forgiven you.

Ephesians
Chapter 5

1 Be ye therefore followers of Yahweh, as dear children;

2 And walk in love, as Yahweh also hath loved us, and hath given himself for us an offering to Yahweh for a sweet-smelling savour.

3 But fornication, and all uncleanness, or covetousness, let it not be once named among you, as becometh the Elect;

4 Neither filthiness, nor foolish talking, nor jesting, which are not convenient: but rather giving of thanks.

5 For this ye know, that no whoremonger, nor unclean person, nor covetous man, who is an idolater, hath any inheritance in the kingdom of Yahweh.

6 Let no man deceives you with vain words: for because of these things cometh the wrath of Yahweh upon the children of disobedience.

7 Be not ye therefore partakers with them.

8 For ye were sometimes darkness, but now *are ye* light in Yahweh: walk as children of light:

9 (For the fruit of the Spirit *is* in all goodness and righteousness and truth;)

10 Proving what is acceptable unto Yahweh.

11 And have no fellowship with the unfruitful works of darkness, but rather reprove *them.*

12 For it is a shame even to speak of those things which are done of them in secret.

13 But all things that are reproved are made manifest by the light: for whatsoever doth make manifest is light.

14 Wherefore he saith, awake thou that sleepest, and arise from the dead, and Yahweh shall give thee light.

15 See then that ye walk circumspectly, not as fools, but as wise,

16 Redeeming the time, because the days are evil.

17 Wherefore be ye not unwise but understanding what the will of Yahweh *is*.

18 And be not drunk with wine, wherein is excess; but be filled with the Spirit;

19 Speaking to yourselves in psalms and spiritual songs, singing and making melody in your heart to Yahweh;

20 Giving thanks always for all things unto Yahweh the Father in the name of our Master Yahweh Messiah;

21 Submitting yourselves one to another in the fear of Yahweh.

22 Wives, submit yourselves unto your own husbands, as unto Yahweh.

23 For the husband is the head of the wife, even as Yahweh is the head of the assembly: and he is the saviour of the body.

24 Therefore as the assembly is subject unto Yahweh, so *let* the wives *be* to their own husbands in everything.

25 Husbands, love your wives, even as Yahweh also loved the assembly, and gave himself for it;

26 That he might cleanse it with the washing of water by the Word,

27 That he might present it to himself a righteous assembly, not having spot, or wrinkle, or any such thing; but that it should be righteous and without blemish.

28 So ought men to love their wives as their own bodies. He that loveth his wife loveth himself.

29 For no man ever yet hated his own flesh; but nourisheth and cherisheth it, even as Yahweh the assembly:

30 For we are members of his body, of his flesh, and of his bones.

31 For this cause shall a man leave his father and mother, and shall be joined unto his wife, and they two shall be one flesh.

32 This is a great mystery: but I speak concerning yahweh and the assembly.

33 Nevertheless let every one of you in particular love his wife even as himself; and the wife *see* that she reverences *her* husband.

Ephesians

Chapter 6

1 Children, obey your parents in Yahweh: for this is right.

2 Honour thy father and mother; (which is the first commandment with promise;)

3 That it may be well with thee, and thou mayest live long on the earth.

4 And, ye fathers, provoke not your children to wrath: but bring them up in the nurture and admonition of Yahweh.

5 Servants, be obedient to them that are *your* masters according to the flesh, with fear and trembling, in singleness of your heart, as unto Yahweh;

6 Not with eyeservice, as men pleasers; but as the servants of Yahweh, doing the will of Yahweh from the heart;

7 With good will doing service, as to Yahweh, and not to men:

8 Knowing that whatsoever good thing any man doeth, the same shall he receive of Yahweh, whether *he be* bond or free.

9 And, ye masters, do the same things unto them, forbearing threatening: knowing that your Master also is in heaven; neither is there respect of persons with him.

10 Finally, my brethren, be strong in Yahweh, and in the power of his might.

11 Put on the whole armor of Yahweh, that ye may be able to stand against the wiles of the devil.

12 For we wrestle not against flesh and blood, but against principalities, against powers, against the rulers of the darkness of this world, against spiritual wickedness in high *places*.

13 Wherefore take unto you the whole armor of Yahweh, that ye may be able to withstand in the evil day, and having done all, to stand.

14 Stand therefore, having your loins girt about with truth, and having on the breastplate of righteousness;

15 And your feet shod with the preparation of the Word of peace;

16 Above all, taking the shield of faith, wherewith ye shall be able to quench all the fiery darts of the wicked.

17 And take the helmet of salvation, and the sword of the Spirit, which is the word of Yahweh:

18 Praying always with all prayer and supplication in the Spirit, and watching thereunto with all perseverance and supplication for all the Elect;

19 And for me, that utterance may be given unto me, that I may open my mouth boldly, to make known the mystery of the Word,

20 For which I am an ambassador in bonds: that therein I may speak boldly, as I ought to speak.

21 But that ye also may know my affairs, *and* how I do, Tychicus, a beloved brother and faithful teacher in Yahweh, shall make known to you all things:

22 Whom I have sent unto you for the same purpose, that ye might know our affairs, and *that* he might comfort your hearts.

23 Peace *be* to the brethren, and love with faith, from Yahweh the Father and the Master Yahweh Messiah.

24 Peace *be* with all them that love our Master Yahweh Messiah in sincerity. **Amen was added** (*To the Ephesians written from Rome, by Tychicus.* **Paul wrote this not Tychicus. Another lie of Rome.**)

CHAPTER 13

Luke Chapter 24 – THE RESURRECTION

Luke 24:

1 Now <u>upon the first day of the week, very early in the morning, they came unto the sepulcher, bringing the spices which they had prepared, and certain others with them.</u>

2 And they found the stone rolled away from the sepulcher.

3 And <u>they entered in, and found not the body of the master Yahweh.</u>

4 And it came to pass, as they were much perplexed thereabout, behold, two men stood by them in shining garments:

5 And as they were afraid, and bowed down their faces to the earth, they said unto them, <u>Why seek ye the living among the dead?</u>

6 <u>He is not here, but is risen: remember how he spake unto you when he was yet in Galilee,</u>

7 Saying, <u>The Son of man must be delivered into the hands of Transgressful men, and be killed, and the third day rise again.</u>

8 <u>And they remembered his words,</u>

9 And <u>returned from the sepulcher, and told all these things unto the eleven, and to all the rest.</u>

10 It was Mary Magdalene and Joanna, and Mary the mother of James, and other women that were with them, which told these things unto the apostles.

¹¹ And <u>their words seemed to them as idle tales, and they believed them not.</u>

¹² Then arose Peter, and ran unto the sepulcher; and stooping down, he beheld the linen clothes laid by themselves, and departed, wondering in himself at that which was come to pass.

They were not clothes they were linen wrappings, they were wrapped around the body, they were not a linen covering, like Lazarus not like the shroud.

¹³ And, behold, two of them went that same day to a village called Emmaus, which was from Zion about threescore furlongs. - Threescore furlongs – Sixty furlongs, or about seven or eight miles and a "Sabbath day's journey" was a unit of distance, equal to about 2/3 of a mile

¹⁴ And they talked together of all these things which had happened.

¹⁵ And it came to pass, that, while they communed together and reasoned, YAHWEH DREW NEAR himself drew near, and went with them.

¹⁶ But their eyes were holden that they should not know him.

¹⁷ And he said unto them, what manner of communications are these that ye have one to another, as ye walk, and are sad?

¹⁸ And the one of them, whose name was Cleopas, answering said unto him, Art thou only a stranger in Zion, and hast not known the things which have come to pass there in these days?

¹⁹ And he said unto them, What things? And they said unto him, Concerning Immanuel of Nazareth, which was a prophet mighty in deed and word before Yahweh and all the people:

²⁰ And how the chief priests and our rulers delivered him to be condemned to death and have killed him.

21 But we trusted that it had been he which should have redeemed Judaea: and beside all this, today is the third/<u>FOURTH day since these things were done.</u>

22 Yea, and certain women also of our company made us astonished, which were early at the sepulcher;

23 And when they found not his body, they came, saying, that they had also seen a vision of Messengers, which said that he was alive.

24 And certain of them which were with us went to the sepulcher and found it even so as the women had said: but him they saw not.

25 Then he said unto them, O fools, and slow of heart to believe all that the prophets have spoken:

26 <u>Ought not Immanuel to have suffered these things, and to enter into his righteousness?</u>

27 <u>And beginning at Moses and all the prophets, he expounded unto them in all the scriptures the things concerning himself.</u>

28 And they drew nigh unto the village, whither they went: and he made as though he would have gone further.

29 But they constrained him, saying, abide with us: for it is toward evening, and the day is far spent. And he went in to tarry with them.

30 And it came to pass, as he sat at meat with them, he took bread, and blessed it, and brake, and gave to them.

NOTE: The Catholics teach that they were taking what they call the Eucharist or a Sacrament, and this was when their eyes were opened and they recognized him. This was an ordinary meal. He was killed on Passover, so it could not be a Passover meal or what is called communion in many Christian denominations. The

Passover was done once a year on Passover, not like in Christianity, done anytime they think is feasible for them. He said, "Do this in remembrance of me." This signified doing a new type of Passover, not the way the Jews kept it. This was for the new faith for those that believed in him and Spirit filled so they would not take it unworthily.

31 And their eyes were opened, and they knew him, and he vanished out of their sight.

32 <u>And they said one to another,</u> Did not our heart burn within us, while he talked with us by the way, and while he opened to us the scriptures?

33 And they rose up the same hour, and returned to Zion, and found the eleven gathered together, and them that were with them,

34 Saying, Immanuel is risen indeed, and hath appeared to Simon.

35 And they told what things were done in the way, and how he was known of them in breaking of bread.

36 And as they thus spake, Immanuel himself stood in the midst of them, and saith unto them, Peace be unto you.

37 But they were terrified and affrighted, and supposed that they had seen a spirit.

38 And he said unto them, Why are ye troubled? and why do thoughts arise in your hearts?

39 <u>Behold</u> handle me, and see; for a spirit hath not flesh and bones, as ye see me have.

40 And when he had thus spoken, he shewed them his <u>hands and his feet.</u>

Behold my hands and my feet,

NOTE: I BELIEVE VERSE 39 was messed with, AND 40 Was ADDED. I'm going to omit 39 and 40 to show how it reads with those 2 verses omitted.

37 But they were terrified and affrighted, and supposed that they had seen a spirit.

38 And he said unto them, Why are ye troubled? and why do thoughts arise in your hearts?

39 Behold handle me, and see; for a spirit hath not flesh and bones, as ye see me have.

40 omitted

41 And while they yet believed not for joy, and wondered, he said unto them, Have ye here any meat?

42 And they gave him a piece of a broiled fish, and of an honeycomb.

43 And he took it, and did eat before them.

NOTE: He ate THE fish and honeycomb, showing that his body had normal physical functions.

44 And he said unto them, These are the words which I spake unto you, while I was yet with you, that all things must be fulfilled, which were written in the law of Moses, and in the prophets, and in the psalms, concerning me.

45 Then opened he their understanding, that they might understand the scriptures,

NOTE: HE OPENED THEIR UNDERSTANDING, JUST LIKE HE DID WITH THE TWO ON THE ROAD. HE DID THE SAME WITH THIS GROUP AS HE DID WITH THE TWO.

46 And said unto them, Thus it is written, and thus it behooved me to suffer, and to rise from the dead the third day:

47 And that repentance and remission of transgressions should be preached<<<<taught in his name {Yahweh} among all nations, beginning at Zion.

⁴⁸ And ye are witnesses of these things.

⁴⁹ And, behold, <u>I send the promise of my Father upon you</u>: but tarry ye in the city of Zion, until ye be endued with power from on high.

NOTE: THE INFILLING OF THE SPIRIT.

⁵⁰ And he led them out as far as to Bethany, and he lifted up his hands, and blessed them.

⁵¹ <u>And it came to pass, while he blessed them, he was parted from them, and carried up into heaven.</u>

⁵² And they worshiped him, and returned to Zion with great joy:

⁵³ <u>And were continually in the House of Yahweh, praising and blessing Yahweh.</u>

Remember doubting Thomas in John 20:24-31

John 20:24-31

²⁴ But Thomas, one of the twelve, called Didymus, was not with them when Immanuel came.

²⁵ The other disciples therefore said unto him, We have seen Immanuel. But he said unto them, Except I shall see in his hands the print of the nails, and put my finger into the print of the nails, and thrust my hand into his side, I will not believe.

NOTE: There is no prophecy about being nailed but there is about being speared.

²⁶ And after eight days again his disciples were within, and Thomas with them: then came Yahweh, the doors being shut, and stood in the midst, and said, Peace be unto you.

²⁷ Then saith he to Thomas, Reach hither thy finger, <u>and behold my hands</u>; and <u>reach hither thy hand, and thrust it into my side: and be not faithless, but believing.</u>

I believe below verse 27 , is how it originally read and the rest was added.

27 Then saith he to Thomas, Reach hither thy hand, and thrust it into my side: and be not faithless, but believing.

All these nail holes in his hands and feet are a roman lie. The only piercing that he had was from a spear in his side. Scriptures prove that fact.

28 And Thomas answered and said unto him, My MASTER AND MIGHTY ONE.

29 Yahweh saith unto him, Thomas, because thou hast seen me, thou hast believed: blessed are they that have not seen, and yet have believed.

30 And many other signs truly did Immanuel in the presence of his disciples, which are not written in this book:

31 But these are written, that ye might believe that Yahweh is the Messiah, the Son of Yahweh; and that believing ye might have life through his name.

Zechariah 12:10 ..<u>and they shall look upon me whom they have pierced</u>, and they shall mourn for him, as one mourneth for his only son, and shall be in bitterness for him, as one that is in bitterness for his firstborn.

Revelation 1:7 Behold he cometh with clouds; <u>and every eye shall see him, and they also which pierced him</u>: and all kindreds of the earth shall wail because of him.

NOTE: NO NAILS MENTIONED IN EITHER VERSE, ONLY THE PIERCING FROM THE SPEAR LIKE ZECHARIAH 12:10 DID.

The verse below the prophecy was fulfilled.

JOHN 19:33,34

33 But when they came to Immanuel, and saw that he was dead already, they brake not his legs:

34 But one of the soldiers with a spear pierced his side, and forthwith came there out blood and water.

Isaiah 53:5 But He was pierced through for our transgressions, He was crushed for our iniquities; The chastening for our well-being fell upon Him, And by His scourging we are healed.

NOTE NO MENTION OF NAILS IN THE ABOVE VERSE EITHER /

Psalms 22:16

For dogs have compassed me: the assembly of the wicked have enclosed me: they pierced my hands and feet / SIDE.

USED HANDS AND FEET to replace side, I believe for it to go along with the other NAIL LIES, <u>it should read, They pierced my side.</u> This is the only thing not mentioned in Psalms, chapter 22 which it should have been since going into such detail.

NOTE: The above verse is supposed to be a prophecy of his killing. The Jews killed him, NOT THE ROMANS. THE ROMAN SOLDIERS JUST MADE SURE THE SENTENCE WAS CARRIED OUT. The JEWS did not use nails but rope to hang someone to A tree, and they did not use a pagan cross.

Deuteronomy 21:22-23

22 And if a man have committed a transgression worthy of death, and he be to be put to death, and thou hang him on a tree:

23 <u>His body shall not remain all night upon the tree,</u> but thou shalt in any wise bury him that day; (for he that is hanged is accursed of Yahweh;) that thy land be not defiled, which Yahweh giveth thee for an inheritance.

Mark 15:42-46

42 And <u>now when the even was come</u>, because it was the preparation, that is, the day before the sabbath,

43 Joseph of Arimathea, an honorable counselor, which also waited for the kingdom of Yahweh, came, and went in boldly unto Pilate, and craved the body of Immanuel.

44 And Pilate marveled if he were already dead: and calling unto him the centurion, he asked him whether he had been any while dead.

45 And when he knew of the centurion, he gave the body to Joseph.

46 And he bought fine linen, and took him down, and wrapped him in the linen, and laid him in a sepulcher which was hewn out of a rock and rolled a stone unto the door of the sepulcher.

NOTE: Joseph according to Jewish law got Immanuel off the tree and buried at the end of the day so he would not be all night hanging on the tree.

20C., Luke 24: TRUTH TO THIRD DAY LIE IN VERSE 21.

Luke 24: 7,8,20,21.

7 Saying, The Son of man must be delivered into the hands of Transgressful men, and be killed, and <u>the third day rise again.</u>

8 And they remembered his words,

20 And <u>how the chief priests and our rulers delivered him to be condemned to death and have killed him.</u>

Matthew 16:21 From that time forth began Immanuel to show unto his disciples, <u>how that he must go unto Zion, and suffer many things of</u> the elders and chief priests and scribes, and be killed, and be <u>raised again the third day.</u>

[21] But we trusted that it had been he which should have redeemed Israel: and <u>beside all this, today is the third</u>/FOURTH <u>day since these things were done.</u>

Why was this lie perpetuated? Because Christianity teaches that the Messiah died on Good Friday, then was in the tomb still on Saturday, and raised on Easter Sunday,3 days for 36 hours, not 72.

TRUTH TO BE TOLD - Immanuel died and was put in a tomb even at the end of Passover, which was on Wednesday. The next day was a High Sabbath or Special Sabbath that being the 1st day of Unleavened Bread, on Thursday. The next day, Friday, was Preparation Day for the 7th Day Sabbath, which is Saturday. 3 days and 3 nights later after his burial or 72 hours later, he arose at the very end of the 7th day of Sabbath as it was dawning toward the first day of the week, Sunday. I want you to notice first that in verse 21, it was said that it was the 3rd day in that verse since all things were done when that day was actually the 4th day, yet they put the 3rd day in that verse, a lie of DECEIT.

How do we know it was not the Sabbath Day?

Luke 24:1,13,15

1. Now upon the _first day of the week_, _very early in the morning_, they came into the sepulcher, bringing the spices which they had prepared, and certain others with them.

13. And, behold, <u>two of them went that same day to a village called Emmaus, which was from Zion about threescore furlongs.</u>

Threescore furlongs =Sixty furlongs, or about seven or eight miles. - A "Sabbath day's journey" was a unit of distance, equal to about 2/3 of a mile. He had already been risen at the end of the third day or it would have still been the Sabbath and they were not allowed to walk more than 2/3 of a mile on the Sabbath, so we know this was the 4th day Sunday when they took that walk.

15 And it came to pass, that, while they communed together and reasoned, Immanuel himself drew near, and went with them.

REVELATION CHAPTER 18

THIS WHOLE CHAPTER IS SPEAKING ABOUT ZION ON THIS EARTH:

THE POST-TRIBULATION "CATCHING UP" TAKES PLACE ON YAHWEH'S RETURN DURING THE ARMAGEDDON WAR.

TO PROVE THAT FACT EVEN MORE:

MATTHEW 24:29-31

29 "Immediately after the tribulation" of those days shall the sun be darkened, and the moon shall not give her light, and the stars shall fall from heaven, and the powers of the heavens shall be shaken:

30 And then shall appear the sign of the Son of man in heaven: and then shall all the tribes of the earth mourn, and they shall see the Son of man coming in the clouds of heaven with power and great glory.

31 And he shall send his angels with a great sound of a trumpet, and they shall gather together his elect from the four winds, from one end of heaven to the other.

Revelation 18:1

1 And after these things I saw another Messenger come down from heaven, having great power; and the earth was lightened with his righteousness.

2 And he cried mightily with a strong voice, saying, Babylon the great is fallen, is fallen, and is become the habitation of devils, and the hold of every foul spirit, and a cage of every unclean and hateful bird.

3 For all nations have drunk of the wine of the wrath of her fornication, and the kings of the earth have committed fornication with her, and the merchants of the earth are waxed rich through the abundance of her delicacies.

4 And I heard another voice from heaven, saying, Come out of her, my people, that ye be not partakers of her transgressions, and that ye receive not of her plagues.

5 For her transgressions have reached unto heaven, and Yahweh hath remembered her iniquities.

6 Reward her even as she rewarded you, and double unto her double according to her works: in the cup which she hath filled fill to her double.

7 How much she hath glorified herself, and lived deliciously, so much torment and sorrow give her: for she saith in her heart, I sit a queen, and am no widow, and shall see no sorrow.

8 Therefore shall her plagues come in one day, death, and mourning, and famine; and she shall be utterly burned with fire: for strong is Yahweh who judgeth her.

9 And the kings of the earth, who have committed fornication and lived deliciously with her, shall bewail her, and lament for her, when they shall see the smoke of her burning,

10 Standing afar off for the fear of her torment, saying, Alas, alas that great city Babylon, that mighty city! for in one hour is thy judgment come.

11 And the merchants of the earth shall weep and mourn over her; for no man buyeth their merchandise any more:

12 The merchandise of gold, and silver, and precious stones, and of pearls, and fine linen, and purple, and silk, and scarlet, and all thyine wood, and all manner vessels of ivory, and all manner vessels of most precious wood, and of brass, and iron, and marble,

13 And cinnamon, and odors, and ointments, and frankincense, and wine, and oil, and fine flour, and wheat, and beasts, and sheep, and horses, and chariots, and slaves, and souls of men.

14 And the fruits that thy soul lusted after are departed from thee, and all things which were dainty and goodly are departed from thee, and thou shalt find them no more at all.

15 The merchants of these things, which were made rich by her, shall stand afar off for the fear of her torment, weeping and wailing,

16 And saying, Alas, alas that great city, that was clothed in fine linen, and purple, and scarlet, and decked with gold, and precious stones, and pearls!

17 For in one hour so great riches is come to naught. And every shipmaster, and all the company in ships, and sailors, and as many as trade by sea, stood afar off,

18 And cried when they saw the smoke of her burning, saying, What city is like unto this great city!

19 And they cast dust on their heads, and cried, weeping and wailing, saying, Alas, alas that great city, wherein were made rich all that had ships in the sea by reason of her costliness! for in one hour is she made desolate.

20 Rejoice over her, thou heaven, and ye apostles and prophets; for Yahweh hath avenged you on her.

21 And a mighty Messenger took up a stone like a great millstone, and cast it into the sea, saying, Thus with violence shall that great city Babylon be thrown down, and shall be found no more at all.

22 And the voice of harpers, and musicians, and of pipers, and trumpeters, shall be heard no more at all in thee; and no craftsman, of whatsoever craft he be, shall be found any more in thee; and the sound of a millstone shall be heard no more at all in thee;

²³ And the light of a candle shall shine no more at all in thee; and the voice of the bridegroom and of the bride shall be heard no more at all in thee: for thy merchants were the great men of the earth; for by thy sorceries were all nations deceived.

²⁴ And in her was found the blood of prophets, and of elect, and of all that were slain upon the earth.

REVELATION CHAPTER 19

Revelation 19:11-21

1 And after these things I heard a great voice of much people in heaven, saying, Halleluyah; Salvation, and honor, and power, unto Yahweh our Mighty One:

2 For true and righteous are his judgments: for He hath judged the great whore, which did corrupt the earth with her fornication, and hath avenged the blood of His servants at her hand.

3 And again they said, Halleluyah. And her smoke rose up for ever and ever.

4 And the four and twenty elders and the four beasts fell down and worshipped Yahweh that sat on the throne, saying, Halleluyah.

5 And a voice came out of the throne, saying, Praise our Yahweh, all ye His servants, and ye that fear him, both small and great.

6 And I heard as it were the voice of a great multitude, and as the voice of many waters, and as the voice of mighty thunderings, saying, Halleluyah: for Yahweh Almighty omnipotent reigned.

7 Let us be glad and rejoice, and give honor to Him: for the marriage of the Lamb is come, and his wife hath made herself ready.

8 And to her was granted that she should be arrayed in fine linen, clean and white: for the fine linen is the righteousness of believers.

9 And he saith unto me, Write, Blessed are they which are called unto the marriage supper of the Lamb. And he saith unto me, These are the true sayings of Yahweh.

10 And I fell at his feet to worship him. And he said unto me, See thou do it not: I am thy fellow servant, and of thy brethren that have the testimony of Yahweh: worship Yahweh: for the testimony of Yahweh is the spirit of prophecy.

11 And I saw heaven opened, and behold a white horse; and he that sat upon him was called Faithful and True, and in righteousness He doth judge and make war.

12 His eyes were as a flame of fire, and on his head were many crowns; and He had a name written, that no man knew, but he Himself.

13 And He was clothed with a vesture dipped in blood: and His name is called The Word of Yahweh.

14 And the armies which were in heaven followed Him upon white horses {spacecraft}, clothed in fine linen, white and clean.

15 And out of His mouth goeth a sharp sword, that with it He should smite the nations: and He shall rule them with a rod of iron: and He treadeth the winepress of the fierceness and wrath of Almighty Yahweh.

16 And He hath on his vesture and on his thigh a name written, King of kings.

17 And I saw an Messenger standing in the sun; and he cried with a loud voice, saying to all the fowls that fly in the midst of heaven, Come and gather yourselves together unto the supper of the great Yahweh;

18 That ye may eat the flesh of kings, and the flesh of captains, and the flesh of mighty men, and the flesh of horses, and of them that sit on them, and the flesh of all men, both free and bond, both small and great.

19 And I saw the beast, and the kings of the earth, and their armies, gathered together to make war against Him that sat on the horse, and against his army.

20 And the beast was taken, and with him the false prophet that wrought miracles before him, with which he deceived them that had received the mark of the beast, and them that worshipped his image. These both were cast alive into a lake of fire burning with brimstone.

21 And the remnant were slain with the sword of Him that sat upon the horse, which sword proceeded out of his mouth: and all the fowls were filled with their flesh.

The Seven Last Plagues are referred to as the Wrath of Yahweh!

Let no one foolishly imagine that they will not occur because the Scriptures must be fulfilled.

Yahweh's people will be saved from His wrath when it is poured out.

1 Thessalonians 5:8–9

8. But since we belong to the day, let us be self-controlled, putting on faith and love as a breastplate, and the hope of salvation as a helmet.

9. For Yahweh did not appoint us to suffer wrath {HIS WRATH} but to receive salvation through our Master, Yahweh Messiah.

Ephesians 5:1-7

1. Be ye therefore followers of Yahweh, as dear children;

2. And walk in love, as the Messiah also hath loved us, and hath given himself for us an offering and a sacrifice to Yahweh for a sweet smelling savour.

3. But fornication, and all uncleanness, or covetousness, let it not be once named among you, as becometh believers;

4. Neither filthiness, nor foolish talking, nor jesting, which are not convenient: but rather giving of thanks.

5. For this ye know, that no whoremonger, nor unclean person, nor covetous man, who is an idolater, hath any inheritance in the kingdom of the Messiah and of Yahweh.

6. Let no man deceive you with vain words: for because of these things cometh the wrath of Yahweh upon the children of disobedience.

7. Be not ye therefore partakers with them.

Romans 13:4

For he is the minister of Yahweh to thee for good. But if thou do that which is evil, be afraid; for he beareth not the sword in vain: for he is the minister of Yahweh, a revenger to execute wrath upon him that doeth evil.

Jeremiah 4:23-27

"I beheld the earth, and, lo, it was without form, and void; and the heavens, and they had no light. I beheld the mountains, and, lo, they trembled, and all the hills moved lightly. I beheld, and, lo, there was no man, and all the birds of the heavens were fled. I beheld, and, lo, the fruitful place was a wilderness, and all the cities thereof were broken down at the presence of Yahweh, and by His fierce anger. For thus hath Yahweh said, The whole land shall be desolate; yet will I not make a full end."

Revelation 11:15

And the seventh Messenger sounded; and there were great voices in heaven, saying, The kingdoms of this world are become the kingdoms of our Yahweh, and his Messiah; who shall reign forever and ever.

Isaiah 34:8,9

8 For it is the day of the Yahweh's vengeance, and the year of recompenses for the controversy of Zion.

9 And the streams thereof shall be turned into pitch, and the dust thereof into brimstone, and the land thereof shall become burning pitch.

10 It shall not be quenched night nor day; the smoke thereof shall go up for ever: from generation to generation it shall lie waste; none shall pass through it for ever and ever.

Revelation 14:10,11

10 The same shall drink of the wine of the wrath of Yahweh, which is poured out without mixture into the cup of his indignation; and he shall be tormented with fire and brimstone in the presence of the righteous Messengers, and in the presence of the Lamb:

11 And the smoke of their torment ascendeth up for ever and ever: and they have no rest day nor night, who worship the beast and his image, and whosoever receiveth the mark of his name.

Revelation 19:2,3

2 For true and righteous are his judgments: for He hath judged the great whore (ZION), which did corrupt the earth with her fornication, and hath avenged the blood of His servants at her hand.

3 And again they said, Halleluyah. <u>And her smoke rose up for ever and ever.</u>

When scriptures speak of smoke rising forever and ever, it just means that whatever scriptures are speaking of when that is said, whatever it is will not ever exist again.

REVELATION CHAPTER 20

1 And I saw a Messenger come down from heaven, <u>having the key of the bottomless pit and a great chain in his hand.</u>

2 And <u>he laid hold on the dragon, that old serpent, which is the Devil, and Satan, and bound him a thousand years,</u>

3 <u>And cast him into the bottomless pit (Grave), and shut him up, and set a seal upon him, that he should deceive the nations no more, till the thousand years should be fulfilled: and after that he must be loosed a little season.</u>

4 And I saw thrones, and they sat upon them, and judgment was given unto them:

12 heads of the 12 tribes and the 12 disciples, will sit on the thrones.

Ruben, Simeon, Levi, Judah, Zebulun, Issachar, Dan, Gad, Asher, Naphtali, Joseph, Benjamin

Luke 22:30 That ye may eat and drink at my table in my kingdom, and sit on thrones judging the twelve tribes of Judaea.

Matthew 19:28 And Immanuel said unto them, Verily I say unto you, That ye which have followed me, (the 12 disciples) in the regeneration when the Son of man shall sit in the throne of his glory/righteousness, ye also shall sit upon twelve thrones, judging the twelve tribes of Judaea.

And <u>I saw the souls of them that were beheaded for the witness of Yahweh Messiah, and for the word of Yahweh,</u> and <u>which had not worshipped the beast, neither his image,</u>

neither had received his mark upon their foreheads, or in their hands; and they lived and reigned with Yahweh Messiah a thousand years.

⁵ But the rest of the dead lived not again until the thousand years were finished. This is the first resurrection.

⁶ Blessed and righteous is he that hath part in the first resurrection: on such the second death hath no power, but they shall be priests of Yahweh and of Messiah, and shall reign with him a thousand years.

⁷ And when the thousand years are expired, Satan shall be loosed out of his prison (the Grave),

⁸ And shall go out to deceive the nations which are in the four quarters of the earth, Gog, and Magog, to gather them together to battle: the number of whom is as the sand of the sea.

⁹ And they went up on the breadth of the earth, and compassed the camp of the saints about, and the beloved city: and fire came down from Yahweh out of heaven, and devoured them.

¹⁰ And the devil that deceived them was cast into the lake of fire and brimstone, where the beast and the false prophet are, and shall be tormented day and night for ever and ever.

¹¹ And I saw a great white throne, and him that sat on it, from whose face the earth and the heaven fled away; and there was found no place for them.

¹² And I saw the dead, small and great, stand before Yahweh; and the books were opened: and another book was opened, which is the book of life: and the dead were judged out of those things which were written in the books, according to their works.

13 And <u>the sea gave up the dead which were in it; and death and the grave delivered up the dead which were in them: and they were judged every man according to their works.</u>

14 And death and grave were cast into the lake of fire. This is the second death.

15 And <u>whosoever was not found written in the book of life was cast into the lake of fire.</u>

REVELATION CHAPTER 21, VERSES 1-5, IS ALL ABOUT NEW ZION.

1 And I saw a new heaven and a new earth: for the first heaven and the first earth were passed away; and there was no more sea.

2 And I John saw the righteous city, NEW ZION, coming down from Yahweh out of heaven, prepared as a bride adorned for her husband.

3 And I heard a great voice out of heaven saying, Behold, the tabernacle of Yahweh is with men, and he will dwell with them, and they shall be his people, and Yahweh himself shall be with them, and be their Mighty One.

4 And Yahweh shall wipe away all tears from their eyes; and there shall be no more death, neither sorrow, nor crying, neither shall there be any more pain: for the former things are passed away.

5 And he that sat upon the throne said, Behold, I make all things new. And he said unto me, Write: for these words are true and faithful.

VERSES 6 AND 7 ARE FOR THE ONES WANTING SALVATION; VERSE 8 FOR THOSE WHO DID NOT WANT SALVATION, AND THEIR END IS THE LAKE OF FIRE.

6 And he said unto me, It is done. I am Alpha and Omega, the beginning and the end. I will give unto him that is athirst of the fountain of the water of life freely.

⁷ He that overcometh shall inherit all things; and I will be his Mighty One, and he shall be my son.

⁸ But the fearful, and unbelieving, and the abominable, and murderers, and whoremongers, and sorcerers, and idolaters, and all liars, shall have their part in the lake which burneth with fire and brimstone: which is the second death.

VERSE 9 TO 27 ARE ALL ABOUT NEW ZION.

⁹ And there came unto me one of the seven Messengers which had the seven vials full of the seven last plagues, and talked with me, saying, Come hither, I will shew thee the bride, the Lamb's wife.

¹⁰ And he carried me away in the spirit to a great and high mountain, and shewed me that great city, the righteous ZION, descending out of heaven from Yahweh,

¹¹ Having the righteousness of Yahweh: and her light was like unto a stone most precious, even like a jasper stone, clear as crystal;

¹² And had a wall great and high, and had twelve gates, and at the gates twelve Messengers, and names written thereon, which are the names of the twelve tribes of the children of Israel:

¹³ On the east three gates; on the north three gates; on the south three gates; and on the west three gates.

¹⁴ And the wall of the city had twelve foundations, and in them the names of the twelve apostles of the Lamb.

¹⁵ And he that talked with me had a golden reed to measure the city, and the gates thereof, and the wall thereof.

16 And the city lieth foursquare, and the length is as large as the breadth: and he measured the city with the reed, twelve thousand furlongs. The length and the breadth and the height of it are equal.

17 And he measured the wall thereof, an hundred and forty and four cubits, according to the measure of a man, that is, of the Messenger.

18 And the building of the wall of it was of jasper: and the city was pure gold, like unto clear glass.

19 And the foundations of the wall of the city were garnished with all manner of precious stones. The first foundation was jasper; the second, sapphire; the third, a chalcedony; the fourth, an emerald;

20 The fifth, sardonyx; the sixth, sardius; the seventh, chrysolyte; the eighth, beryl; the ninth, a topaz; the tenth, a chrysoprasus; the eleventh, a jacinth; the twelfth, anamethyst.

21 And the twelve gates were twelve pearls: every several gate was of one pearl: and the street of the city was pure gold, as it were transparent glass.

22 And I saw no House therein: for the Master Yahweh and the Lamb are the House of it.

23 And the city had no need of the sun, neither of the moon, to shine in it: for the righteousness of Yahweh did lighten it, and the Lamb is the light thereof.

24 And the nations of them which are saved shall walk in the light of it: and the kings of the earth do bring their esteem and honor into it.

25 And the gates of it shall not be shut at all by day: for there shall be no night there.

26 And they shall bring the glory/esteem and honor of the nations into it.

27 And there shall in no wise enter into it any thing that defileth, neither whatsoever worketh abomination, or maketh a lie: but they which are written in the Lamb's book of life.

REVELATION CHAPTER 22 - speaking about Mount Zion when Yahweh is here on this earth. In Chapter 21, VERSE 8, ARE THOSE THAT DID NOT WANT SALVATION AND THEIR END IS THE LAKE OF FIRE after Yahweh taught them.

1 And he shewed me a pure river of water of life, clear as crystal, proceeding out of the throne of Yahweh and of the Lamb.

2 In the midst of the street of it, and on either side of the river, was there the tree of life, which bare twelve manner of fruits, and yielded her fruit every month: and the leaves of the tree were for the healing of the nations.

3 And there shall be no more curse: but the throne of Yahweh and of the Lamb shall be in it; and his servants shall serve him:

4 And they shall see his face; and his name shall be in their foreheads.

5 And there shall be no night there; and they need no candle, neither light of the sun; for the Master Yahweh giveth them light: and they shall reign for ever and ever.

6 And he said unto me, These sayings are faithful and true: and the Master Yahweh of the righteous prophets sent his Messenger to shew unto his servants the things which must shortly be done.

7 Behold, I come quickly: blessed is he that keepeth the sayings of the prophecy of this book.

8 And I John saw these things, and heard them. And when I had heard and seen, I fell down to worship before the feet of the Messenger which shewed me these things.

9 Then saith he unto me, See thou do it not: for I am thy fellowservant, and of thy brethren the prophets, and of them which keep the sayings of this book: worship Yahweh.

10 And he saith unto me, Seal not the sayings of the prophecy of this book: for the time is at hand.

11 He that is unjust, let him be unjust still: and he which is filthy, let him be filthy still: and he that is righteous, let him be righteous still: and he that is righteous, let him be righteous still.

12 And, behold, I come quickly; and my reward is with me, to give every man according as his work shall be.

13 I am Alpha and Omega, the beginning and the end, the first and the last.

14 Blessed are they that do his commandments, that they may have right to the tree of life, and may enter in through the gates into the city.

15 For without are dogs, and sorcerers, and whoremongers, and murderers, and idolaters, and whosoever loveth and maketh a lie.

The ones in verse 15 are the ones being taught by Yahweh and are not allowed in the city only the elect are. Compare verse 8 in chapter 21 to this verse 15.

16 I Yahweh have sent mine Messenger to testify unto you these things in the assemblies. I am the root and the offspring of David, and the bright and morning star.

17 And the Spirit and the bride say, Come. And let him that heareth say, Come. And let him that is athirst come. And whosoever will, let him take the water of life freely.

18 For I testify unto every man that heareth the words of the prophecy of this book, If any man shall add unto these things, shall add unto him the plagues that are written in this book:

¹⁹ And if any man shall take away from the words of the book of this prophecy, Yahweh shall take away his part out of the book of life, and out of the righteous city, and from the things which are written in this book.

²⁰ He which testifieth these things saith, Surely I come quickly. Even so, come, Master Yahweh.

²¹ The Spirit of our Master Yahweh Messiah be with you all.

2 Thessalonians 2:8-12

⁸ And then shall <u>that Wicked be revealed</u>, whom the Lord/YAHWEH shall consume with the spirit of his mouth, and shall destroy with the brightness of his coming:

⁹ <u>Even him, whose coming is after the working of Satan with all power and signs and lying wonders,</u>

¹⁰ And <u>with all deceivableness of unrighteousness in them that perish; because they received not the love of the truth, that they might be saved.</u>

¹¹ And for this cause God/ <u>Yahweh shall send them strong delusion, that they should believe a lie:</u>

¹² <u>That they all might be damned who believed not the truth, but had pleasure in unrighteousness.</u>

I have thought a lot about these verses, and I believe this is the reason why Christians have that feel-good feeling when they are in their churches and why people get that everything is alright feeling with their feeling of having salvation because if they want to believe the lies, then Yahweh sends them strong delusions so they will believe those lies making them believe that they have salvation when they don't. That's why people get so caught up in the lies of Christianity, they go to their services and listen to the preachers who are called of themselves that mess with their emotions, and then they all go home with a high feel good feeling and can't wait to go back and get pumped up again, not realizing it is all part of Satan's deceit, and Yahweh gives the delusions to believe those lies.

THE TIMELINE:

WW3 >>>> 7 Year Peace Plan >>>> Moses and Eliyah bring back the truth - Truth taught to every person on earth - Yahweh's Spirit poured out >>>>> Moses and Eliyah killed midway of Peace Plan >>>> Pope takes power >>>> NO 3rd House of Yahweh, Dome of the Rock will be used >>>> Start of Tribulation Period >>>> Christianity made World Religion - Mark of the Beast given (CROSS) - Yahweh's elect persecuted and killed >>>> Armageddon >> Satan will make himself known and will help the world armies fight Yahweh and his Messengers at Yahweh's return>> Return of Yahweh >>>> Millennial Kingdom on earth >>>> Satan raised from grave to deceive the world one last time >>>> White Throne Judgement >>>> End of this world, it burns up with all the wicked with it >>>> New Heaven and Earth >>>> Yahweh lives on the New Earth with His Elect.

WW3 WILL BE A LIMITED NUCLEAR WAR. IT HAS BEEN PLANNED FOR YEARS.

SALVATION COMES AGAIN DURING THE 7-YEAR PEACE PLAN AFTER WW3:

Tribulation Period

Why run during the Tribulation Period if Yahweh is on your side and a person is Spirit-filled? Yahweh will guide and take care of His people, but when it's time to lay down your life for Him, you will not run.........all those back then were killed off. They went through 11 Emperor persecutions until the last one was killed. Then, the Great Following Away happened when Yahweh took his Spirit of salvation from this earth and became Satan's world totally since that time. This started with Emperor Nero in 54 A.D. to Constantine, which ended about 311 A.D. That is a total of 257 years of persecution and death. Salvation was started at Pentecost up to the great falling away, and the last of Yahweh's elect were killed. Pentecost happened about 37 A.D, 50 days after the Feast of First Fruits which was the next day Sunday after the day of his 7th day Sabbath Resurrection. From there up to 311, which would be about 274 given for salvation.

Yahweh, in the end, is going to do a quick work like the scriptures teach. During the 7-Year Peace Plan, salvation is given at the very beginning of it...then the Tribulation Period is the last half of it.........so that is a 7-year time frame in which Yahweh will complete the final work. So many people believe the Tribulation Period is only for Yahweh's Elect, but those who take the Mark of the Beast are also going to go through their tribulation period for taking the Mark, and Yahweh will make them suffer big time. Yahweh's Elect will die for their testimony that Yahweh is true, just like those back then did. Those who take the Mark will suffer from what Yahweh does to them during the Tribulation Period. THEY ARE BURNED UP AT YAHWEH'S COMING.

CHAPTER 14
THE PAPACY AND ISLAM

To understand you have to go back to the Crusades and find out how the Papacy and Muslims ended the fighting.

A. The Pope & Islam

After researching how the Islamic faith came to be and Rome's obvious involvement in it, history shows that the Vatican arranged the marriage of Mohammed and his wife, who was a Christian. A Catholic denomination did not exist at that time, not until 1559. The bishops helped Mohammed write the Koran and gain his power. This was done by Papal Rome, all to cause the Muslims to hate the Jews and rid the Jews of their land so that Rome can set her churches upon the land in triumph. Of course, history proves it backfired for the Pope, which in turn caused him to war across Europe in the crusades that saw countless deaths for centuries, Christians killing Christians. However lately, it seems Jerusalem is finally within the grasp of Rome once again. The book of Martyrs had nothing to do with Yahweh believers but with Christian believers and pagans, making them killed as martyrs in truth. A pagan lie.

I wondered why Obama went to a Catholic School in a Muslim country. I wondered how the Catholics had churches and schools in Muslim countries when no other denomination had them there, and yet the Muslims were supposed to be anti-Christian, yet they were not against the Catholics. Even Miss America (2010) is a Muslim who went to a Catholic school where she lived, then came to the United States and calls herself a Muslim/Christian. Just like in Jerusalem, there are only Catholic Churches, the Dome of the Rock / Temple of God, which is under Muslim control right now, and the Jewish Synagogues; no other Christian denominations are represented.

Here is why things are as they are: To set it up, the Muslims and the Papacy signed Concordats to stop the fighting, which was still going on with the Ottoman Empire.

"As a result, Muslims were allowed to occupy Turkey in the Christian world, and the Catholics were allowed to occupy Lebanon in the Muslim world. It was also agreed that the Muslims could build Mosques in Christian countries without interference as long as the Roman Universal Church could flourish in Arab countries." This is why when you see a Mosque, there is a Catholic Church next to one across the street or in proximity.

"Muslims agreed to block and destroy the efforts of their common enemy, the Protestant Christians so that Rome could stand as the supreme moral authority, through these Concordats."

"The Vatican engineered a campaign of hatred between the Muslims and the Jews. Before this, they co-existed peaceably." Malachi Martin.

The Jesuits are good at instigating things when it is part of the Papacy's agenda.

When you understand that, you will understand the above thread.

The Muslims helped the Hebrew people escape Spain when the Spanish Inquisition of the Papacy took place. Even today, there are 1,142,000 Muslims living in Israel, being 16% of its population. Muslims live in Israel side by side with the Jewish people in peace.

Let's talk about "Fatima," Portugal, which was named after Muhammad's daughter, and we shall see how the Papacy works. In 1917, the Virgin Mary appeared in Fatima. You may be asking what this has to do with Islam? Note Martin Sheen's statement, "Our Lady's appearances at Fatima marked the turning point in the history of the world's 350 million Muslims. After the death of his daughter, Muhammad wrote that she "is the most holy of all women in Paradise, next to Mary." { Fatima is a lie of Rome.}

2010 - October 23, VATICAN CITY — Bishops from across the Middle East on Saturday urged Israel to end its occupation of Palestinian territories so that a two-state solution could be found swiftly.

In a final communiqué at the end of a two-week-long meeting at the Vatican on the plight of Christians in the Middle East, the bishops also urged Israel not to use the Bible "to wrongly justify injustices," apparently referring to Israel's occupation of the West Bank and Gaza.

Catholic bishops in the Middle East have called on the United Nations to reinforce Security Council resolutions and put an end to the Israeli occupation of Arab lands. The Papacy is over the U.N., so no wonder they did that.

On Saturday, the bishops and patriarchs said the citizens of the Middle East "call upon the international community, particularly the United Nations, to work conscientiously to find a peaceful, just and definitive solution in the region, through the application of the Security Council's resolutions," AFP reported.

On the last day of a two-week synod attended by Pope Benedict XVI, the clergymen released a final statement in which they highlighted the need for the UN to take "the necessary legal steps to put an end to the occupation of the different Arab territories." (The Papacy is over the U.N.)

"The Palestinian people will thus have an independent and sovereign homeland where they can live with dignity and security," they said, noting that Israel would, in return, be able to enjoy peace and security within its "internationally recognized borders."

"The Holy City of [al-Quds] Jerusalem will be able to acquire its proper status, which respects its particular character, its holiness and the religious patrimony of the three religions: Jewish, Christian and Muslim," said the statement, expressing hope that the two-state solution might become a reality.

[al-Quds] Arabic-language daily newspaper based in Jerusalem.

The statement recalled Security Council resolutions requiring Israel to withdraw from territories occupied during the Six-Day War of 1967, including east al-Quds, the West Bank, and the Gaza Strip.

The synod also said they "condemn violence and terrorism from wherever it may proceed as well as all religious extremism."

"We condemn all forms of racism, anti-Semitism, anti-Christianism, and Islamophobia, and we call upon the religions to assume their responsibility to promote dialogue between cultures and civilizations in our region and in the entire world." Anti-Semitism is being taught in the colleges and universities, which are Jesuit controlled and control what is taught in them.

Ayatollah Khomeini bows down and worship the empty throne in Mecca. Islam lacks a throne. Muslims bow down to worship in front of an empty throne.

CHAPTER 15

CHRISTIANITY and ISLAM, SAME TACTICS:

Both religions have:

1. A center city; Rome and Mecca;

2. A primary language for its religious texts and worship: Latin and Arabic;

3. Dictatorial religious leaders: Pope and Caliph (presently absent since 1922);

4. Caliphate - is like the Pope in Christianity, a person that is over secular and religious governments. The Muslims' goal is to reestablish the Caliphate once all the Muslim countries are united all under the head of the Caliph.

5. Holy Wars: Crusades and Jihads;

6. Common enemies: Primarily all racial and religious Jews and especially non-Papal, Protestant Christians;

7. Religious "Holy Men:" Priests and Imams;

8. The goal of "converting the world" by argument or by the sword;

9. Both religions are after world dominion to rule the entire world. One through Socialism and the other through Terrorism.

10. Both wanting to possess the Old City of Jerusalem and Temple Mount when it belongs Scriptural right to the Hebrew/Jew;

11. A hatred for the true Creator and Messiah, Yahweh.

12. Islam tells Muslims that if they die for their religion, they get 70 virgins and go to heaven. Christianity told the Crusaders that if they died for the Crusades, they would go straight to heaven.

*The following helps prove that the problems in the Middle East are of the Papacy to bring about a Muslim Union under the Muslim Brotherhood. The Muslim Brotherhood Mason's run by the Illuminati. ****(forget anti-Papal Shia Islam as it is presently being destroyed)**** (these are the Shiites, these are anti-Pope that are being killed by ISIS)**** This stuff is coming to America when the Pope is ready to get rid of the Protestant denominations and anyone else who does not look to him as full authority. That is why our government is flooding this country with Catholics and Muslims, the very reason the Muslim Brotherhood is now part of our government. This stuff has been going on for centuries if you know anything about the history of the Papacy.*

Everyone knows the Koran says to kill anyone who does not belong to the Muslim religion. The religion of Christianity has killed anyone who did not come over to Christianity throughout history.

Islam uses a Latinized Eesa for the name Jesus, but Eesa in Arabic is the same as Esau in Hebrew, and it was the Papacy who gave the Muslims the name Eesa for Jesus. We know that Jesus came from Rome and Paganism, so only through the Papacy did the Quran end up using that name.

Allah is a moon deity, and Jesus, Christ, Amen, Lord, and God are sun deity names. Adonai of the Jews is also a sun deity name. They worship the created and not the Creator.

All 3 religions, Judaism, Christianity, and Islam, will share the Dome of the Rock / Temple of God, built by Constantine in the 4th Century. Christianity is the Sun, Islam is the Moon, and Judaism is the Star. Islam's Sabbath is on the 6th day, Friday; Jewish or Yahweh's Sabbath is on the 7th day, Saturday; Christianity's Sabbath is on the 1st day of the week, Sunday. Christians pray to the Ceiling; Islam pray to the Floor; Jews pray to the Wall, all in the House of Paganism.

People are taught to believe that Muslims are going to take over the world when it is Christianity and the Pope who will rule over all. This is another reason why I believe that

Nimrod will be brought back to be the last Pope. The Muslims would accept him as the Caliph that they are waiting for since he is an Assyrian and Pope. This would work out for both parties.

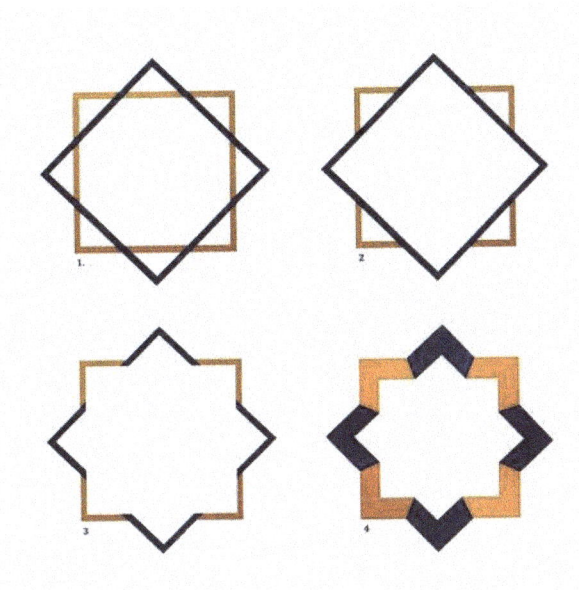

A. STAR OF ISLAM

The 8-pointed Islam star is made with 2 squares overlaid.

The Pope & Islam

I read a couple of books that agreed and stated the Papacy started the Islam religion to get control of the Middle East.

Christianity has over 44,000 different denominations and belief systems, and all the different names they use are nothing but a system of confusion. This is a wake-up call for people to get out of Christianity and see it for what it really is: a Satanic, pagan religious system.

In a recent speech, Pope John Paul said, "Christians and Muslims, we meet one another in faith in the one God...and strive to put into practice...the teaching of our respective holy books. Today, dialogue between our two religions is more necessary than ever. There remains a spiritual bond which unites us and which we must strive to recognize and develop."

Pope John Paul II Kissed the Koran

The latest name Christianity is accepting and has accepted in some denominations is the moon deity of Allah, since they are told it means GOD. GOD is a pagan deity, too.

Netherlands - Roman Catholic Bishop of Breda, Tiny Muskens, says he wants Christians to start calling God "Allah" because he believes such a gesture would promote "rapprochement between Christianity and Islam." Appearing on Dutch television, the 71-year-old cleric said: God, Allah, and Sin are just a few of the moon deity names, so each is interchangeable with one another, and why Christians are easily accepting the name Allah, which is supposed to mean God, well it also means Sin.

"Allah is a very beautiful word for God. Shouldn't we all say that from now on we will name God Allah? ... What does God care what we call him?"

Chrislam is an attempt to produce an ecumenical reconciliation between Christianity and Islam. While it began in Nigeria in the 1980s, Chrislamic ideas have spread throughout much of the world. The essential concept of Chrislam is that Christianity and Islam are compatible, that one can be a Christian and a Muslim at the same time. Chrislam is not an actual religion of its own but rather is a blending of the differences between Christianity and Islam. Let's say 3 people from 3 different cultures that believe in each of those names are talking about their moon deity but never mention the name they use, well they are all thinking that the other two are talking about his moon deity, Sin, and that goes with the other two that use Allah and God for the deities name, believing the same.

With Christians using God for their Sun deity names and Islam using God as their moon deity name, you can see why, though different, they are the same in one another's minds. It is a blending of Nimrod and Semiramis worship.

According to a recent blog post from The Last Crusade, congregations in several metropolitan areas -- Houston, Atlanta, Seattle, and Detroit -- preached sermons and held Sunday school lessons recently on the founder of Islam, Mohammad, whom Muslims consider a prophet. Qurans were also placed in the pews next to Bibles.

For many years now, Paul Crouch, president and founder of TBN, has presented Christians and Moslems as soul mates, as well as the Holy Bible and the Koran as Volume I and Volume II of the same basic religious orientation. Crouch has stated again and again that Christianity and Islam have more in common than what separates them. Chrislam! If you Christians don't see who is behind it all, then you never will.

Just recently, Rick Warren, founder and pastor of Saddleback Community Church in Orange County, California, addressed the convention of the Islamic Society of North America. Warren stated that Muslims and Christians must work together to combat stereotypes, promote peace and freedom, and solve global problems. Christians and Moslems – faith mates, soul mates, and now work mates! Chrislam! No, just Christianity.

Proponents of the movement, which has been dubbed "Chrislam," claim that Christians cannot love their neighbors without having a relationship with them.

NEW BIBLE VERSIONS REMOVE 'FATHER' AND 'SON OF GOD' BECAUSE IT OFFENDS MUSLIMS.

"'Father' and 'Son' Ousted from the Trinity in New Bible Translations," by Hussein Hajj Wario, January 27

A controversy is brewing over three reputable Christian organizations, which are based in North America, whose efforts have ousted the words "Father" and "Son" from new Bibles. Wycliffe Bible Translators, Summer Institute of Linguistics (SIL), and Frontiers are under fire for "producing Bibles that remove "Father," "Son," and "Son of God" because these terms are offensive to Muslims." Concerned Christian missionaries, Bible translators, pastors, and national church leaders have come together with a public petition to stop these organizations. They claim a public petition is their last recourse because meetings with these organizations' leaders, staff resignations over this issue, and criticism and appeals from native national Christians concerned about the translations "have failed to persuade these agencies to retain "Father" and "Son" in the text of all their translations."

Ephesians 4:6,7,8; 11-16

6. One Yahweh and Father of all, who is above all, and through all, and in you all.

7. But unto every one of us is given the Spirit according to the measure of the gift of Yahweh.

8. Wherefore He saith, When He ascended up on high, He led captivity captive, and gave gifts unto men.

11. And He gave some, apostles [the original 12 disciples]; and some, prophets;[those who Yahweh spoke through] and some, teachers [those who taught or gave instruction];

12. For the perfecting of the believers, for the work of the ministry, for the edifying of the body of Yahweh:

13. Till we all come in the unity of the Faith, and of the knowledge of the Son of Yahweh, unto a perfect man, unto the measure of the stature of the fulness of Yahweh:

14. That we henceforth be no more children, tossed to and fro, and carried about with every wind of doctrine, by the sleight of men, and cunning craftiness, whereby they lie in wait to deceive;

15. But speaking the truth in love, may grow up into Him in all things, which is the head, even Yahweh:

16. From whom the whole body fitly joined together and compacted by that which every joint supplieth, according to the effectual working in the measure of every part, maketh increase of the body unto the edifying of itself in love.

In other words, when you first believe, you become a believer, but you are not Spirit-filled yet. So the Spirit-filled believers were the ones who taught the new believers in Yahweh Messiah until Yahweh seen fit to fill them with His Spirit. The Spirit-filled people were taught by the Spirit and knew all things; the believers who were not Spirit-filled had to be taught of Yahweh's ways until their infilling.

Yahweh's people have always done exploits in both Old and New Covenants.

Daniel 11:32

And such as do wickedly against the covenant shall he corrupt by flatteries: but the people that do know their Messiah shall be strong and do *exploits.*

Acts 17:6

And when they found them not, they drew Jason and certain brethren unto the rulers of the city, crying, These that have turned the world upside down are come hither also;

1209-1400, Medieval Inquisition. This is when the breaking away from Rome started, another reason the reformation was started by the Papacy.

The Universal Christian Church of Rome conducted Inquisitions from the Middle Ages onward. Some of these were conducted in collaboration with governmental attacks on people with different religious views that were splitting from the Christian church in Rome, started by Constantine, like the Albigensian crusade in southern France in the Middle Ages, also the Waldensian crusade, the war against the Hussite's in what is now the Czech republic in the 15th century, and the various wars of religion of the 16th and 17th century. Plus, besides fighting themselves, Christians were fighting the Muslims all at the same time in different places.

1209, Pope Innocent III decided it was time to crack down on followers of a religious sect that had become popular in Southern France.

Originally called Albigensians, they came to be more widely known as the Cathars.

229

Catharism, "the pure (ones)," was a Christian dualist movement that thrived in some areas of Southern Europe, particularly northern Italy and southern France, between the 12th and 14th centuries. Cathar beliefs varied between communities because Catharism was initially taught by ascetic priests who had set few guidelines.

Cathars were Christians. But they rejected the authority of the pope and other key aspects of Christianity, so they were deemed heretics by the Church of Rome.

On July 22, 1209, they were celebrating the annual Feast of Mary Magdalene together, a religious holiday observed by various Christians.

Suddenly, the festivities were cut short when an army of "Crusaders" sent by Pope Innocent III showed up outside the walls of the town.

The military leader of the army was Simon de Montfort, a French nobleman highly motivated by the pope's promise that he could keep the land of any heretics he killed.

The Crusaders were accompanied by an official representative of the pope, a French Cistercian monk named Arnaud Amalric (also variously referred to as Arnald Amalric and Arnauld-Amaury).

De Montfort demanded that the leaders of Beziers turn over the town's Cathar heretics to him. They refused. The Crusaders attacked.

According to accounts written decades later, as the attack began, a soldier asked Amalric how they would be able to tell which Beziers townspeople were Catholics and which were Cathars.

Arnaud Amalric answered (in French): "Kill them all and let God sort them out."

De Montfort's army killed almost every man, woman, and child in the town — estimated to be as many as 20,000 people — and burned Beziers to the ground.

As you can see, the Popes sit on Satan's Throne, and they do not care if they kill their own while killing others.

1215, The dogma of transubstantiation was adopted.

Confession was instituted.

1220, The adoration of the Wafer.

1316, The Ave Maria was introduced.

1300 John Wycliffe influenced John Huss (Jan Hus), a priest whose followers were called Hussites. Their rebellion against the Papacy became known as the Hussite Wars.

John Wycliffe, a priest, founded the Lollard movement. It was short-lived, and the Pope ordered Wycliffe's bones exhumed and burned. Intense persecution stamped out his followers and teachings. Wycliffe criticized the abuses and false teachings of Christianity.

Wycliffe criticized the abuses and false teachings of Christianity. He translated Jerome's Latin Vulgate into English, the first translation in over 1000 years

1415, The cup was taken from the laity.

John Huss was burned at the stake. The Hussites made it through for the Reformation.

1439, Purgatory was officially decreed.

ALL THE ABOVE IS WHAT CHRISTIANITY WAS LIKE BEFORE ANY DENOMINATIONS CAME TO BE BEFORE THE REFORMATION. JUST LIKE TODAY'S CATHOLIC DENOMINATION DOES IT NOT? YOU WILL LEARN MORE AS WE GO. This is what our forefathers believed at the above times.

CHAPTER 16

FROM THE REFORMATION FORWARD: BEGINNINGS OF DIFFERENT DENOMINATIONS AND CHURCHES.

Many people in Western Europe were growing increasingly dissatisfied with Christianity, priests, and the Pope.

The protesters were against Christianity, with the Pope over it. They wanted Christianity to line up more with the Scriptures, not realizing they were propagandized and unified, and after the Reformation, many denominations tried to revive the truth to first-century conditions. From there, they started being named after their major beliefs, such as Baptist for Baptism and Pentecostals for believing in the Spirit infilling. Then, some were named after the reformers they followed, like the Lutherans were named after Martin Luther, for following Luther's doctrine; Calvinists for following John Calvin's doctrine, and Catholics for believing they are Universal Christianity. This is how denominations started in Christianity. Since no one really agreed 100% on doctrines, they went with their own freedoms of worship where they would no longer be under the power of the Papacy. They started out just a handful of different denominations and started splitting off from each other until today there are over 44,000 denominations in Christianity. The Satanic lie started with Constantine and why Christianity is a deceitful religion.

1517-1648. The Reformation: It lasted 131 years. The Reformation was a Christian Civil War, Christians killing Christians. I truly believe that the Papacy, using Martin

Luther and other priests, started the Reformation so they could turn the tide and control things to keep people in Christianity.

1517, Martin Luther, in his 95 Thesis never mentioned Catholic or Roman Catholic, just Christianity, just like you will find in other writings of that period. Martin Luther hated the Hebrews with a passion.

1522, Martin Luther founded the Lutheran Church.

1522, **Luther's New Testament**:

To help show how it happened, the Anabaptist, known also as Christian Brethren, did not believe in baby baptism. From these broke off a group called Mennonites, who were followers of Menno Simon, a priest. Then, the Mennonites broke away into a group called Amish, who were followers of Joseph Amman, a priest. The Presbyterians were influenced by John Calvin. What happened during the Reformation Christianity split, those who still believed the Pope was the head of it and the Protestants who did away with the Pope as the head. Just like Christianity splitting East and West during the Great Schism.

1523, the Swiss Reformed Church was founded by Zwingli in Switzerland.

1525, Georg Blaurock, Conrad Grebel, and Felix Manz founded the Anabaptists, which the Mennonites, Hutterites, and the Amish descended from.

1534, **Tyndale's New Testament and Luther's Old Testament**.

1536, the "Act of Supremacy" confirmed King Henry VIII, the Supreme Head of the Church of England in the earth of the Church of England, called "Ecclesia Anglicana," and later the Supreme Governor of the Church of England. Henry VIII found it expedient to replace Papal authority with the supremacy of the English crown. Even though it stayed pretty much the same as the Church of Rome. **Church of England** became the

Anglican Church of England. This came about from Pope Clement VII refusing to annul King Henry's marriage to Catherine of Aragon.

Calvinism was founded by John Calvin in Sweden.

1545-63, Council of Trent. 1559, the Start of the Catholic denomination and the Jesuits to combat the Reformation.

Let's talk about the Catholics or Roman Catholics. When did these titles actually become a denomination? You will never see Catholic or Roman Catholic mentioned any time before the Reformation as a denomination, only the religion of Christianity, because denominations did not exist. Newer writers have tried stating it was Catholic or Roman Catholic as a denomination, but this is not true. When they used catholic, it was just to say that Christianity was the universal religion since it was the State religion started by Constantine and the only religion allowed. All were Christian, even the Jews. Even the Crusades were called the Christian Crusades, not Roman Catholic or Catholic, and the Crusades were from about the 1100s to the 1300s.

Catholic is an adjective derived from the Greek adjective êáèïëéêüò (katholikos), meaning "universal."

The Roman Church was the main church with the authority of the Pope's throne sitting there, and Christianity being the state religion of the empire and was called the universal religion. There became a denomination known as Roman Catholic after the Reformation.

The Roman church, with the Pope as the head of it, remained the most pagan outwardly, so the Protestant Christians will look at her as being apostate and not at the religion of Christianity, which they are all in, as the Apostate and Harlot religion. Many denominations of today think that the Catholic or Roman Catholics are not Christian but a religion in itself. Many of you should wake-up and understand that Christianity is the religion.

Christians are only persecuted where another religion is dominant unless they persecute each other because of their different belief systems in their different denominations. This is why they teach there is a true Christianity and a false Christianity.

1546, the Roman tradition was placed on the same level as Scripture.

1546, The Apocrypha was received into the Canon.

1550-1700, **Spanish Inquisition. Portugal Inquisition**, 16th and early 17th century

1560, John Knox founded the Presbyterian in Scotland.

1571, Counter-Reformation. We are still living in the Counter-Reformation era and will until all the Protestant denominations go back under the Pope's authority like it was before the Reformation Period.

1582, Congregational Church was founded by Robert Brown in Holland

1605, John Smith in Holland, founded the Baptist Church.

John Wesley, who started Methodist, was an Anglican priest. John Smyth, who started the Baptist, was an Anglican priest. Nearly 200 years apart.

1617, The first recorded Seventh Day Baptist meeting was held at The Mill Yard Church in London in 165 under the leadership of Dr. Peter Chamberlen. However many SDBs believe that their origins date to 1617 with John Trask and his wife, but the records for this were lost in a fire.

1628, Michaelis Jones founded the Dutch Reformed Church in the Netherlands.

1647, Founded by George Fox, the Society of Friends / Quakers broke from the "Puritan" movement within the Church of England and coincided with the "Dissenters" movement of England.

1693, founded by Jakob Ammann, the Amish in Switzerland.

1717, Moravians founded by Count Zinendorf in Germany.

1747, Swedenborg Church was founded by Emanuel Swedenborg in Sweden.

1774, the Methodist Church was founded by John & Charles Wesley in England.

1774, the Unitarian Church was founded by Theophilus Lindley in London.

1700s, Protestant Episcopal Church is an offshoot of the Church of England, and was founded by Samuel Seabury in the American Colonies in the 18th Century. Same as Catholics.

1829, The Mormon Church (Latter Day Saints) was founded by Joseph Smith in the U.S.

Jesuit John Peter de Smet also designed the USA 14th Amendment and co-founded the Mormon denomination of Christianity in the early 1800's. Together with High-Level Freemasons, Joseph Smith and Brigham Young were Illuminati members.

Smith claimed that the last prophet to contribute to the book, a man named Moroni, buried it in a hill in present-day New York and then returned to earth in 1827 as an angel, revealing the location of the book to Smith and instructing him to translate and disseminate it as evidence of the restoration of Christ's true church in the latter days.

But Masonry made a mistake. It collectively stood behind the strange disappearance of a man named William Morgan, who was going to publish all the secret rites and symbols and comings and goings of the Masons. His death and disappearance caused a national outcry, and the Masonry began to slip into a far less prominent position in America.

Oh, and the widow of William Morgan? What happened to her?

Why, she ended up being one of Joseph Smith's secret wives."

Where Mormonism Meets Biblical Christianity Face to Face" by Shawn Aaron McCraney, page 222

Joseph Smith, the founder of Mormonism, had 24 wives, one was 14 years old. Smith was convicted of fraud (of being an "imposter"- a con man) in a court of law.

Brigham Young, a high-level Freemason, in 1846 at Council Bluffs, Iowa, had a private meeting with Pierre De Smet, one of the most powerful American Jesuits of the Nineteenth Century. Being the foremost Jesuit of influence among the Indian Nations, De Smet, using Confederate General and 33rd Degree Freemason Albert Pike, incited his Sioux Indians to mass-murder eight hundred White Lutherans of Minnesota.

Mormon and Catholic Churches teamed up and called for Amnesty for Illegal Aliens.

1830s, the Church of Christ was started by Presbyterian ministers Barton Stone and the Scottish immigrant father-son team Thomas and Alexander Campbell, with Methodist, Baptist, and now Presbyterian influence.

1844, It was a Seventh-Day Baptist — Rachel Oakes Preston (1809–1868) — who brought the seventh-day Sabbath understanding to the small Millerite group, which became the SDAs in Washington, New Hampshire. Through her influence, Frederick Wheeler became the first Sabbath-keeping Adventist preacher. This was quickly accepted by the small group that included James and Ellen White. An alliance was formed with other disillusioned "Millerite" groups in the region, and in 1860, this sparse group settled on the name **Seventh-day Adventist.** In 1863, the movement became an official organization.

1865, The Salvation Army was founded by William Booth in London.

Ethiopian Zion Coptic churches are pot smokers. A front for marijuana smuggling.

1870, and of **Charles Taze Russell, a Mason Illuminati Russell bloodline, the founder of Jehovah's Witnesses in the U.S.**. He wrote books about pyramidology and had very complex math and geometry about the importance of its spirituality. He sill believed in his Egyptian cult when he died, thus the pyramid.

Russell was co-founder of the Skull and Bones of Yale University. This elite secret society holds within its membership George H.W. Bush, George W. Bush, Bill Clinton, and Senator John Kerry, as also was Hitler.

The word "Jehovah" came from Germany and a German Priest, and it did not exist before the 16th century, and that is how it got into King James. Their group's very name contains a Catholic "invention," the name "Jehovah."

1879, Christian Science was founded by Mary Baker Eddy in the U.S.

Christianity has Homosexual denominations now. As you should be able to see, Christianity has a denomination for any kind of lifestyle you want to live; if not, then start a new one.

1900, Pentecostalism was founded by Charles Parham along with William Seymore in the U.S. and was arrested for Sodomy with a 21-year-old guy who was also a KKK member.

THERE ARE NO SO-CALLED SPIRIT-FILLED PENTECOSTALS TODAY WITH YAHWEH'S SPIRIT. THEY ARE NOTHING LIKE THE TRUE BELIEVERS IN THE DAYS OF PETER AND PAUL. EVERYTHING WAS DONE IN THE NAME OF YAHWEH, NOT IN THE NAME OF JESUS CHRIST. EVERY TRUE SPIRIT-FILLED BELIEVER BACK THEN WAS CALLED OUT TO BE DISCIPLE TO TEACH THE WORD WITH NO LIES, NOT WITH

ENTICING WORDS FROM MAN'S WISDOM, BUT IN DEMONSTRATION OF THE SPIRIT AND OF POWER WITH MIRACLES. WHAT THEY CALL PENTECOSTALISM TODAY IS NOTHING BUT HYPE AND EMOTIONALISM. THEIR BABBLE IS FROM BABYLON, OF SATAN, NOT FROM YAHWEH.

I was raised in Pentecostalism. I heard the so-called babbling tongues, which are against what the scriptures teach about them. When the interpretation comes after a lot of them, it is all about the Lord, God, Jesus, Christ, and things that go against the scriptures. So when you compare them to what the scriptures really teach, they come from Satan because there is no truth in them. Like all you hear is that he's coming soon. I heard that since I was a kid, and they are looking over the balcony of heaven, another lie, and to pack your bags, I'm coming, sorry, but no bags will be needed to be packed when He comes. They use hype, emotionalism, and sad stories and call it the Spirit moving when people cry and show emotions. Same with the songs they pick to sing, it is all zeroed into emotionalism.

The Apostolic Faith Mission on Azusa Street now considered to be the birthplace of Pentecostalism.

The Los Angeles Times was not so kind in its description:

Meetings are held in a tumble-down shack on Azusa Street, and the devotees of the weird doctrine practice the most fanatical rites, preach the wildest theories, and work themselves into a state of mad excitement in their peculiar zeal. Colored people and a sprinkling of whites compose the congregation, and night is made hideous in the neighborhood by the howlings of the worshippers, who spend hours swaying forth and back in a nerve-racking attitude of prayer and supplication. They claim to have the "gift of tongues" and be able to understand the babel.

Hayford, Jack W.; Moore, S. David (2006). The Charismatic Century: The Enduring Impact of the Azusa Street Revival (August 2006 ed.)

Many existing Wesleyan-holiness denominations adopted the Pentecostal message, such as the Church of God (Cleveland, Tennessee), the Church of God in Christ, and the Pentecostal Holiness Church. The formation of new denominations also occurred, motivated by doctrinal differences between Wesleyan Pentecostals and their Finished Work counterparts, such as the Assemblies of God formed in 1914 and the Pentecostal Church of God formed in 1919. An early doctrinal controversy led to a split between Trinitarian and Oneness Pentecostals, and the latter founded the Pentecostal Assemblies of the World in 1916.

Synan, Vinson (1997). The Holiness-Pentecostal Tradition. Charismatic Movements in the Twentieth Century. Grand Rapids, Michigan: William B. Eerdmans Publishing Company.

He started another Bible School in Houston, Texas, where William Seymour heard the message of the Baptism in the Spirit by speaking in tongues. He took this message to Los Angeles, and the Azusa Street Pentecostal Revival broke out. His story is also in the Pensketches section of this site.

Thousands of Christians visited Azusa Street from around the world in 1906-9 and took the Pentecostal message – and the experience – back to their homes and to the mission field.

Thomas B. Barratt was baptized in the Spirit while staying in New York in November 1906 after hearing news of the Azusa revival. He took the message back to Norway and then over to his native England. Alexander Boddy in Sunderland became the catalyst for a myriad of spiritually hungry seekers, and his invitation to Barratt to visit in 1907 began a British revival. George and Stephen Jeffreys, Smith Wigglesworth, and others received the gift of the Spirit at Sunderland. The first organized Pentecostal missionary agency was birthed in Sunderland as the Pentecostal Missionary Union and the message was taken to the nations.

So why weren't there any so-called Spirit-filled people before this time? This just proves that the true believers were killed off in the days of Peter and Paul, or otherwise, there would always have been Spirit-filled people, which there were not. Yahweh will pour His TRUE Spirit out during the Tribulation Period, the Latter Rain.

1960s and 1970s. Charismatic Catholics, a form of Pentecostalism. Approved by Pope VI in 1975. I remember when they were being taught how to raise their arms when they worshipped and being taught to do other things like the Pentecostal denominations do. It is all about the Papacy's Ecumenical Movement to bring all the Christian denominations back under the control of the papacy.

1933, **Church of God** /1947, **Worldwide Church of God,** founded by Herbert W. Armstrong, in the U.S.

1968, **Metropolitan Community Church**, a predominantly homosexual church, has ordained homosexual candidates for ministry since its founding in 1968. In 1972, the United Church of Christ became the first mainline Protestant denomination in the United States to ordain an openly homosexual clergy. Other churches are the Evangelical Lutheran Church in America (since 2010) and the Presbyterian Church (USA) (since 2012). The Episcopal Church in the United States and the Christian Church (Disciples of Christ) have also allowed the ordination of openly gay and lesbian candidates for ministry for some years. Internationally, churches that have ordained openly lesbian or homosexual clergy include the Church of Scotland, the Church of England, the Church in Wales, the Church of Sweden, the Church of Norway, the Church of Denmark, the Church of Iceland, the Evangelical Lutheran Church of Finland, the Evangelical Church in Germany, the Methodist Church in Britain, the Protestant Church in the Netherlands, the United Protestant Church in Belgium, the Swiss Reformed Church, the United Protestant Church of France, the Evangelical Lutheran Church in Canada, Anglican Church in Canada, the Old Catholic Church, and the United Church of Christ in Japan, US Episcopal Church, in the U.S.

On this chart, I want you to notice it starts out at the bottom as Roman Catholic. In other words Christianity was the Universal which Catholic means religion. Now go up to 1559 on the right side. You will see Roman Catholic again. This is when the denomination of Catholics started at the Council of Trent to counter the Reformation, the same reason the Jesuits were started.

Now, to prove Christianity and its denominations are all a lie compared to what scriptures really teach about true FAITH.

Romans 1:12 That is, that I may be comforted **together with you by the mutual faith both of you and me**.

2 Corinthians 13:11 Finally, brethren, farewell. Be perfect, be of good comfort, be of one mind, live in peace; and Yahweh of love and peace shall be with you.

1 Corinthians 1:10-13

10. Now I beseech you, brethren, by the name of Yahweh Messiah, **that ye all speak the same thing, and that there be no divisions among you; but that ye be perfectly joined together in the same mind and in the same judgment.**

11. For it hath been declared unto me of you, my brethren, **by them which are of the house of Chloe, that there are contentions among you.**

12. Now this I say, that every one of you saith, I am of Paul; and I of Apollos; and I of Cephas; and I of the Messiah.

13. Is the Messiah divided? Was Paul impaled for you? Or were ye baptized in the name of Paul?

I marvel that you so soon are being moved away from Him who called you into the Spirit of Yahweh to another word, **which is not another,** *but some are troubling you and desiring to pervert the Word of Yahweh. But even if we or a Messenger from Heaven preach a word to you beside what we preached to you, let him be accursed. As we said before,*

242

and now I say again, **If anyone preaches a word to you besides what you have received, let him be accursed.** *(Gal 1:6-8)*

Matthew 24:24-25

24. For there shall arise false Messiahs, and false prophets, and shall shew great signs and wonders; insomuch that, if *it were* possible, they shall deceive the very elect.

25. Behold, I have told you before.

Acts 17:6 ...."*These that have* **turned the world upside down**".......

Acts 6:7 *"And the* **Word of Yahweh increased**.*"*

Acts 12:24 *"But the* **Word of Yahweh grew and multiplied**.*"*

Acts 13:49 *"And the* **Word of Yahweh was published throughout all the region**.*"*

Acts 19:20 *"So* **mightily grew the Word of Yahweh and prevailed**.*"*

It's all getting ready to happen once again.

CHAPTER 17

THE ECUMENICAL MOVEMENT

We have seen how Christianity is a Satanic lie and how the people wanted out from under the Pope's authority and, thus, the Reformation. Now we are seeing, according to scriptures and history how they are now going back under the Pope's authority in unity for these end times. It will be even worse during the 3 ½ year Tribulation Period.

<u>VATICAN'S ECUMENICAL MOVEMENT</u>: To bring all religions together, the Protestants are headed back home to Rome.

The Ecumenical Movement is a strategy masterminded by the Papacy to bring about Christian unity. To bring not only every Christian, no matter what denomination, but every religion, atheist or what have you, under the control of the Pope.

Christians think they are being persecuted here in the United States, but it is to make them run back into the arms of the Papacy.

In 1910 forty-six Protestant denominations co-operated in an effort to reunite all the Christian churches in the world, and fifty-five commissions were appointed to attend a world's conference. They were to have been sent in September 1914 to different countries to explain the plan, but the World War delayed it. Another effort was made in 1917, when delegates from "many denominations, including Protestant Episcopal, Baptist, Lutheran, and Presbyterian," met at Garden City, N. Y., where they received a letter from Cardinal Gasparri, Papal Secretary of State and in 1919 three Episcopal bishops were sent to Rome to interview the pope on this question of church union, for Pope Benedict XV had already (1917) started a "move for reunited Christianity."

"Give us good Sunday laws, well enforced by men in local authority, and our churches will be full of worshipers .... A mighty combination of the churches of the United States could win from Congress, the state legislatures, and municipal councils, all legislation essential to this splendid result."–"Homiletic Review," November 1892; quoted in "American State Papers," William A. Blakely, p. 732. Washington, D. C.:1911.

Rev. Sylvester F. Scovel, a leading National Reformer, says:

"This common interest [in Sunday] ought to strengthen both our determination to work and our readiness to co-operate with our Roman Catholic fellow citizens... It is one of the necessities of the situation."– "Views of National Reform, Series One," Bible Students' Library, No. 3, pp. 85, 86. Oakland, Calif.:Jan. 15, 1889.

"Whenever they [the Roman Catholics] are willing to cooperate in resisting the progress of political atheism, we will gladly join hands with them."– "Christian Statesman," Dec. 11, 1884.

The Catholic Lay Congress, held in Baltimore on November 12, 1889, said: "We should seek an alliance with non-Catholics for the purpose of proper Sunday observance."– Quoted in "Religious Liberty in America," C. M. Snow, pp. 283, 284.

The Vatican's ecumenical movement goes beyond the unity of all professing Christians. Their strategy is to bring **all** religions under the power and influence of the papacy. Pope John Paul II has been traveling the world to build bridges to all non-Christian religions. Even Mother Theresa had an ecumenical spirit, as noted in her book *Servants of Love*. She stated, "we went every day to pray in some temple or church. The Archbishop gave us permission to do so. **We prayed with** the **Jews**, the **Armenians**, the **Anglicans**, the **Jains**, the **Sikhs**, the **Buddhists**, and the **Hindus**. It was extraordinary. **All hearts united in prayer to the one true God.**"

Jan. 20, 2003 - While the build-up for war in Iraq continued, and peace protesters staged many rallies, the Vatican sponsored a peace conference attended by representatives of Christianity, Judaism, Islam, Hinduism, Buddhism, Jainism, Zoroastrianism, and Sikhism.

THIS IS ALL ABOUT BRINGING ABOUT ONE Global Religion (Christianity) DURING THE Global Government.

"Rome, when in the minority, is as gentle as a lamb, when in equality is as clever as a fox, and when in the majority is as fierce as a tiger."

The Scriptural Anti-Messiah and False Prophet:

Luther wrote concerning the Papacy, "This teaching [of the supremacy of the pope] shows forcefully that the Pope is the very Antichrist, who has exalted himself above and opposed himself against Christ because he will not permit Christians to be saved without his power, which, nevertheless, is nothing, and is neither ordained nor commanded by God. This is, properly speaking, to exalt himself above all that is called God. . . . The Pope, however, prohibits this faith, saying that to be saved, a person must obey him" (Smalcald Articles, II, IV, 10-12).

"The pope is of so great dignity, and so exalted, that he is not a mere man, but as it were God." (Ferraris Ecclesiastical Dictionary)

"To believe that our Lord GOD the Pope has not the power to decree as he is decreed is to be deemed heretical." (The Gloss Extravagantes o.f Pope John XXII Cum inter, Tit. XIV, Cap. IV. Ad Callem Sexti Decretalium, Paris, 1685)

"The Pope and God are the same, so he has all power in Heaven and earth." (Pope Pius V, quoted in Barclay, Chapter XXVII, p. 218, Cities Petrus Bertanous)

"The Pope is not only the representative of Jesus Christ, but he is Jesus Christ, Himself, hidden under the veil of human flesh." — Catholic National, July 1895.

Pope Boniface VIII, *Unam Sanctam*, Nov. 18, 1302: "Now, therefore, **we declare, say, determine, and pronounce that for every human creature, it is necessary for salvation to be subject to the Roman pontiff.**"

Papal Bull - Unam Sanctum: "Furthermore, we declare, we proclaim, we define that it is absolutely necessary for salvation that every human creature be subject to the Roman Pontiff." (Declaratio quod subesse Romano Pontifici est omni humanae creaturae de necessitate salutis)

From Pope Leo XIII

Encyclical Letter

June 20, 1894 :

"We hold upon this earth the place of God Almighty."

"All must be subject to him (the pope) who has had all things put under him (the pope)." Evangelical Christendom, Jan 1, 1895, page15

"The pope is of so great dignity, and so exalted, that he is not a mere man, but as it were God." Ferraris Ecclesiastical Dictionary.

"No man may enter (into the kingdom) unless he is led by the Sovereign Pontiff, and only if they be united to him can men be saved." Pope John XXIII at his coronation, Nov.4, 1958.

"Hence the pope is crowned with a triple crown, as king of heaven and of earth." Lucius Ferraris, Prompta Bibliotheca, 1763 Volume VI, papa II, page26

"This judicial authority will even include the power to forgive sin." The Catholic Encyclopedia, Vol XII, page265

Pope St. Gregory the Great: **"The holy universal Church teaches that it is not possible to worship God truly except in her and asserts that all who are outside of her will not be saved."**

"The Pope and God are the same, so he has all power in Heaven and earth." — Pope Pius V, quoted in Barclay, Chapter XXVII, p. 218, "Cities Petrus Bertanous".

Los Angeles Times, December 12, 1984, quoted Pope John Paul II as saying, "Don't go to God for the forgiveness of sins. Come to me." "And God himself is obliged to abide by the judgment of his priest and either not to pardon or to pardon, according as they refuse to give absolution, provided the penitent is capable of it." — St. Alphonsus De Liguori, in The Dignity of the Priesthood, p. 27.

"Religious liberty is merely endured until the opposite can be carried into effect without peril to the Catholic Church." -Bishop O'Conner of Pittsburg.

"Even if the Pope were Satan incarnate, we ought not to raise up our heads against him but calmly lie down to rest on his bosom. He who rebels against our Father is condemned to death, for that which we do to him we do to Christ: we honor Christ if we honor the Pope; we dishonor Christ if we dishonor the Pope. I know very well that many defend themselves by boasting: "They are so corrupt and work all manner of evil!" But God has commanded that, even if the priests, the pastors, and Christ-on-earth were incarnate devils, we be obedient and subject to them, not for their sakes, but for the sake of God, and out of obedience to Him." (St. Catherine of Siena, SCS, p. 201-202, p. 222, quoted in Apostolic Digest, by Michael Malone, Book 5: "The Book of Obedience," Chapter 1: "There is No Salvation Without Personal Submission to the Pope").

Ignatius Loyola himself declared the purpose of the Order was to: ." . . win to God [the Pope of Rome], not only a single nation, a single country but all nations, all the kingdoms of the world."

"The Pope is not simply the representative of Jesus Christ. On the contrary, <u>he is Jesus Christ Himself</u>, under the veil of the flesh." (Evangelical Christendom, January 1, 1895, pg. 15, published in London by J. S. Phillips)

"Against this background of love towards the Holy Church, 'the pillar and bulwark of the truth' (1 Tim 3:15), we readily understand the devotion of Saint Francis of Assisi for '<u>THE LORD POPE</u>,' the daughterly outspokenness of Saint Catherine of Siena towards the one whom she called '<u>SWEET CHRIST ON EARTH</u>.'" (Pope John Paul II, Apostolic Exhortation on the Consecrated Life and Its Mission in the Church and in the World, to the bishops and clergy, religious orders and congregations, societies of apostolic life, secular institutes, and all the faithful, given in Rome, at Saint Peter's, March 25, 1996)

"The Pope is of so great dignity, and so exalted that he is not a mere man, <u>but as it were God</u> and the vicar of God." (Ferraris Ecclesiastical dictionary)

"All names which in the Scriptures are applied to Christ, by virtue of which it is established that He is over the church, <u>all the same names are applied to the Pope</u>." (On the Authority of the Councils, book 2, chapter 17)

"<u>The Pope and God are the same</u>, so he has all power in Heaven and earth." (Pope Pius V, quoted in Barclay, Chapter XXVII, p. 218, "Cities Petrus Bertanous)

"To believe that our <u>Lord God the Pope</u> has not the power to decree as he is decreed, is to be deemed heretical." (the Gloss "Extravagantes" o.f Pope John XXII Cum inter, Tit. XIV, Cap. IV. Ad Callem Sexti Decretalium, Paris, 1685) .

"Hence the Pope is crowned with a triple crown, as <u>king of heaven and of earth and of the lower regions</u>." (Ferraris, «Prompta Bibliotheca,» 1763, Volume VI, 'Papa II,' p.26)

"The Saviour Himself is the door of the sheepfold: 'I am the door of the sheep.' Into this fold of Jesus Christ, <u>no man may enter unless he be led by the Sovereign Pontiff; and only if they be united to him can men be saved</u>, for the Roman Pontiff is the Vicar of Christ and

His personal representative on earth." (Pope John XXIII, in his homily to the Bishops and faithful assisting at his coronation on November 4, 1958)

"This is our last lesson to you: receive it, engrave it in your minds, all of you: by God's commandment, <u>salvation is to be found nowhere but in the Church</u>; the strong and effective instrument of <u>salvation is none other than the Roman Pontificate</u>." (Pope Leo XIII, Allocution for the 25th anniversary of his election, February 20, 1903; Papal Teachings: The Church, Benedictine Monks of Solesmes, St. Paul Editions, Boston, 1962, par. 653)

The goal of the Company of Jesus (Jesuits) is to consolidate all of the world's wealth (including all land and labor) and all power (both spiritual and temporal) into their hands. By these means, the Order then seeks to compel all nations to submit to the earthly government of the Roman "White Pope." J. A. Wylie wrote in his nineteenth-century release, The History of Protestantism, Vol. II, Book Fifteen, pp. 387, 388, 393, 398, 412, and 399, concerning the Jesuits: The Vatican has stated at various times that "the Pope is for total disarmament; the Pope is for the elimination of the sovereignty of the nation states; the Pope is also stating that property rights are not to be considered true property rights. The Pope believes that only the Vatican knows what is right for man. I would love to see the day that Yahweh destroys this Satanic Institution. It is coming very soon!

"By the end of this decade we will live under the first One World Government that has ever existed in the society of nations ... a government with absolute authority to decide the basic issues of human survival. One world government is inevitable." - Pope John Paul II.

The Pope wanted the One World Order up and running by he year 2000, but as you can see, this is 2015, so they are 15 years behind schedule with a lot of catching up to do. **Now they are saying 2025. This is now 2024.**

Daniel 11:45

And he (Pope) shall plant the tabernacles of his palace between the seas (Dead Sea and Mediterranean Sea) in the righteous mountain; yet he (Pope) shall come to his end, and none shall help him.

Isaiah 33:22 For Yahweh is our Judge (Judicial), Yahweh is our Lawgiver (Legislative), Yahweh is our King (Executive); He will save us--As you can see Yahweh is a government in Himself, so when the One World Order comes, we will know what government to serve, not the Anti-Messiah's, but the true Messiah, Yahweh.

Daniel 7:26 But the court will sit, and his power will be taken away and completely destroyed forever. Then, the sovereignty, power, and greatness of the kingdoms under the whole heaven will be handed over to the saints, the people of the Most High. His kingdom will be an everlasting kingdom, and all rulers will worship and obey Him."

"He Who Does Not Remember History Is Condemned To Repeat It" - Georges Santayana Satan's seat is in Rome right now, but will be moved to Jerusalem when the Papacy regains its power and will rule the world.

Chapter 16 of The Life and Death of NSSM 200: How the Destruction of Political Political Will Doomed a US Population Policy by Stephen D Mumford (Center for Research on Population and Security, 1996).

This reality has not been lost on the Vatican. When the Bishop's Pastoral Plan for Pro-Life Activities was promulgated, Rome preempted the ecumenical initiative and began making major investments to promote ecumenism. In the last few years, Vatican interests in ecumenism have escalated sharply. "Evangelicals and Catholics Together," issued in March 1994 as an unofficial document, called on these two groups to recognize each other as Christians and to work together on common issues, such as abortion and pornography.

Catechism (doctrines) of the Catholic Church

841 The Church's relationship with the Muslims.

"The plan of salvation also includes those who acknowledge the Creator, in the first place amongst whom are the Muslims; these profess to hold the faith of Abraham, and together with us, they adore the one, merciful God, mankind's judge on the last day."

Most of the Protestants leaders in the USA are ready to bury the hatchet with Rome:

"Heads of **American Protestant** and Eastern Orthodox churches who were meeting with Pope John Paul II on Friday hailed their first broadly representative discussion as a landmark on the road to greater unity...The Rev. Donald Jones, a United Methodist and chairman of the University of South Carolina religious studies department termed it, 'the most important **ecumenical** meeting of the century.' The Rev. Paul A. Crow Jr., of Indianapolis, ecumenical officer of the Christian Church (Disciples of Christ), called it a 'new day in ecumenism' opening a future in which **God 'is drawing us together.'"** *The Montgomery Advertiser, Sept. 12, 1987*

Billy Graham:

"In 1949 [two Roman Catholic Knights of Malta] William Randolph Hearst, head of a large publishing empire, and Henry Luce, chief of another, Time, Inc., were both worried about Communism and the growth of liberalism in the United States. . . Billy Graham, an obscure evangelist [opened his poorly attended Crusade for Christ tent meetings in Los Angeles. . . in the same week Russia tested its first atomic bomb. This fresh menace gave Graham his text: "Communism is inspired and directed by the Devil himself, who has declared war against Almighty God. Did you know that the Communists are more rampant in Los Angeles than any other city in America?"]. Hearst and Luce interviewed the obscure preacher and decided he was worthy of their support. Billy Graham became an almost instantaneous national and, later, international figure preaching anti-Communism. In late 1949, Hearst sent a telegram to all Hearst editors: "Puff Graham." The editors did — in

Hearst newspapers, magazines, movies, and newsreels. Within two months, Graham was preaching to crowds of 350,000" (Ben Bagdikian, The Media Monopoly, p. 39 ff). Illuminus Rockefeller was supportive of Graham's New York Crusade, and his Chase-Manhattan Bank helped him out.

Billy Graham understood that a successful mass ministry would require professional salesmanship and he carefully cultivated contacts in the major media with an eye to marketing his product. He does not, however, have an understanding of the faith of Jesus Christ. "Notwithstanding his professed calling, it is apparent that Graham worked the corridors of Congress as well as the private rooms of the White House, sometimes overtly, sometimes quietly, in secret letters and private phone calls. And, quite contrary to Time's assertion, it seems that Graham did more to abet segregation than to end it, actively opposing Martin Luther King Jr.'s use of civil disobedience while endorsing aggressive police tactics and punitive laws."

Henry Luce, Illuminist and Order of Skull & Bones initiated, supervised, and helped fund one of Billy Graham's first crusades in New York City. The Illuminati have long worked behind the scenes to influence and control the Christian establishment.

Super-rich elitist William Randolph Hearst, Catholic Knights of Malta high-up, told his national newspaper chain to "puff" Billy Graham and make him a household name.

It was Luce, along with Hearst who are said to be most influential in making Graham the chief spokesman of Protestant Christianity. This is odd when one considers that both Hearst and Luce were members of a devout Catholic order that openly declares its purpose is "service to ... the Holy Father (i.e. the pope)

"I've found that my beliefs are essentially the same as those of orthodox Roman Catholics." *McCall's, January 1978. He also, called Pope John Paul II: "The greatest* religious leader of the modern world." *The Saturday Evening Post, January-February 1980*

1984, when Ronald Reagan signed the Concordat with the Papacy, men like Billy Graham and Jerry Falwell meekly accepted and defended the establishment of United States political ties with the Vatican.

It was Luce, along with Hearst who are said to be most influential in making Graham the chief spokesman of Protestant Christianity. This is odd when one considers that both Hearst and Luce were members of a devout Catholic order that openly declares its purpose is "service to ... the Holy Father (i.e., the pope)."2 Was it their intent to create a kind of "Protestant Pope" to guide the beliefs of non-Catholics? Whether they intended this or not, that is exactly what Billy Graham would become.

I remember when Billy Graham had to get permission from the Pope to preach in Europe and if any Catholics were saved. In his meetings, he had to turn them back over to the Catholic church.

Oral Roberts was a charismatic faith healer, a 33rd-degree Mason, and a lodge brother of his close friend Billy Graham before his death.

Paul Crouch: "I'm eradicating the word Protestant even out of my vocabulary...I'm not protesting anything... [it's] time for Catholics and non-Catholics to come together as one in the Spirit and one in the Lord." *"Praise the Lord" program, Trinity Broadcasting Network, Oct 17, 1989*

Paul Crouch: wears priest's shirts with the Roman collar all the time. *Paul & Jan Crouch*: Crouch often denies being a Protestant, saying, "I'm not protesting anything." TBN has had two-hour specials singing the praises of the late ***Pope John Paul II*** and ***Mother Teresa***, of whom Jan Crouch has said that in her presence, all she could do is bow.

Paul Crouch: wears priest's shirts with the Roman collar all the time.

Robert Schuller: "It's time for Protestants to go to the shepherd [the pope] and say, "What do we have to do to come home?" *Los Angeles Herald Examiner, September 19, 1987, Religion page*

In the side entrances to his Crystal Cathedral are giant bronze statues of Schuller's heroes. On the one side are his primary heroes – one statue of himself (self-love and all that) across from one of **Norman Vincent Peale**. At the other entrance is Billy Graham across from the statue of Roman Catholic TV pioneer **Bishop Sheen**.

The Crystal Cathedral's Reverend Robert Schuller, 33rd-degree Mason

Bishop Vann was chosen to lead the Roman Catholic Diocese of Orange County, California, by Pope Benedict XVI in September, but Monday's installation made it official. Vann succeeds Tod Brown, who held the post through some of the diocese's most tumultuous times, including the priest sex abuse scandal. Brown said in a statement that though the diocese has made progress in the last 14 years, including last year's $57.5-million purchase of the Rev. Robert H. Schuller's Crystal Cathedral in Garden Grove, "much work remains to be done. Vann will face a $100-million capital campaign, which will go toward parish renovations, school funding, and upgrades to the high-profile Crystal Cathedral for Catholic worship. Monday's <u>event was attended by bishops from across the country, as well as such local religious personalities</u> as Rick Warren — pastor of the giant Saddleback Church — and Schuller.

David Wells: "If Catholicism is to become more Catholic in the future, which is what I expect under the present pope, then theological differences will become sharper, but our alliances with Catholics against the secular culture can become deeper. , for one, am ready for the trade-off." *Eternity Magazine, Sept. 1987.***Bill McCartney:** "It has become clear to me what God has in mind for Promise Keepers. The answer is found in the Sermon on the Mount: 'Blessed are the peacekeepers, for they are the sons of God.' A peace-maker is one who brings warring factions together. The reason there isn't a Catholic men's group filling stadiums around the country is because God wants us together."

Joel Osteen **also met with the Pope, saying, "I love the fact that he's made the Church more inclusive, not trying to make it smaller, but to try to make it larger — to take everybody in. So, that just resonates with me."**

Lee Grady: *Charisma Magazine's* editor who frequently promotes ecumenical relationships with Roman Catholics. Lee is a big defender of the Catholic charismatic renewal and embraces any of them who speak in tongues. **Chuck Colson:** One of the originators and signers of the ECT (Evangelicals and Catholics Together) document that promises not to target Catholics for evangelism. Of course, Colson is married to a practicing Roman Catholic and sees no problem with it.

Jack & Rexella Van Impe - Rexella: "So Protestants should love Protestants, we should love Catholics, Catholics should love Protestants, we should love the Greek Orthodox." **Jack**: We're all members of the one body. All the different denominations represent these different fingers. But some folks won't let us do this: get together."

Binny Hinn: Hinn proudly stated, "My upbringing, of course, was Catholic in that I attended the Catholic school in Jaffa, Israel. And so my mentality basically is a Catholic mentality. When I was born again, I was Catholic in my ways. I was very Catholic in my ideas, in my behavior." (Christianity today, Sept3, 1991.)

Benny Hinn sang the praises of the Roman Catholic Church and made arrangements for TBN president Paul Crouch to have a face-to-face introduction to the late Pope John Paul II. He has boasted of sharing communion with the nuns who frequent his meetings. Hinn is critical of those in the church who point out the unbiblical errors that rightly divide Christians and Catholics.

Benny Hinn was exposed as a fraud by various TV news programs.

Hinn, like Paul Crouch, wears a shirt with a Roman collar.

Hinn has long been infatuated with the late faith healer Kathryn Kuhlman. Jamie Buckingham wrote that she was happiest when there were Roman Catholic priests on the platform with her.   There were a lot of Catholic priests in her audience, as there are in his.

Benny Hinn worked for Kathryn Kuhlman, and that is why he acts and talks like she did.

Ecumenical healer whose rallies were frequently attended by a variety of priests and nuns, some of whom she would have on her television broadcast.

Many claim that **Kathryn Kuhlman** was an undercover agent working for the Roman Catholic church, indirectly gathering information from the inside about the Pentecostals, the Ecumenical and Charismatic movements. She was a witch, a master of hypnosis, and had incredible psychic abilities. Kuhlman was associated with the Legion of Mary. Although Kathryn Kuhlman was supposedly a Protestant heretic, she was blessed by the Pope. This, of course, is strictly forbidden under the canon law of the church unless you are Catholic. She was a Catholic witch under a special oath.

Rick Warren: A CFR member, he is on the CFR-established Religious Round Table, and it is the Papacy that started the Social Justice/Reform agenda.   Warren is also pushing the Papacy's Echenimical Movement to bring all religions and denominations together under the Pope's authority. He is also for a One World Order.

"Rick Warren spends much of his time fighting for social justice and participating in political groups and discussions. He believes everyone must work together for peace—that all religions must unite and, with the help of the global government, solve poverty and corruption.**J. L. Packer**": "Protestant and Catholic charismatic teaching on the Christian life is to all intents and purposes identical. Is this not significant for the Christian future?" *J. I. Packer, Christianity Today, June 22, 1992*

Rick and Kay Warren of Saddleback Church; the Most Rev. Kevin Vann, bishop of the Roman Catholic Diocese of Orange; and the National Alliance on Mental Illness-Orange

County (NAMI-OC) on Friday co-hosted the "Gathering on Mental Health and the Church" at Saddleback Church in Southern California, featuring religious, health and psychology professionals who reinforced the need to work together to address critical mental health issues.

James Dobson: *Catholics have served on his board and are frequently his guests on his radio program "Focus on the Family." His books can easily be found in Catholic bookstores.*

Dr. Rodney R. Romney, former Senior Pastor of the First Baptist Church of Seattle, is a person frequently quoted as an example of a New Age Christian. He very candidly revealed what was conveyed to him in his contemplative prayer periods. The 'source of wisdom' he was in contact with told him the following:

I want you to preach this oneness, to hold it up before the world as my call to unity and togetherness. In the end, this witness to the oneness of all people will undermine any barriers that presently exist.

Beach's encounter with the Roman Pontiff came as a member of the Christian World Communions and following a special luncheon at the Vatican." *Review* Nov. 8, 2001 [Note: The Seventh-day Adventist church is the member, not Beach individually. Beach was representing the Adventist church.]

Neal C. Wilson: "Although it is true that there was a period in the life of the **Seventh-day Adventist Church** when the denomination took a **distinctly anti-Roman Catholic** viewpoint...that attitude...has **now been consigned to the historical trash** heap so far as the Seventh-day Adventist Church is concerned. *Neal C. Wilson, former president of the* **Seventh-day Adventist** *General Conference, 1974*

You must watch the following all the way through:

http://cogcw.org/2014/04/10/doug-batchelor-analyzes-popes-recent-threat-of-unity-or-else/

'We Are Brothers,' Pope Declares in Heartfelt Message to Pentecostals'

FORT WORTH, Texas — Pope Francis sent a video message to a gathering of U.S. Pentecostal leaders, voicing his "yearning" that separation between Catholics and other Christians may end.

"We have a lot of cultural riches and religious riches. And we have diverse traditions," he said. "But we have to encounter one another as brothers."

"Let's give each other a spiritual embrace and let God complete the work that he has begun," he said, adding that "the miracle of unity has begun."

Pope Francis' message was delivered to a meeting of the Fort Worth, Texas-based Kenneth Copeland Ministries by Pentecostal Bishop Tony Palmer, who had recorded it on an iPhone in a Jan. 14 meeting with the Holy Father. Palmer knew Pope Francis from his time in Argentina when he was archbishop of Buenos Aires. At the end of Pope Francis' message, the audience gave the Pope a standing ovation, and Pentecostal minister Kenneth Copeland encouraged the audience to respond to the Pope's words.

However, Palmer spoke of did not speak of a return to God, but a return to the Catholic Church. As Palmer expounded, saying, "If you're born again, you're all Catholics."

James Robinson: "Pope Francis, let me just say to you that I see Jesus in you, and in Christ, we are brothers, we are family. Thank you for speaking the language of love that all may come to know him and love him and love one another.

Palmer, on the left end, was killed in a head-on motorcycle accident. The others had better wake-up and find the real truth.

Kenneth Copeland:

"Come on, the man asked us to pray for him," Copeland said with enthusiasm.

"Oh, Father ... we answer his request," Copeland prayed. "And since we know not how to pray for him as we ought, other than to agree with him in his quest and his heart for the unity of the body of Christ ... we come together in the unity of our faith. Halleluiah!"

He said the congregation prayed for the Pope "in the Spirit" and received "words that are not our own."

Copeland and the congregation then began to SPEAK IN TONGUES.

Kenneth Copeland's Response to Request by Pope Francis:

Recently, I received a message from Pope Francis in which he asked that, as a ministry and part of the Body of Christian believers, we pray for him. In 1 Timothy 2:2, the Bible teaches that we are to pray "for all that are in authority." It is scriptural that we do so. Therefore, it is our duty to honor the Pope's request and, as a Body of believers, join our faith with his by coming together in unity and agreeing with him in his quest for what is in his heart: the unity of the Body of Christ. So, in obedience to our Lord and His Word, we join our faith with that of Pope Francis as we pray with and for him that he will receive the righteous desire of his heart, according to the words of Jesus in Mark 11:24: "That whatsoever things you desire when you pray, believe you receive them, and you shall have them." Our desire, along with that of Pope Francis, is in the fourth chapter of the book of Ephesians: "Till we all come in the unity of the faith and of the knowledge of the Son of God unto a mature man unto the measure of the stature of the fullness of Christ." This is very important to us all as the Body of Christ.

Join us in prayer for unity in the Body of Christ throughout the world!

Jesus is Lord!

Kenneth Copeland Ministries

Bill Bright, **Pat Robertson,** and **Chuck Colson** <u>signed the Evangelicals And</u> <u>Catholics Together document</u> that claims that *Evangelicals and Catholics are preaching* *the same gospel.* Pat Robertson met with His Holiness Pope John Paul II...[he] described their meeting as warm. "I think this meeting was historic," said Robertson, who joined with other Christian religious leaders [including **Don Argue** of the National Association of Evangelicals and **James I. Packer**] in greeting the Pope at the New York residence of His Eminence, John Cardinal O'Connor.

Hank Hanegraaff, Jack Van Impe, Norm Geisler, and many other evangelicals are presently fueling the ecumenical affair with Rome.

This is exactly what will happen to countries that do not join the One World Order. They will be taken by force, so it isn't any wonder why the Pope will rule over secular and religious governments at this time. Satan is a deceiver and a murderer. Rome is Satan's seat.

This will be a slow, deceitful process until they get control. Then, that is when you see the big changes in control and murder.

1 Corinthians 1:27 But Yahweh hath chosen the foolish things of the world to confound the wise, and Yahweh hath chosen the weak things of the world to confound the things which are mighty.

POPE FRANCIS SAYS ATHEISTS CAN DO GOOD AND GO TO HEAVEN TOO!

LOS ANGELES, CA (Catholic Online) 5/30/13 - The Holy Father is full of surprises, born of true and faithful humility. On Wednesday, he declared that all people, not just Catholics, are redeemed through Jesus, even atheists.

However, he did emphasize there was a catch. Those people must still do good. In fact, it is in doing good that they are led to the One who is the Source of all that is good. In essence, he simply restated the hope of the Church that all come to know God through His Son, Jesus Christ.

Francis based his homily on the message of Christ to his disciples taken from the Gospel of Mark. Francis delivered his message by sharing a story of a Catholic who asked a priest if atheists were saved by Christ.

"They complain," Francis said, "If he is not one of us, he cannot do good. If he is not of our party, he cannot do good." He explained that Jesus corrected them, "Do not hinder him, he says, let him do good."

The disciples, Pope Francis explained, "were a little intolerant," closed off by the idea of possessing the truth, convinced that "those who do not have the truth cannot do good." "This was wrong... Jesus broadens the horizon." Pope Francis said, "The root of this possibility of doing good - that we all have - is in creation."

"Even them, everyone, we all have the duty to do good, Pope Francis said on Vatican Radio.

"Just do good," was his challenge, "and we'll find a meeting point."

From a brochure of the General Commission on Christian Unity and Interreligious Concerns of the United Methodist Church.

HIS NAME IS YAHWEH, AND HE IS MANKIND'S TRUE MESSIAH

Look at the preachers who got caught doing so many different things, from sexual perversion to tax evasion, from homosexuality to murder, fraud, etc, and then went right back into the ministry. It's all about the money and how people follow them. Look at all the faith healers who are and were found to be phonies. This world has been deceived, and people keep deceiving themselves by listening to and following these guys and women.

It will be the Christians who kill the people of Yahweh. Christianity will become the One World Religion with the Pope ruling over it.

Psalms 116:13 I will take the cup of salvation and call upon the name of Yahweh.

Isaiah 12:2 Behold, Yahweh is my salvation; I will trust, and not be afraid: for Yahweh is my strength and my song; he also is become my salvation.

Isaiah 52:6 Therefore My people shall know My name; Therefore, they shall know in that day That I am He who speaks: `Behold, it is I.

Isaiah 45:22 Look unto me and be ye saved, all the ends of the earth: for I am Yahweh, and there is no one else.

Revelation 19:6 And I heard as it were the voice of a great multitude, and as the voice of many waters, and as the voice of mighty thunderings, saying,

Hallelujah: for Yahweh omnipotent reigneth,

CHAPTER 18
THE NAME YAHSHUA:

I must show you this Yahshua name study since I told the story about my brother Neal in chapter 12.

Since Christians use Jesus's name for their salvation, I ask Christians, who did Jesus inherit his name from? No one can answer that question. Inheritance comes from someone else, not yourself.

Anyone who believes the Father's name is Yahweh but uses the name they think the SON was named at birth for their salvation, I ask the same question them. Who did your Yahshua inherit his name from? They cannot answer it truthfully but will give a long explanation of that name, proving it is not the Father's name. The answer to this question is what this study is all about.

Who did the SON inherit his name from? His Father, Yahweh. Yahweh is the Messiah. The Son is the Father in the FLESH.

This name Yahshua came from so-called scripture scholars and hearsay. There is no historical or scriptural evidence for the name of Yahshua, but there is for the name of Yahweh.

Why would Yahweh, the Father, who gave his name to his only begotten son, also give it to someone else? The son inherited the name of the Father, which is above every name. That name is Yahweh, and there is no way he will accept a watered-down version of a name that's supposed to be His.

I would like to add something else to the name of Yahshua. They say it means Yahweh, our salvation, which I have no argument with, for it is the meaning of this name. Now, I will show you why it is not the Messiah's name. The name Yahshua is too confining in that it could never mean anything else but what it means. I'll show you what I'm talking about. In the Old Covenant, Yahweh was called by the following:

Genesis 22:14 - Yahweh-yirah = Yahweh will provide

Exodus 17:15-16 - Yahweh-nissi = Yahweh is my banner

Judges 6:23-24 - Yahweh-shalom - Yahweh is peace

Exodus 15:26 - Yahweh-ropheka - Yahweh, our healer

Jeremiah 23:6 - Yahweh-tsidkenu = Yahweh our righteousness

Jeremiah 23:5-6

Behold, the days come, saith Yahweh, that I will raise unto David a righteous Branch and a King shall execute judgment and justice in the earth. In his days Judah shall be saved, and Israel shall dwell safely: and **THIS IS HIS NAME WHEREBY HE SHALL BE CALLED, "YAHWEH OUR RIGHTEOUSNESS."**

From the above verses, you can see that they show his name, Yahweh, and the offices, which are provider, banner, and peace. As you can see, his name never changes, only the office. If you take what he was called in Judges, Yahweh-shalom, and make it Yahshalom, this name could never mean anything more than Yahweh is peace. Here again, Yahshalom, being a name in itself, is not the name of Yahweh. When Yahweh returns to redeem his people, he will be to them Yahweh the redeemer or Yahweh-Gaal. Jeremiah 34:16 says that Zion will be called Yahweh-tsidkenu or Yahweh our righteousness.

Surely you can see by now that Yahshua is a name and is not the name of the Messiah. The Messiah's name is Yahweh, and he is Yahweh-shua or Yahweh, our salvation. His name never changes, only the office. You do not take his name Yahweh and add shua to it like this Yahwehshua; by doing this, you have made a compound name that is completely different from the original and here again made it confining.

YAHSHUA means this - YAHWEH SALVATION

YAHWEH-SHUA is this - YAHWEH SALVATION

The Assemblies of Yahweh and other Messianic movements will tell you that Yahshua has Yahweh's name in it because it begins with YAH. This is an error to destruction. Yahweh is the Father's name which **the son inherited, the name above all names.** Yahshua is a name like anyone else's name, and it is not the Father's name. There is no salvation in the name Yahshua just because it means Yahweh's salvation.

That is why he was named Immanuel at birth, just like the scriptures teach, because Yahweh would have foreseen the problems with his name being Yahshua at birth, especially when **He was out to magnify HIS OWN NAME above all names.**

The reason they believe this is that they think the name Jesus is a translation of the name Yahshua. This is proven to be a downright lie because they are two separate names with two different meanings. This is exactly like Messiah and Christ; they do not mean the same thing and are not the same thing.

What it all comes down to is people need to think for themselves and not what the world wants them to believe. Your salvation is in your own hands, not in the hands of others unless you put it there.

People who believe the Messiah's name is Yahshua, like the Assemblies of Yahweh, will see no difference with the name Jesus in Christianity.

They say:

Acts 19:3   **Baptized in the name of Yahshua,** the Messiah.

Since Father, Son and Spirit are Titles, the apostles understood His saving name is **YAHSHUA**. That is why they gave immersion in the name of **YAHSHUA** Messiah. (**Another lie of theirs**.)

Their lie:

Acts 4:12   <u>Yahshua</u>, the <u>**only name under heaven which saves.**</u>

The truth:

<u>Matthew 28:19</u> Go ye therefore, and teach all nations, <u>**baptizing them in the name of the Father, and of the Son, and of the Spirit**</u>.

DO YOU REALIZE IF THEY WOULD HAVE REPLACED THE TRUE BIRTH-GIVEN NAME THAT, THEY WOULD BE CALLING ON BOB FOR THEIR SALVATION WHEN THE BIRTH-GIVEN NAME HAS NO SALVATION IN IT, EVEN THE TRUE BIRTH-GIVEN NAME DOESN'T.

ONE NAME: YAHWEH. The <u>**Father was never called Yahshua or the Christian name Jesus.**</u>

Scriptures teach the name they were baptized in, and the only name that brings salvation is YAHWEH. So, by the Scriptures, you see who is in error.

<u>**Below also comes from the Yahweh/Yahshua people. Watch how they twist the truth into a lie.**</u>

All personal names in the Hebrew language have their own specific meaning. "**YAH**" is the short or poetic form for "<u>**YAHWEH,**</u>" the **name that is to be called upon to be SAVED**, the **name that is forever,** and the **name that is a memorial for all generations**. The Hebrew word "**shua**" means **salvation**. Putting them together, you have "**Yahshua,**" meaning "**YAHWEH'S Salvation**. **YAH**shua is true "**YAHWEH SALVATION**," for **He saves His people from their transgressions, as stated in the above scripture!** Therefore, He truly does have His **Father's name, the ONLY sacred name by which we must be saved!** (Sacred a sun deity name.)

Just an ordinary name with its meaning:

YAHSHUA **means this** - YAHWEH SALVATION

Truth = Name and Office:

YAHWEH-SHUA is this - YAHWEH SALVATION

Immanuel was the birth-given name and has nothing to do with salvation. He inherited the Father's name, Yahweh, and why Yahweh is the Messiah's name.

Acts 17:3 Opening and alleging that **the Messiah must needs have suffered, and risen again from the dead; THAT THIS IMMANUEL, WHOM I PREACH UNTO YOU, IS YAHWEH.**

I'd like to talk about something. I see so many of you saying Yahshua is the Messiah. Just like the Christians saying Jesus is the Messiah. What is the difference between Christians and those who use Yahshua, Yeshua, or whatever they think the birth-given name was for salvation? The answer is NONE. The baby that was born to become the Messiah, his real birth-given name was Immanuel proven by prophecy of scriptures. The birth-given name, no matter what people may think it was, has nothing to do with salvation.

The Father's name is Yahweh; the first thing He did in Creation was created FLESH for Himself. So He could dwell among men and reveal Himself through the Flesh and the Spirit. The Father's name is Yahweh; the Flesh of the Father was called Yahweh because the Spirit took on the Flesh. Yahweh of the Old is the Messiah of the New. That's why the scriptures say over and over there is no savior besides Yahweh, and He would not give any esteem to any other name. This is why His name is the only name given for salvation.

Everything in the New was done in the Father's name, Yahweh. Immanuel came in the Father's name. Everything he did was to esteem the Father and His Name. This is why Immanuel inherited the name above all names. Scriptures prove Yahweh's name is the name above all names over and over. Immanuel inherited the Father's Name, Yahweh.

The name Immanuel was for everyday living and tax purposes, it had nothing to do with the healings and miracles or salvation.

So when those of you who say Yahshua is the Messiah's name, you are actually Anti-Messiah. Because that is not and never was the Messiah's name, his name is Yahweh and why Yahweh is the Messiah's name and no other. There are very few people today who realize who the Messiah truly is and what his one and only name is.

Read the scriptures, and you will find that only Yahweh is coming back; Yahweh's wrath will be poured out on all the non-believers, **also called the LAMBS WRATH, because HE IS YAHWEH the Father in the FLESH.**

It's not a Messianic Faith. It is FAITH IN YAHWEH, who is the Messiah. Yahweh, the Father, took on the Flesh to become the **OFFERED LAMB**. People must come to that knowledge.

The birth-given name has nothing to do with salvation, no matter what it was.

A LETTER THAT I WROTE TO THE FAITH MAGAZINE, AN ASSEMBLY OF YAHWEH 1/5/06

I read "The Savior True Name" article in "The Faith " dated 10-12, 2005. I believe you have gotten yourselves into a name game like the Jehovah's Witnesses. Jehovah's Witnesses know his name is Yahweh, yet if they came out and said they were no longer going to use the name Jehovah for his true name, Yahweh, they would lose their congregation. I have read some of their articles about the names and they twist it right back to Jehovah.

In your latest article about the Messiah's name you come out and say **his name is YAHWEH**. I will quote from your article on page 9 and watch the 3 little words **that take you from the truth.**

".......and since we know **the name of the Father is "Yahweh,"** therefore, **the name of the Son must also be "Yahweh" "in some form"**.

"IN SOME FORM," you added this to make the truth a lie. This is what takes you from the truths that you state on the previous page (page 8) from scripture. Why? That lets you explain **why you use the name Yahshua instead of his true name, "Yahweh."** There is **only NAME that was given for salvation**, and **that name was and is "YAHWEH." there is NO OTHER**.

The **name given to him at birth HAS NOTHING TO DO WITH SALVATION. ONLY the one HE INHERITED from the FATHER, THE NAME of YAHWEH. Scriptures prove this over and over. No one has shown me yet where the birth-given name is the one that brings salvation because scripture does not teach this. It really does not matter what his name was at birth, except for truth's sake.**

The Messiah Himself tells you what the name is, WHY? Because He is the Father in the FLESH, there is no other name but YAHWEH. So, you in the Yahweh assemblies use the name game of Yahweh and Yahshua, you tell the truth of the name Yahweh then you twist it back to Yahshua. I have read many articles on the name game from different assemblies, and all of you use the same name game. Then, it takes you forever to dissect the name Yahshua to explain why you use it for salvation instead of the name Yahweh.

The name Yahweh was for salvation and for baptism, the name you call upon. Not the name Yahshua, Yeshua, Immanuel, Jesus, Joshua, or any other that people try to use for their salvation. When you start using Yahweh's name for all the previous reasons I have mentioned, then and only then will you stop using the Yahshua name for your salvation and use Yahweh's name.

I believe you know the truth, so I ask you this: are you afraid to teach the truth because you might lose your congregation because you have gotten yourselves in a name game you can't get out of, as the Jehovah's Witnesses, which I have seen the Yahweh assemblies come against a lot on their name thing?

What you have done was take the so-called birth-given Christian name Jesus and change it to Yahshua, then teach what the Christians teach about the name. I can go a whole lot deeper into this, but I will not. All I can say is I hope Yahweh will open the eyes of someone in your assembly, teach the truth about the name and quit playing the name game.

Sincerely,

THESE ASSEMBLIES OF YAHWEH ARE NOT TEACHING THE TRUTH ABOUT YAHWEH MESSIAH. THEY ARE JUST LIKE THE CHRISTIANS USING THE NAME THEY THINK WAS THE BIRTH-GIVEN NAME FOR SALVATION. THEY ARE KEEPING PEOPLE IN THE LIE WHILE TRYING TO BECOME LIKE THE JEWS, YET REMAINING CHRISTIAN. NOT REALIZING THAT SALVATION IS NOT AVAILABLE TODAY FOR THE GENTILES OR THE JEWS AND WHY THERE ARE SO MANY FALSE TEACHINGS.

A. JUSTIFICATION BY WORKS OR JUSTIFICATION OF THE SPIRIT THROUGH FAITH?

Simply put, to justify is to declare righteous, this is done by the infilling of Yahweh's Spirit, He is Spirit.

James 2: 18,24

18 Yea, a man may say, thou hast faith, and I have works: shew me thy faith without thy works, and I will shew thee my faith by my works.

24 You see that a person is justified by works and not by faith alone.

271

Titus 3:7 - That being justified by his Spirit, we should be made heirs according to the hope of eternal life.

Romans 5:1-2

1 Therefore being justified by faith, we have peace with Yahweh through our Master Yahweh Messiah:

2 Through him we have also obtained access by faith into this salvation in which we stand, and we rejoice in hope of the righteousness of Yahweh.

Galatians 3:24 - Wherefore the law was our schoolmaster to bring us unto Yahweh, that we might be justified by faith.

1 john 3:9 Whoever has been born of Yahweh does not transgress, for His seed remains in him; and he cannot transgress, because he has been born of Yahweh.

1 Corinthians 6:11 And such were some of you. But you were washed, you were sanctified, you were justified in the name of the Yahweh Messiah and by the Spirit.

JAMES 2:1 My brethren, have not the faith of our Master Yahweh Messiah, *the Master* of righteousness, with respect of persons.

2 For if there come unto your assembly a man with a gold ring, in goodly apparel, and there come in also a poor man in vile raiment;

3 And ye have respect to him that weareth the gay clothing, and say unto him, Sit thou here in a good place; and say to the poor, Stand thou there, or sit here under my footstool:

TREAT ALL MEN THE SAME NO MATTER HOW POOR OR RICH; YAHWEH IS NO RESPECTER OF PERSONS TO WHO HE GIVES HIS SPIRIT. HE GOES BY THEIR FAITH IN HIM, AND THE WORKS WILL FOLLOW WITH THE FAITH. YOU MUST HAVE THE FAITH TO HAVE THE WORKS.

B. OUTER DARKNESS AND LAKE OF FIRE, THE DIFFERENCE:

Darkness is death, so there is no weeping and gnashing of teeth when a person is dead. But there will be in the Lake of Fire.

This is how the lies were perpetuated. "Outer Darkness/death" comes before the "Lake of Fire." After the Lake of Fire, a person seizes to exist.

So, you should be able to see that they put "outer darkness" in place of the "Lake of Fire" in the following two verses.

Read the below two verses the first time using "outer darkness" and what was put in those verses, then read them the second time using "the Lake of Fire," and you will see right off that what I am saying is true.

Matthew 25:30 And cast ye the unprofitable servant into "outer darkness" / "the Lake of Fire," there shall be weeping and gnashing of teeth.

Matthew 22:13 Then said the king to the servants, bind him hand and foot and take him away, and cast him into "outer darkness" / "the Lake of Fire," there shall be weeping and gnashing of teeth.

Matthew 13:42 And shall cast them into a furnace of fire: there shall be <u>wailing and gnashing of teeth.</u>

Luke 13:27-28

27 But he shall say, I tell you, I know you not whence ye are; depart from me, all ye workers of iniquity.

28 There shall be weeping and gnashing of teeth, when ye shall see Abraham, Isaac, and Jacob, and all the prophets, in the kingdom of Yahweh, and you yourselves thrust out.

Jeremiah 13:16 Give honor to Yahweh, before He cause darkness, and before your feet stumble upon the dark mountains, and, while ye look for light, he turn it into the shadow of death, and make it gross darkness.

Job 10:21 Before I go whence I shall not return, even to the land of darkness and the shadow of death;

Job 17:13 If I wait, the grave is mine house: I have made my bed in the darkness.

Job 34:22

There is no darkness, nor shadow of death, where the workers of iniquity may hide themselves.

Psalms 88:6

Thou hast laid me in the lowest pit, in darkness, in the deeps.

1 Samuel 2:9

He will keep the feet of his Elect, and <u>the wicked shall be silent in darkness;</u> for by strength shall no man prevail.

CHAPTER 19

NO WANT FOR YAHWEH'S PEOPLE:

People must come to realize the fact that Yahweh will take care of His people during the Tribulation, and even when they suffer death at that time, they will feel no pain and they will have no fear. NOTE: You hear a lot of preachers telling people to store food and other things up to get through the Tribulation Period because there is not going to be any food at that time. The truth comes out during the beginning of the 7-Year Peace Plan after WW3, and this study will prove to those who believe in Yahweh Messiah at that time that Yahweh will take care of their needs, food, or what have you. Those who try to save their lives will lose it. Those who lose their life will save it. Why is that? Because the Mark of the Beast is given at that time, only Yahweh's Elect will not take the Mark. Yahweh will feed them, heal them, and protect them up to when they will give their lives to prove that Yahweh is true, just like those in the days of the Apostles did and including them.

Persecution of Yahweh's people is coming, and His Spirit will lead His people in all things, even unto death. Fear not if you have Yahweh's Spirit at that time. In the **King James Version** of the scriptures, the phrase "**fear not**" appears 500 **times**.

Psalms 84:11-12

11. <u>For Yahweh is a sun and shield</u>: Yahweh will give protection and honor: no good thing will he withhold from them that walk uprightly.

12. O Yahweh of hosts, blessed is the man that trusteth in thee.

NOTE: <u>I believe that Psalms 84:11 is about a sun and shield, meaning is found in Psalms 78:14.</u>

Psalms 78:14 <u>In the daytime also he led them with a cloud, and all the night with a light of fire.</u>

Matthew 6:11 Give us this day our daily bread.

Joshua 1:9 - Have I not commanded you? Be strong and courageous. Do not be frightened, and do not be dismayed, for Yahweh is with you wherever you go."

Proverbs 29:25 - The fear of man lays a snare, but whoever trusts in Yahweh is safe.

Matthew 21:21,22

21 Immanuel answered and said unto them, Verily I say unto you, If ye have faith, and doubt not, ye shall not only do this which is done to the fig tree, but also if ye shall say unto this mountain, Be thou removed, and be thou cast into the sea; it shall be done.

22 And <u>all things, whatsoever ye shall ask in prayer, believing, ye shall receive.</u>

Luke 5:4-7

4 Now when he had left speaking, he said unto Simon, Launch out into the deep, and let down your nets for a draught.

5 And Simon answering said unto him, Master, we have toiled all the night, and have taken nothing: nevertheless at thy word I will let down the net.

6 And when they had this done, they enclosed a great multitude of fishes: and their net brake.

7 And they beckoned unto their partners, which were in the other ship, that they should come and help them. And they came, and filled both the ships, so that they began to sink.

Luke 9:1-3

1. Then he called his twelve disciples together, and gave them power and authority over all devils, and to cure diseases.

2. And he sent them to preach the kingdom of Yahweh, and to heal the sick.

3. And he said unto them, Take nothing for your journey, neither staves, nor scrip, neither bread, neither money; neither have two coats apiece.

When the 12 Tribes left Egypt, not one of them was sick or crippled they all walked under their own power, even the old people.

1 Kings 17:2 Then the word of Yahweh came to Elijah: **3** "Leave here, turn eastward and hide in the Kerith Ravine, east of the Jordan. **4** You will drink from the brook, and I have directed the ravens to supply you with food there." **NOW HOW NEAT IS THAT?**

Luke 9:13-17

5 loaves 2 fishes, fed about 5,000 people and there remained with broken pieces, 12 baskets.

Luke 10:1-4 sent the 70 out without purse wallet shoes .

Luke 22:35

35 And he said unto them, When I sent you without purse, and scrip, and shoes, lacked ye any thing? And they said, Nothing.

Hebrews 11:6 But without faith it is impossible to please Him: for he that cometh to Yahweh must believe that He is, and that He is a rewarder of them that diligently seek him.

Philippians 4:5-13

5 Let your moderation be known unto all men. Yahweh is at hand.

6 Be careful about nothing; but in everything by prayer and supplication with thanksgiving let your requests be made known unto Yahweh.

7 And the peace of Yahweh, which passeth all understanding, shall keep your hearts and minds through Messiah Yahweh.

8 Finally, brethren, whatsoever things are true, whatsoever things are honest, whatsoever things are just, whatsoever things are pure, whatsoever things are lovely, whatsoever things are of good report; if there be any virtue, and if there be any praise, think on these things.

9 Those things, which ye have both learned, and received, and heard, and seen in me, do: and Yahweh of peace shall be with you.

10 But I rejoiced in the Lord greatly, that now at the last your care of me hath flourished again; wherein ye were also careful, but ye lacked opportunity.

11 Not that I speak in respect of want: for I have learned, in whatsoever state I am, therewith to be content.

12 I know both how to be abased, and I know how to abound: everywhere and in all things I am instructed both to be full and to be hungry, both to abound and to suffer need.

13 I can do all things through Yahweh which strengtheneth me.

Psalms 115:13,14

13 <u>He will bless them that fear Yahweh, both small and great</u>

14 <u>Yahweh shall increase you more and more, you and your children.</u>

Psalms 84:11-12

11. <u>For Yahweh is a sun and shield</u>: Yahweh will give sanctification and esteem: no good thing will he withhold from them that walk uprightly.

12. O Yahweh of hosts, blessed is the man that trusteth in thee.

NOTE: I believe that Psalms 84:11 about a sun and shield meaning is found in Psalms 78:14.

Psalms 78:12-16; 19-32

12 He did miracles in the sight of their ancestors in the land of Egypt, in the region of Zoan.

13 He divided the sea and led them through; He made the water stand up like a wall.

14 <u>He guided them with the cloud by day and with light from the fire all night.</u>

15 <u>He split the rocks in the wilderness and gave them water as abundant as the seas;</u>

16 <u>He brought streams out of a rocky crag and made water flow down like rivers.</u>

19 They spoke against Yahweh; they said, <u>"Can Yahweh really spread a table in the wilderness?</u>

20 True, <u>He struck the rock, and water gushed out, streams flowed abundantly, but can he also give us bread?</u> <u>Can he supply meat for his people?"</u>

21 Therefore <u>Yahweh heard this, and was wroth</u>: So a fire was kindled against Jacob, And anger also came up against Israel;

22 <u>Because they believed not in Yahweh, And trusted not in his salvation:</u>

23 Though <u>He had commanded the clouds from above, And opened the doors of heaven,</u>

24 And <u>had rained down manna upon them to eat, And had given them of the corn of heaven.</u>

25 <u>Man did eat Messenger's food: He sent them meat to the full.</u>

26 <u>He caused an east wind to blow in the heaven: And by his power he brought in the south wind.</u>

27 <u>He rained flesh also upon them as dust, And feathered fowls like as the sand of the sea:</u>

28 And <u>He let it fall in the midst of their camp, Round about their habitations.</u>

29 So <u>they did eat, and were well filled: For He gave them their own desire;</u>

30 They were not estranged from their lust. But while their meat was yet in their mouths,

31 The wrath of Yahweh came upon them, And slew the fattest of them, And smote down the chosen men of Israel.

32 <u>For all this they transgressed still, And believed not for his wondrous works.</u>

Psalms 105:40-41

40 <u>The people asked, and He brought quails, and satisfied them with the bread of heaven.</u>

41 <u>He opened the rock, and the waters gushed out; they ran in the dry places like a river.</u>

1 Kings 17:15-17

15 <u>She went away and did as Elijah had told her. So there was food every day</u> <u>for Elijah and for the woman and her family.</u>

16 For <u>the jar of flour was not used up and the jug of oil did not run dry, in</u> <u>keeping with the word of Yahweh spoken by Elijah.</u>

17 And it came to pass after these things, that the son of the woman, the mistress of the house, fell sick; and his sickness was so sore, that there was no breath left in him.

18 And she said unto Elijah, What have I to do with thee, O thou man of Yahweh? art thou come unto me to call my transgression to remembrance, and to slay my son?

19 And he said unto her, Give me thy son. And he took him out of her bosom, and carried him up into a loft, where he abode, and laid him upon his own bed.

20 And he cried unto Yahweh, and said, O Yahweh my Almighty, hast thou also brought evil upon the widow with whom I sojourn, by slaying her son?

21 And he stretched himself upon the child three times, and cried unto Yahweh, and said, O Yahweh my Almighty, I pray thee, let this child's soul come into him again.

22 And Yahweh heard the voice of Elijah; and the soul of the child came into him again, and he revived.

23 And Elijah took the child and brought him down out of the chamber into the house, and delivered him unto his mother: and Elijah said, See, thy son liveth.

24 And the woman said to Elijah, Now by this I know that thou art a man of Yahweh, and that the word of Yahweh in thy mouth is truth.

Psalms 1:2-3

2. but his delight is in Yahweh's law. On His law he meditates day and night.

3. He will be like a tree planted by the streams of water, that brings forth its fruit in its season, whose leaf also does not wither. Whatever he does shall prosper.

Psalms 3:5-8

5. I laid myself down and slept. I awakened; for Yahweh sustains me.

6. I will not be afraid of tens of thousands of people who have set themselves against me on every side.

7. Arise, Yahweh! Save me, my Yahweh! For you have struck all of my enemies on the cheek bone. You have broken the teeth of the wicked.

8. Salvation belongs to Yahweh. Your blessing be on your people.

Psalms 9:9-10

9. Yahweh will also be a high tower for the oppressed; a high tower in times of trouble.

10. Those who know your name will put their trust in you, for you, Yahweh, have not forsaken those who seek you.

Psalms 29:11 Yahweh will give strength unto his people; Yahweh will bless his people with peace.

Psalm 37:25 I have been young, and now am old; yet have I not seen the righteous forsaken, nor his seed begging bread.

A. NO PAIN IN DEATH DURING THE TRIBULATION PERIOD

STEPHEN IS AN EXAMPLE OF THIS:

Acts 6: 8-9

8 And Stephen, full of faith and power, did great wonders and miracles among the people.

9 Then there arose certain of the synagogue/**CITY** which is called the synagogue/**CITY** of the Libertines, and Cyrenians, and Alexandrians, and of them of Cilicia and of Asia, disputing with Stephen.

ACTS 7:5-60

54 On hearing this, the members of the Sanhedrin were enraged, and they gnashed their teeth at him.

55 But **Stephen, full** of the Spirit, **looked intently into heaven and saw** the righteousness of Yahweh **standing at the right hand** of Yahweh.

56 " Look," he said, "I see heaven open and the Son of Man standing at the right hand of Yahweh.

57 Then they cried out with a loud voice, and stopped their ears, and ran upon him with one accord,

58 They dragged him out of the city and began to stone him. Meanwhile the witnesses laid their garments at the feet of a young man named Saul.

59 while **they were stoning him, Stephen appealed,** "Yahweh, **receive my spirit."**

60 Falling on his knees, he cried out in a loud voice, "Yahweh, do not hold this transgression against them." And when he had said this, he fell asleep.

HE WAS STANDING UP BEING STONED, HIS MIND WAS ON YAHWEH. He seemed to be in no pain or fear while being stoned, then he died quickly.

CHAPTER 20
JUDAEA OR ISRAEL?

A. THE WORD "ISRAEL" IN THE SCRIPTURES, HOW DID IT GET THERE?

Since Judaea is the true name and where the term Jew comes from, Judah, you cannot get Jews out of Israel. This is the conclusion that I produced in my research of that word. Jerome had to be the one that exchanged the word Judaea for Israel to have Israel in the Old and New Testaments that are Covenants in truth. He added more lies to Constantine's propagandized New Testament, and he followed the lead of Constantine, naming the New Covenant the New Testament. Why Jerome named the Old Covenant the Old Testament is a good example of how Israel replaced Judaea and the Testament replaced Covenant came about in all the translations since Jerome's Latin Vulgate to make people believe those lies and many more, all for deceit. Jerome was the root of all the translations that we have today and the first to have both the Old and New Testaments in it. Judaea was not named Israel until after WW2; they took Israel from the scriptures to give it the name it is called today, not realizing it is a lie of Satan. How was it done? The Papacy, any time they want to change scriptures to fit a new belief, all they do is bring out new translations to get them to bring about the deceit and act like the new add-on or word switch was always there, but also all the translations will end up not agreeing with one another and will end up saying different stuff to cause even more confusion, unbelievable? Why do they call it Judaism, Christianity Today, and Judaeo-Christianity in 1939?

Israel asks a question: Is Ra El? Speaking of Amen Ra, a sun deity name in the worship of Nimrod.? The name had to do with the worship of the sun. Some of the Jews at one time were worshipers of the sun, as proven by scripture, and Christianity is based on sun worship and why the word Israel has to do with sun worship.

Ezekiel 8:15-17

15 Then said he unto me, Hast thou seen this, O son of man? Turn thee yet again, and thou shalt see greater abominations than these.

16 And he brought me into the inner court of the Yahweh's House, and behold, **at the door of the House of Yahweh, between the porch and the altar, were about five and twenty men, with their backs toward the House of Yahweh, and their faces toward the east; and they worshipped the sun toward the east.**

17 Then he said unto me, Hast thou seen this, O son of man? Is it a light thing to the house of Judah that they commit the abominations which they commit here? For they have filled the land with violence and have returned to provoke me to anger: and, lo, they put the branch to their nose.

Yahweh has a lot of wrath built up against Nimrod for starting pagan sun worship and the Babylonian religious system and why. I believe Nimrod will be the last Pope when Yahweh pours his wrath out during the Tribulation Period, so he must live through it and the wrath that is poured out at Yahweh's return. This is why he wants Nimrod to be there at the time he pours his wrath out so Nimrod will be there to see it and to feel his wrath and, of course, his end in the Lake of Fire.

Acts 7:43 Yea, ye took up the tabernacle of Moloch [Nimrod], and the star of your deity Remphan, figures which ye made to worship them: and I will carry you away beyond Babylon.

Moloch is Nimrod, who goes by many different names from many diverse cultures, Saturn, Jupiter, Sol, and Baal, to name a few of them, and a lot of other names in his worship that are Satanic and who destroys and devour little children, Abortion today.

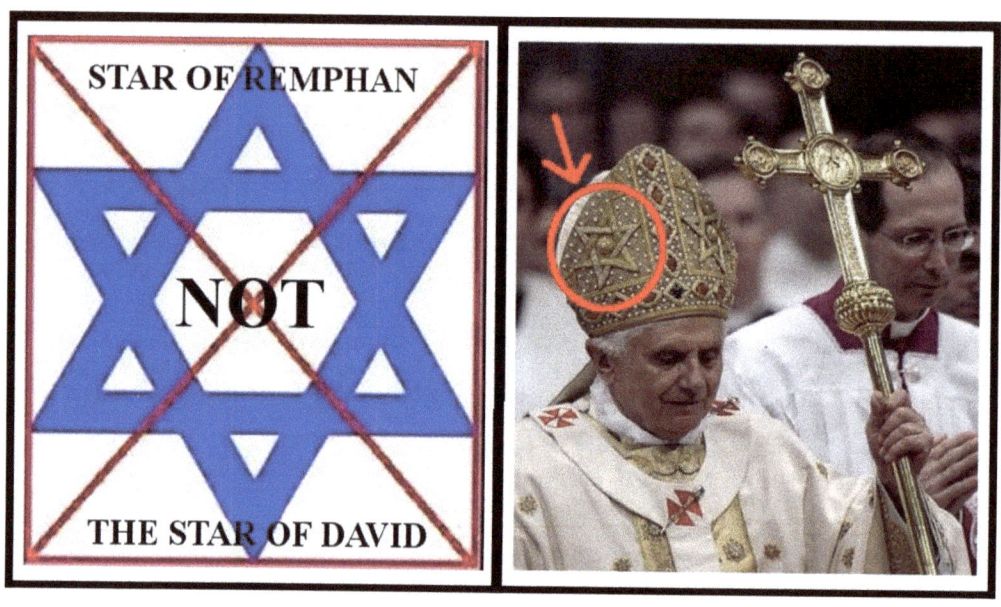

The Hexagram was also used to represent Saturn, which has been identified as the name for "Satan." This indicates that anyone killed in the name of Israel is a sacrifice to Satan.

MANY WANTED THE MENORAH ON THE FLAG INSTEAD OF THE STAR TO REPRESENT **THE JEWS TO BE ON THEIR FLAG, THE OLDEST JEWISH SYMBOL.**

CHAPTER 21

Murder by Abortion

Roe verses Wade was overturned, but it did not stop Abortions. It was turned over to the States to set up their own laws for Abortions. They even passed a law that States do not have to say how many Abortions they do. The liberal States like New York and California do not say how many they do. Abortions are here to stay. Once doors are opened, they are a whole lot harder to get closed, being sacrificed to Moloch in a different way in this sick Satanic world. One day, people just might come to the reality that this Satanic world is all about death. If humanity can kill babies, there is nothing that they won't do, and why this world will just keep getting more Satanic.

Today, 80% of Blacks have babies out of wedlock.

55 to 60% of Hispanics have babies out of wedlock.

25% of Whites have babies out of wedlock.

AT THE TIME THIS STUDY WAS DONE.

THESE 3 FOLLOWING VERSES IN ECLECCLESIASTES ROMANS AND PROVERBS, I BELIEVE, ARE THE BEST ONES NOT TO HAVE AN ABORTION OR ABORTIONS. YOU ARE MURDERING INNOCENT LIFE!

Ecclesiastes 11:5 As <u>you do not know the way the spirit comes to the bones in the womb of a woman with child, so you do not know the work of Yahweh who makes everything.</u>

THESE 2 FOLLOWING VERSES IN ROMANS AND PROVERBS I BELIEVE ARE THE BEST ONES FOR NOT DOING ABORTIONS.

<u>Romans 1:28-32</u>

28 And <u>even as they did not like to retain Yahweh in their knowledge, Yahweh gave them over to a reprobate mind, to do those things which are **not convenient;**</u>

29 <u>Being filled with all unrighteousness,</u> fornication, **wickedness,** covetousness, maliciousness; **full of** envy, **murder**, debate, **deceit**, malignity; whisperers,

30 Backbiters, haters of Yahweh, **despiteful**, proud, boasters, **inventors of evil things**, disobedient to parents,

31 Without understanding, Covenant breakers, **without natural affection**, implacable, **unmerciful**:

32 Who knowing the judgment of Yahwek, that they which commit such things are worthy of death, not only do the same, but have pleasure in them that do them.

Proverbs 6:16-19

16 These six things doth the LORD hate: yea, seven are an abomination unto him:

17 A proud look, a lying tongue, and hands that shed innocent blood,

18 An heart that deviseth wicked imaginations, feet that be swift in running to mischief,

19 A false witness that speaketh lies, and he that soweth discord among brethren.

~ There are six things that Yahweh hates, seven that are an abomination to him: haughty eyes, a lying tongue, and **hands that shed innocent blood**, **a heart that devises wicked plans**, feet that make haste to **run to evil**, a **false witness who breathes out lies**, and one who sows discord among brothers.

"I've noticed that everybody that is for abortion has already been born." ~Ronald Reagan

There is no such thing as an illegitimate child

The parents are the ones that are illegitimate.

Illegitimate:

1. not authorized by the law; not in accordance with accepted standards or rules.

The parents are the ones by the law who are the guilty ones and who are supposed to be married. Think about it: ILLEGIT - I (my) - MATE = ILLEGAL MATE.

1. not legal

2. not logically admissible

3. without justification

289

The child is the one who receives the title "ILLEGITMATE" and the "DEATH SENTENCE" by the parent or parents of that child, who are really the guilty ones.

If you throw a match on some gas, you know it will ignite. If you have sex, you know a baby will be produced. That is just the way things are made to be. So quit blaming and sentencing a baby for your own greedy and lustful actions.

Total number of abortions in the U.S. 1973-2011: 54.5 million

234 abortions per 1,000 live births (according to the Centers for Disease Control)

Abortions per year: 1.2 million

Abortions per day: 3,288

Abortions per hour: 137

9 abortions every 4 minutes

1 abortion every 26 seconds

http://www.all.org/nav/index/heading/OQ/cat/MzQ/id/NjA3OQ/

The number of abortions provided by Planned Parenthood has increased from 305,310 in 2007 to 324,008 in 2008, while adoption referrals are down to 2,405 in 2008 from 4,912 in 2007. Their fact sheet also reveals that the number of prenatal clients dropped from 10,914 in 2007 to 9,433 in 2008.

An unborn baby grabs the doctor's hand.

Clinton Stands By Her Praise of Eugenicist Margaret Sanger

Apr 15, 2009, • By KEVIN VANCE

After the founder of the American Birth Control League, which changed its name Planned Parenthood in the 1940s, last month Secretary of State Hillary Clinton accepted Planned Parenthood's Margaret Sanger Award, named after the founder of the American Birth Control League, which changed its name to Planned Parenthood in the 1940s.

Mrs. Sanger, of course, wasn't the benevolent advocate for human rights that Clinton's remarks make her out to be. In fact, Sanger's "vision" for birth control seems to be united to a eugenic vision. In the October 1921 issue of The Birth Control Review, Sanger wrote that "the campaign for Birth Control is not merely of eugenic value but is practically identical in ideal with the final aim of Eugenics."

Look who joined the ranks of Clinton, no other than Catholic Nancy Pelosi, the spokesperson for the U.S. Bishops.

Pelosi compares illegal immigrant kids to "baby Jesus"

I reference the conference of bishop's statement in which they say baby Jesus was a refugee from violence. Let us not turn away these children and send them back into a burning building. That is the bishops, so we must do this in a way that honors our values but also protects our border and does so in a way that the American people understand more clearly.

But don't protect the unborn in America. She is a double-standard witch, just like Hillary is.

On March 27th, 2014 - during the Lenten season, Democratic Minority Speaker of the House, Catholic Nancy Pelosi, was awarded the Margaret Sanger Award, an award presented annually to recognize leadership, excellence, and outstanding contributions to the reproductive health and rights movement. She joins Hillary Clinton in the Sanger Slaughter Hall of Fame.

At her gala Sanger Slaughter acceptance speech, pious Pelosi accused pro-lifers of being dumb. "When you see how closed their minds are or oblivious or whatever it is–dumb–then you know what the fight is about," declared Pelosi.

Number of blacks killed by lynching in the U.S. between 1864 and 1968:

4,946 (47.7 per year).

- Between 1882 and 1968, 3,446 Blacks were lynched in the U.S. That number is surpassed in less than 3 days by abortion.
- 1,452 African American children are killed each day by abortion.
- 3 out of 5 pregnant African American women will abort their child.
- Number of black babies killed by abortion between 1973 and 2010: 17,237,000 (currently 574,000 per year) Ratio of black babies killed by abortion to blacks killed by lynching:

3,485 to 1

- And what political party supports the killing of black and white babies? Democrats!

Planned Parenthood is a liberal organization that was conceived with one purpose: To eradicate the black population in America. "Planned Parenthood's legacy of racism & eugenics is firmly established through its founder Margaret Sanger." blackgenocide.org/sanger.html

Per the NY Daily News, 2/23/2011, federal statistics show blacks make up about 13% of the American population and account for 36.4% of U.S. abortions. "...our future is in jeopardy as a genocidal plot is carried out through abortion," said the Rev. Stephen Broden, an official with the anti-abortion group Life Always.

This past December, Planned Parenthood released its new 2012-2013 annual report and revealed it received $1.5 Million in Taxpayer Funds every day during 2012-2013 in the form of grants, contracts, and Medicaid reimbursements, an increase of 5% to a total of $1,21 billion (about $370 per person in the US) in its fiscal year ending June 30, 2013. ..of that, 45%, or $540.6 million, was provided by taxpayer-funded government health services grants, and a total of 327,166 abortions were performed in the year ended on September 30, 2012.

- Margaret Sanger was a Catholic.
- In some States, 1 out of 2 Black babies are aborted. Otherwise, it's between 1/3 and 1/2. The government is behind it.
- Hillary Clinton is behind having parental rights taken away from parents, another U.N. agenda of Rome.

96.3% of Planned Parenthood's services to women in 2008 were abortions, and the other 3.7% were adoptions and prenatal care. In 2008 and 2009, Planned Parenthood performed more than 650,000 abortions! We are sacrificing our children to Moloch!

- Planned Parenthood President Cecile Richards complained that cutting off the $350 million a year that PP receives from U.S. Taxpayers would harm women who are coming to Planned Parenthood for "access to basic health care such as mammograms..." But a young woman called PP of Georgetown, and they said: "We do not provide mammograms... We're mostly a surgical facility."
- Abbey Johnson, who used to work for Planned Parenthood, has a new book, Unplanned. She writes: "As a Planned Parenthood clinic manager, I was directed to double the number of abortions our clinic performed in order to drive up revenue. In keeping with that goal, Planned Parenthood headquarters recently issued a directive mandating that all of its affiliates provide abortions by 2013."
- Planned Parenthood Reports 333,964 Babies Killed - They are now selling the parts to aborted babies.
- As sick as this makes me look at it, people need to see and stop this madness.
- THIS IS HOW THEY KILL A LIVE BIRTH ABORTION! - SEVERING THE BRAINSTEM AND SPINAL CORD!

· Many of the women who have abortions end up committing suicide. So, they get double indemnity.

Elliot Institute Presents New Findings at International Women's Health Conference

A new Elliot Institute study has found that women who have had abortions are more likely to commit suicide than those who have given birth.

The study examined Medi-Cal records for more than 173,000 low-income California women who had abortions or gave birth in 1989. Linking these records to death certificates, the researchers found that women who had state-funded abortions were 2.6 times more likely to die of suicide compared to women who delivered their babies.

The average annual suicide rate per 100,000 women was 3.0 for delivering women, compared to 7.8 for aborting women. The national average suicide rate for women between the ages of 15 and 44 is 5.2 per 100,000 women (about the seating capacity of the Los Angeles Memorial Coliseum). This shows that aborted women have a higher suicide rate than women in general while giving birth actually reduces women's suicide risk.

"The data clearly shows what we have long suspected: that abortion is harmful rather than helpful to women," said Elliot Institute director Dr. David Reardon, one of several researchers working on the study.

They also presented studies that found higher rates of depression, mental illness, miscarriages, and substance abuse among post-abortive women compared to women who gave birth.

· If it isn't a baby, then you aren't pregnant, so what are you aborting? ~Author Unknown
· Think about just how many Christians work for Planned Parenthood.
· 17% of abortions were done with abortion pills in 2010.
· The birth control pill was invented by a Catholic doctor.

Besides abortion, they use other means to control population growth, which are birth control pills, homosexuality, which is also a form of birth control, and sterilization in many forms. Contraception includes barrier methods, such as condoms or diaphragms, hormonal contraception, and contraceptives.

If all these babies are not wanted, why become animals to get rid of them? Why would they get pregnant in the first place? Have people been dummied down so far that they can't learn it's by having sex that you get pregnant, and there are responsibilities that go along with doing that?

Drugs play a big part in this. We have been fighting a drug war for 40 years, and all it is to this government is a big money maker. Plus, it helps again to tear down the morality of a country.

YOU HAVE THE RIGHT TO CHOOSE THE ANTIDOTE TO ABORTION... Yep, you have the right to choose to keep your legs shut or not... With that choice, you have already chosen whatever comes of it (cause and effect), even if that means sharing your body with your child. After all, you shared it with some guy who made the making of that baby possible.

A. What Scriptures Teach

Proverbs 6:16,17

16. There are six things which Yahweh hates; Yes, seven which are an abomination to him:

17. Haughty eyes, a lying tongue, and hands that shed innocent blood;

This country is over 70% Christian, and besides Abortion, they have legalized Drinking, Gambling, Homosexual Marriage in some states, and Homosexual Adoptions. They are trying now to legalize Dope and Prostitution.

If a baby is conceived through rape, then kill the rapist and adopt the baby. Just because the government legalized abortion, it still does not make it right.84% of American abortion patients identify themselves as Christians. Christians not only fill the sidewalks in front of abortion clinics as protesters but the patient beds in abortion clinics as well.

Ecclesiastes 11:5

5. As you do not know the way the spirit comes to the bones in the womb of a woman with child, so you do not know the work of Yahweh who makes everything.

Jeremiah 1:5

5. Before I formed thee in the belly I knew thee; and before thou camest forth out of the womb I sanctified thee, and I ordained thee a prophet unto the nations.

Psalm 139:13-16

13 For thou hast possessed my reins: thou hast covered me in my mother's womb.

14 I will praise thee; for I am fearfully and wonderfully made: marvellous are thy works; and that my soul knoweth right well.

15 My substance was not hid from thee, when I was made in secret, and curiously wrought in the lowest parts of the earth.

16 Thine eyes did see my substance, yet being unperfect; and in thy book all my members were written, which in continuance were fashioned, when as yet there was none of them.

Luke 1:41-42

41. And it came to pass, that, when Elisabeth heard the salutation of Mary, the babe leaped in her womb; and Elisabeth was filled with the Spirit:

42. And she cried out with a loud voice and said, "Blessed are you among women, and blessed is the fruit of your womb!

Luke 1: 14-15

14. You will have joy and gladness, and many will rejoice at his birth.

15. For he will be great in the sight of Yahweh; and he will drink no wine or liquor, and he will be filled with the Spirit while yet in his mother's womb. [OBJ]

Genesis 25:22-23 Jacob and Esau

22. But the children struggled together within her; and she said, "If it is so, why then am I this way?" So, she went to inquire of Yahweh.

23. Yahweh said to her, "Two nations are in your womb; And two peoples will be separated from your body; And one people shall be stronger than the other; And the older shall serve the younger."...

Isaiah 44:2

Thus says Yahweh who made you And formed you from the womb, who will help you, 'Do not fear, O Jacob My servant; And you Jeshurun whom I have chosen.

THE KILLING OF BABIES WILL NEVER STOP; HUNDREDS OF THOUSANDS ARE STILL BEING KILLED EVERY YEAR, EVEN AFTER THE OVERTURNING OF ROE VERSES WADE IN THE U.S. YOU MUST REMEMBER THAT ABORTIONS ARE BEING DONE ALL OVER THE WORLD. IT IS PART OF POPULATION CONTROL FOR THE GLOBAL GOVERNMENT. THIS SATANIC WORLD IS ALL ABOUT DEATH. THINK ABOUT THIS: THE U.S. GOVERNMENT LETS MILLIONS UPON MILLIONS OF ILLEGAL ALIENS COME INTO THIS COUNTRY AND EVEN HELPS THEM DO IT. THEN LET THE TAXPAYERS PAY FOR THEM ALL. THIS IS ALSO AN AGENDA, AS WELL AS ABORTIONS. LIKE TRUMP NOW SAYS ABOUT ALL THE ILLEGAL ALIENS THAT CAME INTO THIS COUNTRY CAN NOW BECOME CITIZENS. HE IS AFTER THE

GANGS AND THOSE SET FREE FROM PRISONS TO COME HERE FROM THE PRISONS. THEY ALWAYS WORK AROUND GETTING RID OF THE ILLEGALS WHILE OTHERS COME INTO THIS COUNTRY LEGITAMENTLY. KILL OUR BABY CITIZENS SO THEY CAN MAKE ROOM AND TAKE CARE OF MILLIONS OF ILLEGALS. THEY WILL MAKE THE PAPACY MORE MONEY FROM LIVING HERE AND TAKING JOBS AND GOVERNMENT HAND OUTS TO THESE PEOPLE, ALL ABOUT OPEN BORDERS AND MAKING THIS COUNTRY PRODOMINITELY CATHOLIC.

A SENATOR ON A RADIO PROGRAM SAID," ANY COUNTRY THAT WANTS AID FROM THE U.S. MUST AGREE TO ABORTIONS TO RECEIVE AID."

CHAPTER 22

COMPARING THE CHRISTIAN JESUS TO THE TRUTH OF IMMANUEL:

JESUS	IMMANUEL
1. Son of God, a pagan deity	1. Son of Yahweh
2. Carried the Cross	2. Carried a yoke
3. Died by Roman Law	3. Died by Jewish Law
4. Died on a Cross	4. Died on an Olive Tree
5. Crucified, 3 nails were used	5. Hung with rope tied to wrists
6. 3 separate Crosses were used	6. All 3 suspended on the same Olive Tree
7. Died on Good Friday	7. Died on the Wednesday Passover
8. Rose on Sunday	8. Rose at the end of the Sabbath
9. 36 hours in the grave.	9. 72 hours in the grave.
10. 2 nights / 1 day in the grave.	10. 3 nights / 3 days in the grave.
11. Inherited his own name.	11. Inherited the Father's name
12. Became Jesus Christ.	12. Became Yahweh Messiah.
13. Christ means good	13. Messiah means anointed

14. Died for Sins

14. Died for Transgressions

15. Jesus, an Anti- Messiah name

15. Yahweh, the true Messiah's name

16. Is a Latinized Greek name

16. Immanuel is a Hebrew name.

17. Jesus Christ are 2 sun deities.

17. The name Immanuel is not pagan

18. Your end, the Lake of Fire.

18. Your end, Eternal Life.

19. Born on December 25.

19. Born on Nisan 1.

20 Born in Bethlehem of Judah.

20. Born in Bethlehem of Galilee.

CHAPTER 23

YAHWEH AND HIS MESSIAH:

INCARNATION –Yahweh took on the flesh, who is Spirit, to be made visible to man and to become the offered Lamb for the transgressions of man.

Romans 1:5

Through Him and for his name's sake, we received the Spirit and apostleship to call people from among all the Gentiles to the obedience that comes from faith.

When Scriptures speak of Yahweh and His Messiah, He is speaking of the flesh. Yahweh, the Father is Spirit. No man has ever seen the Father. It is only through the Son, which is the Father manifested in the flesh, that He can dwell among man. The Father had to take on the flesh to become the offered Lamb. That's why you must believe in the son because you must believe He is the Father in the flesh. That's why no one can come to the Father but by Him (speaking of the son.)

Acts 18:28

28. For he mightily convinced the Jews and that publicly, showing by the scriptures that Yahweh was the Messiah.

Now, to prove by scripture: The following scriptures prove that Yahweh is the Messiah.

Isaiah 42:8

8. I am Yahweh; that is MY NAME; and my esteem will I not give to another.

Isaiah 43:11

11. I, even I, am Yahweh; and beside me there is no savior.

Psalms 83:16-18

16. Fill their faces with shame; that they may SEEK THY NAME, O YAHWEH.

17. Let them be confounded and troubled forever; yea, let them be put to shame, and perish:

18. That MEN MAY KNOW THAT THOU, WHOSE NAME ALONE IS YAHWEH, ART THE MOST HIGH OVER ALL THE EARTH.

John 5:43

43. I come in my Father's name, and ye receive me not: if another shall come in his own name, him ye will receive.

Hebrews 1:4

4. Being made so much better than the Messengers, as he hath by inheritance obtained a more excellent name than they.

Philippians 2:9

9. Wherefore Yahweh also hath highly exalted him, and given Him a name which is above every name.

Matthew 28:19

19. "Go ye therefore, and teach all nations, baptizing them in the name of the Father, and of the Son, and of the Spirit."

1. It says NAME not NAMES, the name is YAHWEH.

2, Father, Son, Spirit are offices of Yahweh.

3. Yahweh is ONE not three.

Micah 5:2 But thou Bethlehem Ephratah, though thou be little among the thousands of Judah, yet out of thee shall he come forth unto me that is to be ruler in Israel; whose goings forth have been from of old, from everlasting.

Psalms 90:1-2

1. Yahweh, thou hast been our dwelling place in all generations.

2. Before the mountains were brought forth, or ever thou hadst formed the earth and the world, even from everlasting to everlasting, thou art Yahweh.

Isaiah 9:6

6. For unto us a child is born, unto us a son is given: and the government shall e upon his shoulder: and his name shall be called Wonderful, Counselor, The Almighty, THE EVERLASTING FATHER, The king of Peace.

Here again, these are the names of his offices. Yahweh is his name.

Jeremiah 23:5-6

5. Behold, the days come, saith Yahweh, that I will raise unto David a righteous Branch, and a King shall reign and prosper, and shall execute judgment and justice in the earth.

6. In his days Judah shall be saved, and Judaea shall dwell safely: and this is his name whereby he shall be called, YAHWEH OUR RIGHTEOUSNESS.

Mark 13:13

13. And ye shall be hated of all men for my name's sake: but he that shall endure unto the end the same shall be saved.

Micah 4:5

5. For all people will walk everyone in the name of his deity, and we will walk in the name of Yahweh, our Almighty for ever and ever.

Isaiah 52:6

6. Therefore, My people shall know my NAME: therefore they shall know in that day that I am he that doth speak: behold, it is I.

1 John 4:1-3

1. Beloved, believe not every spirit, but try the spirits whether they are of Yahweh because many false prophets are gone out into the world.

2. Hereby know ye the Spirit of Yahweh: Every spirit that confesseth that Yahweh the Messiah is come in the flesh is of Yahweh.

3. And every spirit that confesseth not that Yahweh the Messiah is come in the flesh is not of Yahweh: and this is that spirit of ANTI-MESSIAH, whereof have heard that should come; and even now already is it in the world.

1 John 2:18   Little children, it is the last time: and as ye have heard that ANTI-MESSIAH shall come, even now are there many ANTI-MESSIAHS; whereby we know that it is the last time.

2 John 1:77.

"For many deceivers are entered in the world, who confess not that Yahweh the Messiah is come in the flesh. This is a deceiver and a ANTI-MESSIAH."

1 John 2:22-23

22. Who is a liar but he that denieth that Yahweh is the Messiah: He is ANTI-MESSIAH, that denieth the Father and the Son.

23. Whosoever denieth the Son, the same hath not the Father: but he that acknowledgeth the Son hath the Father also.

Zechariah 14:9

9. And Yahweh shall be king over all the earth: in that day shall there be one Yahweh and His name one.

DO YOU REALIZE THAT ROME AND CHRISTIANITY HAVE MADE SCRIPTURES VOID OF SALVATION?

Proverbs 30:4

John 1:1-3

1. "In the beginning was the WORD, and the WORD WAS WITH YAHWEH, and the WORD WAS YAHWEH.

2. The same was in the beginning with Yahweh.

3. All things were made through Him, and without Him was not anything made that has been made.

Colossians 1:15-17,19

15. **Who is the IMAGE OF THE INVISIBLE YAHWEH,** the first born of all creation;

16. For in him were all things created, in the heavens and upon the earth, things visible and things invisible, whither thrones or dominions or principalities or powers; all things have been created through Him, and to Him.

17. And He is before all things, and in him all things consist.

19. For it was the good pleasure of the Father that in Him should all the fulness dwell;

Colossians 2:9,

9. For in Him all the fullness of the Majesty on high bodily.

Titus 2:13

13. looking for the blessed hope and the appearing of the esteem of our great Sovereign, and our Savior Yahweh.

John 1:30

30. This is He of whom I said, "After me cometh a Man who is preferred before me, for He was before me."

Exodus 23:21

20. Behold, I send an Messenger before thee, to keep thee in the way, and to bring thee into the place which I have prepared.

21. Beware of Him, and obey his voice, provoke him not; for He will not pardon your transgressions: FOR MY NAME IS IN HIM.

John 10:30

30. "I and the Father are one."

John 14:1-3,6-9

1. Let not your heart be troubled: ye believe in Yahweh, believe also in me.

2. In my Father's house are many mansions: if it were not so, I would have told you. I go to prepare a place for you.

3. And if I go and prepare a place for you, I will come again, and receive you unto myself; that where I am, there ye may be also.

6. Immanuel saith unto him, I am the way, the truth, and the life: no man cometh unto the Father, but by me.

7. If ye had known me, ye should have known my Father also: and from henceforth ye know him and have seen him.

8. Philip saith unto him, Master, shew us the Father, and it sufficeth us.

9. Immanuel saith unto him, Have I been so long time with you, and yet hast thou not known me, Philip? he that hath seen me hath seen the Father; and how sayest thou then, Shew us the Father?

John 17:5

5. "Now, O Father, esteem Me with Your Own Self, with the esteem which I had with You before the world was."

Revelation 1:8,

8. "I am the Alpha and the Omega," says the Sovereign Yahweh, "who is and who was and who is to come, Yahweh."

Revelation 22:13

13. I am the Aleph and the Taw, the first and the last, the beginning and the end."

{Isaiah 41:4; Isaiah 44:6}

Romans 3:29

29. Or is Yahweh the Almighty of the Jews only? Is he not the Almighty of Gentiles also? Yes, of the Gentiles also:

Acts 1:20,21

20. The sun shall be turned into darkness, And the moon into blood, Before the day of Yahweh come, That great and notable day:

21. And it shall be, that whosoever shall call on the name of Yahweh shall be saved.

Acts 4:12

Neither is there salvation in any other: for there is none other name under heaven given among men, whereby we must be saved

We have inherited the lies of our forefathers, and it is now time to open and cleanse our minds of all those lies we inherited. Yahweh is coming soon. I know you've heard that forever, well, not in Yahweh's name, but in other names used in place of Yahweh, the true Messiah. The Old Covenant tells who the true Messiah is and His NAME. The New Covenant must be in harmony with the Old Covenant or something is very wrong. Well, people, something is very wrong. You must study to show yourselves approved and that means studying the things that will lead you to the truth.

Matthew 10:32-39

32. Whosoever therefore shall confess me before men, him will I confess also before my Father which is in heaven.

33. But whosoever shall deny me before men, him will I also deny before my Father, which is in heaven.

34. Think not that I am come to send peace on earth: I came not to send peace, but a sword.

35. For I am come to set a man at variance against his father, and the daughter against her mother, and the daughter-in-law against her mother-in-law.

36. And a man's foes shall be they of his own household.

37. He that loveth father or mother more than me is not worthy of me; and he that loveth son or daughter more than me is not worthy of me.

38. And he that taketh not his burden, and followeth after me, is not worthy of me.

39. He that findeth his life shall lose it; and he that loseth his life for my sake shall find it.

Malachi 2: 16

16. Then they that feared Yahweh spoke one with another; and Yahweh listened, and heard, and a book of remembrance was written before Him, for them that feared Yahweh, and that thought upon His NAME.

NO OTHER NAME LIKE YAHSHUA or YESHUA, LIKE SOME ARE TRYING TO SAY.

The New Covenant has scriptures quoted from the Old Covenant; some are direct quotes, and others are paraphrased with the name Yahweh in them, so to prove that the name "Yahweh" should also be in the New Covenant, here we go.

Isaiah 45: 21-24 – THE TRUTH

"And there is no other Mighty One besides Me, a righteous Mighty One and a Savior; there is none except Me. Turn to Me, and be saved, all the ends of the earth; for I am Yahweh, and there is no other. I have sworn by Myself, the Word has gone forth from My mouth in righteousness and will not turn back, that to Me every knee will bow, every tongue will swear allegiance, they will say of Me, 'Only in Yahweh are righteousness and strength.' Men will come to Him, and all who were angry with Him shall be put to shame."

Philippians 2: 9-11 – THE LIE

9. Therefore God exalted him to the highest place and gave him the name that is above every name, 10. that at the name of Jesus every knee should bow, in heaven and on earth and under the earth, 11 and every tongue confess that Jesus Christ is Lord, to the glory of God the Father.

Philippians 2: 9-11 – THE TRUTH

9. Therefore Yahweh exalted him to the highest place and gave him the name that is above every name,

10. that at the name of YAHWEH every knee should bow, in heaven and on earth and under the earth,

11. and every tongue confess that YAHWEH MESSIAH IS MASTER, to the esteem of YAHWEH the Father.

Do you want to believe Satan's Christian LIE or the truth of Yahweh that the scriptures really teach? It's your decision, and you are responsible for your own salvation, no one else but you.

In Isaiah 43: 11 Yahweh said, "I, even I, am Yahweh, and there is no savior besides Me.

Joel 2: 32

"Everyone who calls on the Name of Yahweh will be delivered."

Acts 2:21. – THE LIE

And it shall come to pass, that whosoever shall call on the name of the Lord shall be saved.

Do you see what they did from the above 2 scriptures? So take "the LORD" out and put YAHWEH in. Anywhere "the Lord or LORD is, the name of Yahweh goes." This will start you into the real truth of His Name.

Acts 2:21.

And it shall come to pass, that whosoever shall call on the name of Yahweh shall be saved.

By doing this, the scriptures of the New will harmonize with the scriptures of the Old.

Romans 10:13 – THE LIE

For whosoever shall call upon the name of the Lord shall be saved.

See once again the same scripture repeated from Joel 2:32, repeated in the New.

Romans 10:13 – THE TRUTH

For whosoever shall call upon the name of Yahweh shall be saved.

Acts 4:12

Neither is there salvation in any other: for there is NONE OTHER NAME UNDER HEAVEN GIVEN AMONG MEN, WHEREBY WE MUST BE SAVED.

Now, did those above verses ever mention the name JESUS? NO. So, which version are you going to accept for the name used? The truth of Yahweh's name, or the lie of the LORD, you only have two picks, which one will you choose, LORD or Yahweh? When your scriptures say "the Lord Jesus Christ," Yahweh's name goes where "the Lord" is, and "Jesus Christ" was added.

Scriptures say there is only ONE NAME for salvation. Which one will you choose for yours?

As you should be able to see, all they had to do was take Yahweh's Name out of the scriptures to make them VOID of salvation. Even where they put the name Jesus in some places should be the name Yahweh. Otherwise, it should be Immanuel.

REVELATION CHAPTER 18

THIS WHOLE CHAPTER IS SPEAKING ABOUT ZION, THE CITY CALLED JERUSALEM TODAY:

18 And after these things I saw another Messenger come down from heaven, having great power; and the earth was lightened with his righteousness.

2 And he cried mightily with a strong voice, saying, Babylon the great is fallen, is fallen, and is become the habitation of devils, and the hold of every foul spirit, and a cage of every unclean and hateful bird.

3 For all nations have drunk of the wine of the wrath of her fornication, and the kings of the earth have committed fornication with her, and the merchants of the earth are waxed rich through the abundance of her delicacies.

4 And I heard another voice from heaven, saying, Come out of her, my people, that ye be not partakers of her transgressions, and that ye receive not of her plagues.

5 For her transgressions have reached unto heaven, and Yahweh hath remembered her iniquities.

6 Reward her even as she rewarded you, and double unto her double according to her works: in the cup which she hath filled fill to her double.

7 How much she hath glorified herself, and lived deliciously, so much torment and sorrow give her: for she saith in her heart, I sit a queen, and am no widow, and shall see no sorrow.

8 Therefore shall her plagues come in one day, death, and mourning, and famine; and she shall be utterly burned with fire: for strong is Yahweh who judgeth her.

9 And the kings of the earth, who have committed fornication and lived deliciously with her, shall bewail her, and lament for her, when they shall see the smoke of her burning,

10 Standing afar off for the fear of her torment, saying, alas, alas that great city Babylon, that mighty city! for in one hour is thy judgment come.

11 And the merchants of the earth shall weep and mourn over her; for no man buyeth their merchandise anymore.

12 The merchandise of gold, and silver, and precious stones, and of pearls, and fine linen, and purple, and silk, and scarlet, and all thyine wood, and all manner vessels of ivory, and all manner vessels of most precious wood, and of brass, and iron, and marble,

13 And cinnamon, and odors, and ointments, and frankincense, and wine, and oil, and fine flour, and wheat, and beasts, and sheep, and horses, and chariots, and slaves, and souls of men.

14 And the fruits that thy soul lusted after are departed from thee, and all things which were dainty and goodly are departed from thee, and thou shalt find them no more at all.

15 The merchants of these things, which were made rich by her, shall stand afar off for the fear of her torment, weeping and wailing,

16 And saying, alas, alas that great city, that was clothed in fine linen, and purple, and scarlet, and decked with gold, and precious stones, and pearls!

17 For in one hour so great riches come to naught. And every shipmaster, and all the company in ships, and sailors, and as many as trade by sea, stood afar off,

¹⁸ And cried when they saw the smoke of her burning, saying, What city is like unto this great city!

¹⁹ And they cast dust on their heads, and cried, weeping, and wailing, saying, alas, alas that great city, wherein were made rich all that had ships in the sea by reason of her costliness! for in one hour is she made desolate.

²⁰ Rejoice over her, thou heaven, and ye apostles and prophets; for Yahweh hath avenged you on her.

²¹ And a mighty Messenger took up a stone like a great millstone, and cast it into the sea, saying, thus with violence shall that great city Babylon be thrown down, and shall be found no more at all.

²² And the voice of harpers, and musicians, and of pipers, and trumpeters, shall be heard no more at all in thee; and no craftsman, of whatsoever craft he be, shall be found any more in thee; and the sound of a millstone shall be heard no more at all in thee;

²³ And the light of a candle shall shine no more at all in thee; and the voice of the bridegroom and of the bride shall be heard no more at all in thee: for thy merchants were the great men of the earth; for by thy sorceries were all nations deceived.

²⁴ And in her was found the blood of prophets, and of elect, and of all that were slain upon the earth.

Revelation 18:10,17,19,21

10. IN ONE HOUR IS THY JUDGMENT COME.

17. IN ONE HOUR...RICHES COME TO NOUGHT.

19. IN ONE HOUR IS SHE MADE DESOLATE.

21. WITH VIOLENCE ZION IS THROWN DOWN.

THE END OF ZION HERE ON EARTH, THAT IS CALLED JERUSALEM TODAY.

Revelation 18:22-23

22 And the voice of harpers, and musicians, and of pipers, and trumpeters, shall be heard no more at all in thee; and no craftsman, of whatsoever craft *he be*, shall be found any more in thee; and the sound of a millstone shall be heard no more at all in thee;

23 And the light of a candle shall shine no more at all in thee; and the voice of the bridegroom and of the bride shall be heard no more at all in thee: for thy merchants were the great men of the earth; for by thy sorceries were all nations deceived.

Jeremiah 4:6 Set up the standard toward Zion: retire, stay not: for I will bring evil from the north, and a great destruction.

ZION IS THE LAST DAY BABYLON:

Revelation 18:2 And he cried mightily with a strong voice, saying, Babylon the great is fallen, is fallen, and is become the habitation of devils, and the hold of every foul spirit, and a cage of every unclean and hateful bird.

ZION LAYS DOWN WITH THE PAPACY AND BECOMES THE CAPITAL CITY OF THE WORLD

Papacy Agendas, for a Global Government: Illegal Alien Agenda, Universal Healthcare Agenda, Catholic Take Over of Public Schools Agenda, Taking over all

Healthcare and Hospitals Agenda, Earth Warming Agenda, Spreading the Wealth Agenda, U.N. Authority Agenda, 10 World Unions Agenda, One World Order Agenda, Social Justice or Reform Agenda, Homosexual Agenda, Muslim Agenda, Gun Control Agenda, Planned Third World War 3 Agenda, the next big event and the last years before we meet our Creator, World Government, World Religion, World Army, International Police Force, World Central Bank and Monetary System Agenda, World Court, Global Taxation, Homosexual Agenda/LGBT/ Transgender Sex Changes, World Currency, Population Control Agenda, Common Core Agenda, Downfall of the United States Agenda. No more Property Ownership Agenda. These are all the Vatican's agendas for a World Government.

CATHOLICS WILL END UP TAKING OVER THE HOSPITALS' AND SCHOOLS' AGENDA

We were forewarned:

Abraham Lincoln,

"I am not happy about the rebirth of the Jesuits. Swarms of them will present themselves under more disguises ever taken by even a chief of the Bohemians, as printers, writers, publishers, school teachers, etc. If ever an association of people deserved eternal damnation, on this earth and in hell, it is this society of Loyola."(John Adams, 1816). Abraham Lincoln said: "If the Protestants of the North and the South could learn what the priests, nuns, and monks, who daily land on our shores, under the pretext of preaching their religion, were doing in our schools and hospitals, as emissaries of the Pope and the other despots of Europe, to undermine our institutions and alienate the hearts of our people from our Republic.

ABRAHAM LINCOLN, I conceal what I know on that subject from the knowledge of the nation, for if the people knew the whole truth, this war would turn into a religious war, and it would, at once, take a tenfold more savage and bloody character, it would become merciless as all religious wars are. It would become a war of extermination on both sides. The Protestants of both the North and the South would surely unite to exterminate the priests and the Jesuits if they could hear what Professor Morse has said to me of the plots made in the very city of Rome to destroy this Republic and if they could learn how the priests, the nuns, and the monks, which daily land on our shores, under the pretext of preaching their religion, instructing the people in their schools, taking care of the sick in the hospitals, are nothing else but the emissaries of the Pope, of Napoleon, and the other despots of Europe, to undermine our institutions, alienate the hearts of our people from our constitution, and our laws, destroy our schools, and prepare a reign of anarchy here as they have done in Ireland, in Mexico, in Spain, and wherever there are any people who want to be free, etc." **SO TRUE MORE SO TODAY!**

Med as the ministers of righteousness, whose end shall be according to their works.

Matthew 24:24

24: For there shall arise false Messiahs (Jesus, Lord, God, Christ, Allah, Buddha, Adonai, etc., and false prophets, (Preachers, Ministers, Evangelist, Priests, Rabbi's, etc.) and shall show great signs and wonders; insomuch that, if it were possible, they shall deceive the very elect.

Revelation 12:4,5,7,8,9

4. And his tail drew the third part of the stars of heaven, and did cast them to the earth: and the dragon stood before the woman which was ready to be delivered, for to devour her child as soon as it was born.

5. And she brought forth a man child, who was to rule all nations with a rod of iron: and her child was caught up unto Yahweh, and to His throne.

Now, in the next verse 7, watch what happens AFTER the child is caught up unto Yahweh and His Throne.

7. And there was war in heaven: Michael and his Messengers fought against the dragon; and the dragon fought and his messengers,

8. And prevailed not; NEITHER WAS THEIR PLACE FOUND ANY MORE IN HEAVEN.

9. And the great dragon WAS CAST OUT, that old serpent, called the Devil, and Satan, which DECEIVETH THE WHOLE WORLD: HE WAS CAST OUT into the earth, AND HIS MESSENGERS WERE CAST OUT WITH HIM.

See how Satan has deceived the WHOLE WORLD since the days of Peter and Paul?

John 8:24-28

24. I said therefore unto you, that ye shall die in your transgressions: for if ye believe not that I am He (YAHWEH), ye shall die in your transgressions.

28. Then said Immanuel unto them, When ye have lifted up the Son of man, then shall ye know that I am He (YAHWEH), and that I do nothing of myself; but as my Father hath taught me, I speak these things.

John 14:7,8

7. If ye had known me, ye should have known my Father also: and from henceforth ye know him, and have seen him.

8. Philip told him, "Master, show us the Father, and that will satisfy us."

9. Immanuel saith unto him, Have I been so long time with you, and yet hast thou not known me, Philip? he that hath seen me hath seen the Father; and how sayest thou then, Shew us the Father?

Philippians 2:6

Who, being in the form of Yahweh, thought it not robbery to be equal with Yahweh:

318

You must get out of Christianity, it will be the One World Religion, and Yahweh Messiah is calling a people out for His Name's sake.

Matthew 10:36 And a man's foes shall be they of his own household.

CHAPTER 24

A.   . THE 3 1/2 YEAR TRIBULATION PERIOD

⁶ And he opened his mouth in blasphemy against Yahweh, to blaspheme his name, and his tabernacle, and them that dwell in heaven.

⁷ And it was given unto him to make war with the Elect, and to overcome them: and power was given him over all kindred's, and tongues, and nations.

⁸ And all that dwell upon the earth shall worship him, whose names are not written in the book of life of the Lamb slain from the foundation of the world.

⁹ If any man have an ear, let him hear.

¹⁰ He that leadeth into captivity shall go into captivity: he that killeth with the sword must be killed with the sword. Here is the patience and the faith of the Elect.

¹¹ And I beheld another beast coming up out of the earth; and he had two horns like a lamb, and he spake as a dragon.

NOTE: The Papacy is a Religious / Secular Government. This is what the two horns like a lamb means.

¹² And he exerciseth all the power of the first beast before him, and causeth the earth and them which dwell therein to worship the first beast, whose deadly wound was healed.

IT'S THE SAME BEAST. I believe the second time around, the Black Pope will be over the secular government, and the White Pope will be over the religious government. The Black Pope will enforce the worship of the White Pope.

13 And he doeth great wonders, so that he maketh fire come down from heaven on the earth in the sight of men,

14 And deceiveth them that dwell on the earth by the means of those miracles which he had power to do in the sight of the beast; saying to them that dwell on the earth, that they should make an image to the beast, which had the wound by a sword, and did live.

B.   THE POPE IS THE IMAGE OF THE BEAST

15 And he had power to give life unto the image of the beast, that <u>the image of the beast</u> should both speak, and cause that as many as would not worship the image of the beast should be killed.

Definition of IMAGE:

1. noun

A physical likeness or representation of a person, animal, or thing photographed, painted, sculptured, or otherwise made visible.

5. form; appearance; resemblance:

THE POPE IS THE IMAGE OF THIS RELIGIOUS GOVERNMENT BEAST!!!!!

"Even if the Pope were Satan incarnate, we ought not to raise up our heads against him but calmly lie down to rest on his bosom. He who rebels against our Father is condemned to death, for that which we do to him we do to Christ: we honor Christ if we honor the Pope; we dishonor Christ if we dishonor the Pope....(St. Catherine of Siena, SCS, p. 201-202, p. 222, quoted in Apostolic Digest, by Michael Malone, Book 5:

"The Book of Obedience", Chapter 1: "There is No Salvation Without Personal Submission to the Pope").

Ignatius Loyola himself declared the purpose of the Order was to..." win to God [the Pope of Rome], not only a single nation, a single country but all nations, all the kingdoms of the world."

C.   MARK OF THE BEAST

[16] And he causeth all, both small and great, rich and poor, free and bond, to receive a mark in their right hand, or in their foreheads:

Turzovka, Czechoslovakia, 1958 - page 331, FROM AN APPARITION OF MARY AND WHAT SHE HAD SAID,

<u>"All my children will receive and carry the sign of the cross on their foreheads."</u>

<u>"This sign will only my chosen ones will see."</u>   (Could this mean it will only be seen with some special light used by certain Christians to see if people have the Mark?)

Dozule, France - page 332

<u>All those who come to repent at the foot of the Glorious Cross </u>(this apparition is referred to as the Glorious Cross) <u>will be saved.</u>

<u>Notice:</u> The Mark of the Beast cannot be given until after the truth about Yahweh's Messiah killed has been taught throughout the world to every person so that they have the opportunity to accept salvation or reject it. This happens during the 7-Year Peace Plan. When the MARK is enforced when the Tribulation Period begins, the last part or 3 1/2 years of the 7-Year Peace Plan between the Papacy and Judaea.

The Sign of the Cross is the symbol of a Christian, the symbol of Christianity, that is to say, it is the outward sign which distinguishes the Christian from other men. The reason why Christianity will become the One World Religion and the Cross will be the Mark of the Beast, the Papacy. Who will rule the world from Zion?

If we go back to what Pope Urban said, "Since Jerusalem is the one and only holy city, and Christianity is the one and only true religion, then he (Pope) should rule over Jerusalem."

The *Jewish Encyclopedia* says:

"The cross as a Christian symbol or "seal" came into use at least as early as the second century (see "Apost. Const." iii. 17; Epistle of Barnabas, xi.-xii.; Justin, "Apologia," i. 55-60; "Dial. cum Tryph." 85-97); and the marking of a cross upon the forehead and the chest was regarded as a talisman against the powers of demons (Tertullian, "De Corona," iii.; Cyprian, "Testimonies," xi. 21-22; Lactantius, "Divinæ Institutiones," iv. 27, and elsewhere). Accordingly, the Christian Fathers had to defend themselves, as early as the second century, against the charge of being worshipers of the cross, as may be learned from Tertullian, "Apologia," xii., xvii., and Minucius Felix, "Octavius," xxix. Christians used to swear by the power of the cross (see Apocalypse of Mary, viii., in James, "Texts and Studies," iii. 118)." TRUTH BE TOLD THE CROSS AS A SYMBOL OF CHRISTIANITY STARTED WITH CONSTANTINE IN THE 4TH CENTURY. THE PAGANS USED IT BEFORE THAT TIME AS A SYMBOL FOR THE SUN BY THE PAGANS. CONSTANTINE, A SUN WORSHIPER, USED THE SUN SYMBOL THAT HE SAID HE SAW IN THE SKY THAT SAID WITH THIS SIGN CONQUER. ANN STARTED BEING USED AS A SYMBOL OF CHRISTIANITY.

This is very interesting to talk about some guy named John Leary, a so called prophet of the Catholic Church. Of course, they deny it. But this is one of his voiced opinions on the CROSS: *"We will know the people that will be with us as*

323

they will be marked with a cross on their foreheads. Those without a cross will not be with us."

D. UNDERSTANDING THE NUMBER 666

The reason the Scriptures speak negatively about the number 666 is that it symbolizes the power of the person who has that number to have power over all the deities, which in the case of the POPE is their claim to be the almighty and to have authority over Yahweh and his law. The word Catholic means universal and originated with astrology rather than with the Christian Church (Vance, page 8).

Going deeply back into Babylonian astrology, we find the real reason for the sanctity of the number 36. The Babylonians divided each of the 12 houses in the zodiac into three rooms, making 36 in all. They then divided the entire remainder of the sky into 36 constellations and appointed the ruling god of each constellation to rule over one of the 36 rooms of the zodiac. Since the spirits of the departed were believed to go to and dwell in the stars - a teaching still much alive today, there was, therefore, not a spirit in the heavens, not a star in the sky, which was not represented in the 36 rooms of the zodiac, and to swear by the number 36 was to swear by every god in the heavens above, as well as by all the spirits of the departed. The 36 gods were called decans because each ruled over 10 degrees of the zodiacal circle and over 10 days of the 360-day year.

The number 666 itself was a symbol of its authority over all the deities, even including the highest of the deities. This is because the number 666 contained the numbers of all the deities that formed the sum, and **the sum itself was perceived as having power over all the deities.**

Historians have noted that at one point, it seemed almost the entire city of Rome [Roman Empire] converted virtually overnight to Christianity.

Revelation 13:17 And that no man might buy or sell save he that <u>had the mark</u>, or <u>the name of the beast</u>, or <u>the number of his name</u>.

[18] **Here is wisdom. Let him that hath understanding count the number of the beast: for it is the number of a man, and his number is Six hundred three score and six.**

<u>The number 666 itself was a symbol of its authority over all the deities, even including the highest of the deities.</u> This is because the number 666 contained the numbers of all the deities that formed the sum, and <u>the sum itself was perceived as having power over all the deities.</u>

This was supposed to provide extra protection, including from the sun god, since this god's sum was present on the amulet. The one above has the god of the sun standing on the lion. This indicated the sun's position in the constellation of Leo during the hot days of August. The back is inscribed "Nachyel," meaning "intelligence of the sun," and the numbers 1 to 36.

The second illustration is also a solar seal, but it honors the star Basilisco, which was the diminutive form of the Greek basileus (king), thus meaning the same as the Latin regulus. Regulus is the only first-magnitude star in the constellation of Leo. The sun and the moon are again clearly seen on this amulet and on the reverse side is the same arrangement of numerals with the actual figure 666 given as the total.

Deuteronomy 4:19

"And lest thou lift up thine eyes unto heaven, and when thou seest the sun, and the moon, and the stars, *even* all the host of heaven, shouldest be driven to worship them, and serve them, which Yahweh thy Mighty One hath divided unto all nations under the whole heaven."

E.   THE POPE HAS THIS NUMBER: 666.

Daniel 9:27 And he shall confirm the covenant with many for one week: and in the midst of the week he shall cause the offering and the oblation to cease, and for the overspreading of abominations he shall make it desolate, even until the consummation, and that determined shall be poured upon the desolate.

NOTE: The Papacy will make a 7-year peace Plan with the world and Judaea to get control of Zion. After 31/2 years the Pope will no longer go along with the Peace Plan. The rest of the last 31/2 years of this Peace Plan will be the Tribulation Period. This is when the Pope will make Christianity the One World Religion, and the Christians will kill the believers in Yahweh Messiah at this time.

Daniel 11:45 And he shall plant the tabernacles of his palace between the seas in the righteous mountain; yet he shall come to his end, and none shall help him.

NOTE: The Pope moves to the Dome of the Rock, which is a facade for the "TEMPLE OF GOD." The Dome of the Rock is in ZION, between the Mediterranean and Dead Seas.

CHAPTER 25

MY PERSONAL STORY

I knew at an early age something was wrong with Christianity, and that stuck with me. The funny thing about Christianity is that they have a denomination to fit anyone's lifestyle, and if you do not like any of them, you can start your own like the homosexuals have done. This is how Satan keeps people within Christianity. I was raised in Pentecostalism. There came a time early on in my studies when I thought the Pentecostals were the only ones who had the truth, just because they believed in the infilling of the Spirit, which I have always believed, just not what they were saying it was. Yet I knew something was not right with them either, but I still believed in the name of Jesus. Once I found out that Yahweh was the Father's name and studied out and proved the son inherited the Father's name and why he became Yahweh the Father in the Flesh, thus Yahweh Messiah. That is when I started telling everybody that ALL Christianity was a lie, and that is when the truth started opening and why I am where I am today. People have been brainwashed into the name of Jesus that they fear going against it. I felt like that, just part of the brainwashing to make you believe that lie. Now I cringe when hearing that name. But only the truth to the lie of that name will set you free from the Christian bondage. Yet you have these so-called Messianic Movements that use Yahshua, Yehshua, Yahoshua, or other spellings, also thinking because of their Christian upbringing that the birth given name, no matter what, you think was the name for salvation. That is another big, fat Christian lie. So, they don't realize they are just as bad as the Christians, and why do so many of them think they must now speak Hebrew or act like they are a Jew to feel more righteous than Everyone else? It is one big Satanic mess. Plus, people have always been taught that there is a true

Christianity and a false Christianity and why people think there are some good ones and all the other ones are not really Christians.

I have been to a couple of crazy churches that scared kids to death. I know I was one of them. People running around the isles, jumping up on chairs, rolling around on the floor, I always thought it was the workings of Satan, not of the Spirit. I never read about any of it in the scriptures with Spirit-filled people acting like that along with their gibberish babel tongues. I never read that in Scripture. They were thinking the Spirit was making them do that. To me, it seemed like they were always trying to outdo one another to prove which one had more of the Spirit infilling. It was the small country churches that seemed to act more like that. I have seen many of the top healing Evangelists growing up in the 50's and heard many excuses because people were not healed. All this stuff thoroughly confused my young mind, and listening to the preaching of all the Hell Fire preachers scaring people half to death to get them saved. Plus, about all the back-sliding stuff. This stuff, I believed, started planting the seed in me, wanting to know the truth about it all. I have seen so many Christians I have known growing up that backslid in their language and even with me. Made me think, why can't G/d keep anyone when it seems everyone goes in and out of Christianity, the only place to go where you think there is salvation, yet you cannot leave it for long. What does a person do? You are taught it is the only place to receive salvation. After all, who wants to be burned alive and never to exist again, right? So, I started studying for the truth to everything that I was taught, I have studied a lot of different subjects through the years to find truth and was out to prove everything that I was taught to be true or not. It turned out that everything I was taught was lies, and how they were being taught was different from what the truth to them was. I have done some deep studies, and as the doors opened to the truth, I just kept walking through the doors as they were opened, knowing that if I quit doing that, then no other doors would open until I walked through the last door given to me. I have gained so much knowledge in my years of studying that I can say, after debating educated scholars and they could not come against the truth with their Christian education to make them scholars, then I am a self-made scholar. Many prophecies and other things were opened too without taking any college courses or seminary studies, which are controlled by the Jesuits so that everyone would teach the same basic belief system in Christianity.   Speaking of Seminary, it comes from the Latin *seminarian,* pertaining to seed," from semen, the planting of seed. I have debated a few scholars, and they ended up being rooted in the teachings of Christianity, so they were easy. Even college professors that many of them agreed with me on certain subjects. My Christian upbringing gave me the knowledge of what these so-called Christian Scholars would use in their debate, the basics. I have also debated many preachers from many different denominations of Christianity on different chat sites. --

At this point, I need to tell you about my brother Neal, who had a friend whose parents were attending an Assembly of Yahweh that I recall as being in Michigan. He went to the place and talked with them and received a bunch of their literature. He lived in Indiana at that time and still does. I lived in Kentucky. He sent me a bunch of their literature about the name Yahweh and the name Yahshua that they used in place of Jesus' name. I remember talking to him on the phone, and I was against it because I was brainwashed, as is the rest of Christianity, in the name of Jesus. I remember running across the name Yahweh when I was studying Moses, and Moses used the name Yahweh, He told me to go through my history books and search out the names. He knew that I had a lot of history books. I remember in a different conversation with him, I told him that I could not find anything on the name Yahshua, but I had found a lot on the name of Yahweh, so I started using Yahweh as the Father's name and still used Jesus for the son's name. With that info, I started studying the scriptures again, looking into the current information on the name Yahweh in the scriptures, and paid more attention to the name Immanuel. After a month or two, I had proven that his name was not Jesus, but it was Immanuel, and that the birth given name was not used for salvation because Immanuel inherited the name above all names, the Father's name, Yahweh and finally after a lot more studying figured out that Immanuel actually became the Father in the flesh, Yahweh Messiah, Yahweh was the only name given to man for salvation. This is when I knew not to listen to any Christians ever again about their Jesus, the only name for salvation taught by Christianity. When I started studying the names and figured out the name Jesus was a lie along with other ones and that Yahweh was the Father's name and the Messiah inherited the Father's name, that is really when things started opening up for me and found that the birth given name had nothing to do with salvation, then knowing the Jesus birth given name was actually a pagan lie is when I studied out Immanuel as the birth given name. Christianity has brainwashed people with the name Jesus, and they fear going against it even as I had until I proved that it has nothing to fear except for your brainwashing and lack of knowledge of the truth.

To make a long story short, This is the third book I have put together from my hundreds of studies on the many different subjects in scriptures that I have done, and happy with the knowledge of what is coming and whether I live or die, I know either way there will be a time that salvation will be obtainable in either condition that I may be in, dead or alive.

I had a Pentecostal preacher from Memphis, TN, tell me that he could kill me because I was a heretic. That is just how frustrated he got with me. The Papacy made that word famous during the Dark Ages. Now you can see why it will be the Christians killing the Elect of Yahweh who are Spirit-filled. They will be the ones killed for not going over to Christianity when Christianity was made the Global Religion by the Papacy during the Tribulation Period. I even had a thing that continuously went across my computer screen one time that said, "We will hunt you down until we find you, and when we find you, we will kill you." I used to debate 5 or 6 preachers at a time on Christian Chat, and one by one, they would leave frustrated after finding out they could not come against the truth. How do you know when you have found the truth? When nothing can come against it and it only builds on itself.

One last thing: when I started putting my studies together, I had to write them all out by hand. I thought an electric typewriter would be faster, so I started typing them all, I took typing in high school. Then, years later, computers came out, and typing came to good use once again. Before there was an internet, I had a computer to type them all out on the computer and saved them on it then printed them out, making a book with those office binders. When the internet came along, I had to retype every study on the website. There were between twenty to thirty studies that I had at that time and the first website I had them on shut down the website, so I lost that one and opened another one. I forget how many years I had that one, but they sold it last year, and I lost that website and all my studies with it. I found a lot of them that I had stored in other places, but not all of them. I had a couple hundred studies by then. As you can see, I had a lot of difficulties with my studies and a rough road along the way, but I never quit. I had a drive for people needing to know what I must share. I had a mission that I could never quit or give up on. With these books I can now make a dream my reality. My mother told me one time that "She had seen the Spirit in all her kids except for me." They must have all at one time individually in her Pentecostalism received the babbling tongues that to them is when you receive the Spirit infilling according to her, and I was the only one that did not. Today, I am very thankful that I did not. She also told someone in my family that she had never seen anyone who knew so much about the Old Testament, that I knew more than she did, and it took her years to learn. I also remember telling her, "I must be reading a different Bible than she was because what I was reading did not agree with what I was taught. Compare the teachings with what different preachers are teaching about the same subjects within my books. Gary W. Stanfield. 2024

Below is someone that I met on Christian Chat over 20 years ago, and this is what she told someone about me and what I believed. We had many conversations about beliefs and what I believed in with Yahweh Messiah. I always enjoyed talking with her. It was the name she used on Christian Chat, not her last name anyway. We never had to debate. Simply good conversations, she was more curious and interested in what my beliefs were.

I would see her on other Christian sites, and she was very talkative., I am sure she has passed on by now. Below is what she said to another person on Christian Chat about me.

<u>Yvonne Ray</u>

"I have studied the Bible and religions - including Christianity and world religions - for almost sixty years. I have four doctorate degrees in the field of theology. But I have never encountered anyone with such unique beliefs in my life as him."

Yahweh's Truth is incredibly unique compared to Christianity and the other world religions.

Ephesians 6:12 For we wrestle not against flesh and blood, but against principalities, against powers, against the rulers of the darkness of this world, against spiritual wickedness in high places.

A Satisfied Soul

"Consume the Word, satisfy your soul."